BICYCLING
VANCOUVER
ISLAND
& The Gulf Islands

SIMON PRIEST
Maps by Kimberley Klint

Douglas & McIntyre
Vancouver/Toronto

To our parents who provided the first bicycles:
Michael Priest
Valerie Anne Priest
Dale Klint
Sharon Klint

Douglas & McIntyre Ltd., 1615 Venables Street, Vancouver, British Columbia V5L 2H1

Canadian Cataloguing in Publication Data

Priest, Simon.
   Bicycling Vancouver Island and the Gulf
Islands

Bibliography: p.
ISBN 0-88894-420-9

1. Bicycle touring – British Columbia – Vancouver Island – Guide-books. 2. Bicycle touring – British Columbia – Gulf Islands – Guide-books. 3. Vancouver Island (B.C.) – Description and travel – Guide-books. 4. Gulf Islands (B.C.) – Description and travel – Guide-books. 5. Vancouver Island (B.C.) – Maps. 6. Gulf Islands (B.C.) – Maps. I. Klint, Kimberley. II. Title.
GV1046.C3P74 1984   917.11'34   C84-091056-8

Cover photograph by Lloyd Sutton, Photo/Graphics
Design by Barbara Hodgson
Typeset by Ronalds Printing
Printed and bound in Canada by D.W. Friesen & Sons

CONTENTS

PREFACE

A few years ago when Steve Whan and I were teaching bicycle touring and repair courses in the Greater Vancouver area, our students' final assignment was to plan and execute a weekend trip without the assistance of an instructor. The main obstacle that students encountered was a lack of accurate, current information to assist them in planning their tour. They complained that neither existing guidebooks nor available maps were specific enough to provide details important to a cyclist.

Thus we decided to develop a new kind of guidebook for people wishing to travel by bicycle in British Columbia: one that offered options on where to go; that provided key information, such as camping availability, traffic conditions, terrain grades and supply and repair stores; and that took a flexible approach to bicycle touring.

This guide to bicycling Vancouver Island is planned as the first in a series of cycle tours around the province of British Columbia. We have chosen to begin with the Vancouver Island area because of its great diversity of environments, from the rocky cliffs of the Gulf Islands in the east to the long sandy beaches of the Pacific Rim in the west, from the urban bustle of Victoria in the south to the wild forests of the Nimpkish in the north. The eight regions described here are laced together by roads well-suited to bicycle travel, and each has a particular appeal. Cyclists can seek out historical sites and museums, travel beneath towering mountain ranges and alongside coastal waters, visit man-sculptured gardens and cathedral-like first-growth forests. For those who live off-island, bicycling is the most satisfying way of experiencing island life. Island dwellers will find that they too are more in touch with their surroundings when they set out to see it on two wheels.

If you are a mainland visitor, British Columbia and Washington State both provide ferry service to the island, and B.C. ferries also connect many of the Gulf Islands. The map on page 6 depicts the areas covered in this volume. Come, bring your friends, and explore Vancouver Island, where tranquillity is always just around the corner.

ACKNOWLEDGEMENTS

This project has passed through many stages of revision and reflects the hard work of many unrewarded friends who cared enough to check information thoroughly, were willing to explore every last side road, to cycle in all types of weather, and to pose endlessly for pictures. I hope their joy in experiencing British Columbia's best by bike has been rewarding and that they are as proud of the result as I am.

Special thanks to:

Anne Alfred	Catherine Ostler
Sherri Audet	Beth Peterson
Lesley Cerny	Angela Smailles
Ron Graham	Danielle Soulodre
Daphne Guerney	Rob Staschuk
Leanne Guerney	Susan Staschuk
Kimberly Hornsby	Deborah Tacholsky
Kimberley Klint	Angela Tambosso
Debbie Lister	Janet Wauthier
Melanie Mason	Steve Whan
Marsh Ney	Cathy Winter

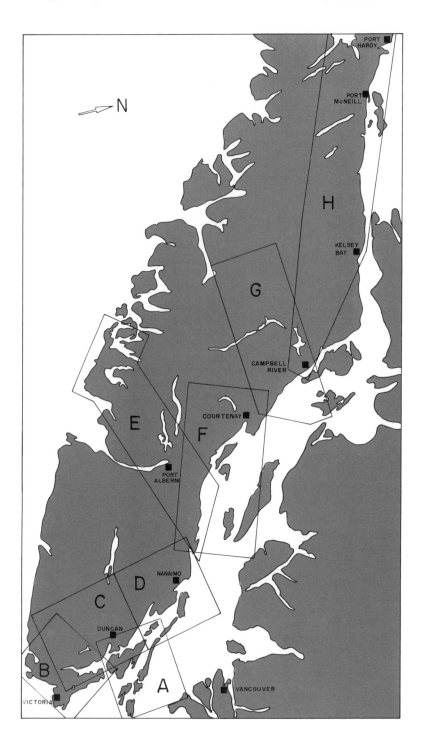

N

PORT HARDY

PORT McNEILL

H

KELSEY BAY

G

CAMPBELL RIVER

COURTENAY

E

F

PORT ALBERNI

NANAIMO

D

C

DUNCAN

B

A

VANCOUVER

VICTORIA

REGIONAL INDEX

HOW TO USE THIS BOOK

The 108 tours of this guidebook are arranged so that the cyclist may combine several tours into a personalized trip. All the tours are connected to one another and many start where others finish.

To plan your trip, simply choose an area that you wish to visit, then study the tours that connect your starting point with your destination. Each numbered tour covers three geographic locations, rates the tour according to difficulty, and gives its one-way distance. A brief overview of the tour follows, including highlights, special information regarding the traffic and terrain to be encountered, and where repairs and supplies can be obtained in nearby communities.

Once you have selected the combination of tours that will comprise your trip, draft a rough itinerary for your bicycle expedition. This schedule should be flexible enough to allow for unexpected route changes and extra time spent taking side trips and exploring points of interest. Plan your trip to include rest stops and campgrounds. Make note of places you wish to visit and areas where you need to use extra care. Arrange the trip so that sections with potentially heavy traffic volume and/or steep grades are travelled when you are rested — or at a time — often early morning — when traffic congestion is minimal.

Remember to leave a copy of your intended schedule with a responsible person who will summon help should you not return by an agreed time or date.

THE TOURS

To make your trip a safe and enjoyable one, study each tour's checkpoints. These outline important items along the route such as start and finish locations, junctions for shortcuts and side trips, uphill and downhill grades, potential dangers that require particular caution, and campgrounds and points of interest along the way. You may wish to do some research of the area you plan to visit at your public library and check with your local tourism office for additional information.

THE MAPS

Each tour has an accompanying map that details the route along the listed checkpoints. The following legend lists the symbols used on each map:

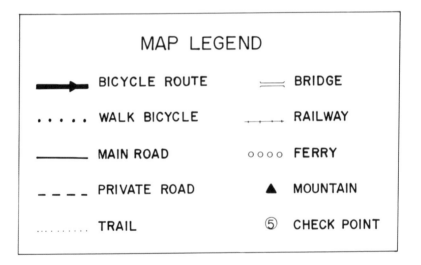

Each map is drawn to a scale of 1:100,000. This means that one centimetre on the map is equivalent to 100,000 centimetres on the ground. The maps are the focal point of this guide and serve as the primary means of finding your way along a route. The checkpoints are secondary and are designed to be used in conjunction with the map. You may find it convenient to copy the map and checkpoints of a tour before you head out.

THE RATING SCHEME

Each tour in this book is rated on a scale of 1 to 10 and is assigned an evaluation based on this scale. This scheme takes into account two important factors: Terrain and Traffic.

Terrain relates directly to the number and grade of hills found along the tour route. Traffic considers the potential volume of cars and trucks that may be encountered.

Three types of terrain are identified: flat land (easy grade), rolling hills (moderate grade), and steep hills (difficult grade). The three types of traffic and road conditions you will encounter are: back roads (low volume), main roads (medium volume) and highways (high volume). These categories are shown in the diagram below:

THE RATING SCHEME	TRAFFIC		
	Back Road Low Volume	Main Road Medium Volume	Highway High Volume
T Flat Land E Easy Grade	1	3	6
R R Rolling Hills A Moderate Grade	2	5	8
I Steep Hills N Difficult Grade	4	7	9

10 is reserved for extreme cases of continuous steep hills and highway conditions

If, for example, the tour you are interested in is rated (5), expect to travel on main roads among rolling hills. Such a tour would be further rated as "Intermediate" according to the following groups: BEGINNER = 1 2 3; INTERMEDIATE = 4 5 6; ADVANCED = 7 8 9. Since these divisions are purely subjective, experiment with a few tours before placing yourself at a particular level. The rating will also change with the amount of equipment you take on a tour, the condition of your bicycle, and your own cycling abilities. You can make positive changes in your endurance by challenging and conquering steeper hills. And you can become more skilled at riding in traffic by practising in traffic. Experience is the best teacher, and the way to get experience is simply to get out there and pedal. HAPPY TOURING!

CHECKLIST

ESSENTIAL ITEMS for Day Trips

Wear comfortable tracksuit and running shoes.

Take:
- Day pack or handlebar bag
- Water bottle and lunch
- Lock and chain
- Helmet and gloves
- Wool sweater
- Warm jacket or windbreaker
- Rain suit or poncho
- First aid kit and personal medication
- Flashlight and batteries
- Pocket knife
- Matches and candle
- Sun lotion and bug repellent

Tools:
- Pump and tire gauge
- Spare inner tube and patch kit
- Brake and gear cables
- Tire irons
- Crescent wrench
- Screwdrivers
- Needlenose pliers
- Allen keys
- Spoke wrench
- Spare nuts and bolts
- Spare outer tire

ADDITIONAL ITEMS for Overnight Trips

Take:
- Rear panniers/saddlebags
- Front panniers/saddlebags
- Tent with waterproof fly
- Sleeping bag and mattress
- Stove and fuel
- Cooking pots and pans
- Eating utensils
- Biodegradable soap and scrubber
- Food and drink
- Extra clothing including a change of shoes and socks

Tools: (shared among group members)
- Vise-grip pliers
- Freewheel remover
- Various length spokes
- Chain tool and spare links
- Spare brake pads or blocks
- Lightweight chain lubricant
- Vaseline or bearing grease
- Cleaning rag and solvent
- Pipe wrench
- Small hammer
- Metal files
- Extra tires and tubes

SOME WORDS ON SAFETY

A bicycle is a marvellous way to see the sights and experience the outdoors first hand. However, as with any vehicle, when travelling you are vulnerable to certain risks. To minimize those risks:
— Wear a helmet.
— Dress appropriately, and be prepared for the worst weather.
— Know how to keep your bicycle in proper working order, and how to repair breakdowns on the road.
— Gain experience riding in traffic so that you are not panicked by travelling on main roads with many cars.
— Slow your pace on gravel roads and exercise caution at road and railway crossings.
— Avoid hurrying to your destination; enjoy the adventure.

Under British Columbia law, a bicycle is a motor vehicle. You are subject to the same regulations as cars and trucks — and have the same rights and responsibilities. Occasionally, there are additional local rules that apply strictly to bicycles. If you are not already familiar with these rules, take the time to inquire at a local police office with regard to the law as it pertains to you.

A course in bicycle touring and maintenance is well worth taking for the confidence it instills. Start off by cycling with other experienced cyclists; read books on cycling and put the knowledge gained into practice. For information on courses, clubs, books and the law, contact:

Bicycle HOTLINE
(24 hours) (604) 731-7433

THE BICYCLING ASSOCIATION OF BRITISH COLUMBIA
Suite 332-1367 West Broadway, Vancouver, B.C. V6H 4A9
(604) 737-3034

REGION A   THE GULF ISLANDS

The first ten tours cover the area collectively known as the Gulf Islands. This group of approximately one hundred islands is located on the west side of the Strait of Georgia and is well serviced by ferries. The five main islands of Saltspring, Galiano, Mayne, Pender and Saturna may be reached by ferries from Swartz Bay (near Victoria) and Tsawwassen (near Vancouver). Occasional transfering between islands may be necessary, and often this enables the cyclist to visit all of the islands during a single extended trip. Provincial camping is permitted on only three islands: Pender, Galiano and Saltspring, so plan your trip to avoid getting stranded on an island with no accommodations.

The main attraction of the Gulf Islands is their scenic beauty and natural marine environment. The many sandstone cliffs dotted with Arbutus trees and the backdrop of distant snowcapped peaks offer picturesque scenes that are a lure to photographers. The accessible beaches abound in marine life, so it is well worth taking along a local tide table and a guidebook to identify the fascinating creatures found in tidepools and on mudflats at low tide.

Please take care not to damage the environment or to alter the very beauty you seek to explore and enjoy.

Tour Ratings
Beginner: 4, 6, 7, 8, 9
Intermediate: 1, 2, 5, 10
Advanced: 3

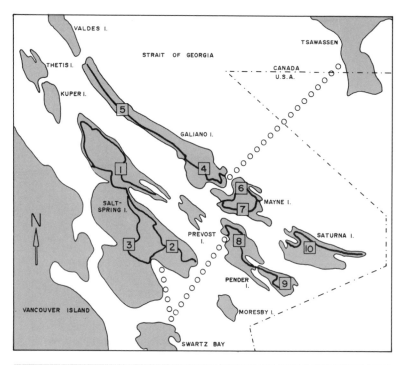

Gulf Islands: Cyclists pause to admire the view from Bluff Park, Galiano Island.

1

LONG HARBOUR FERNWOOD VESUVIUS	RATING: Intermediate (2 to 5) DISTANCE: 23.6 km/14.7 mi

HIGHLIGHTS: Walker Hook; beach at Fernwood; views from Sunset Drive; local pub at Vesuvius; farmlands and cottages along the way.

TRAFFIC: Heavy near ferry terminals at sailing times.

TERRAIN: Rolling hills with two or three steep hills.

REPAIRS: Bicycle shop in Ganges.

SUPPLIES: Corner stores in Vesuvius and Fernwood, supermarkets in Ganges.

CONNECTIONS: Tours 2 & 3. Ferries at Long Harbour and Vesuvius.

CHECKPOINTS

km *(mi)*

0.0 *(0.0)* START   Long Harbour Ferry Terminal (1). Wait for the traffic to go first. Rolling hills ahead following Scott Road.

4.4 *(2.7)* JUNCTION   Turn right and stay right on Robinson Road. A left leads into downtown Ganges (2).

6.0 *(3.7)* CAUTION   Steep descent followed by uphill. Road is bumpy and narrow. Turn right at the top of the hill.

7.8 *(4.9)* INTEREST   A dirt road leads right to Walker Hook (3); continue straight on, following the paved road along the shore.

11.3 *(7.1)* INTEREST   Fernwood beach and pier (4) with public access. Good views across Trincomali Channel to Galiano Island.

13.8 *(8.6)* UPHILL   Steep ascent on North Beach Road. Turn right onto North End Road at the top of the hill.

16.7 *(10.4)* JUNCTION   Turn left on Sunset Drive. A right leads downhill to Southey Point (5); public access is limited.

22.0 *(13.8)* CAUTION   Steep downhill followed by steep uphill to Vesuvius.

23.1 *(14.4)* JUNCTION   Turn right on Vesuvius Bay Road. A left leads to Ganges.

23.6 *(14.7)* FINISH   Vesuvius Ferry Terminal (6). Marked beach access.

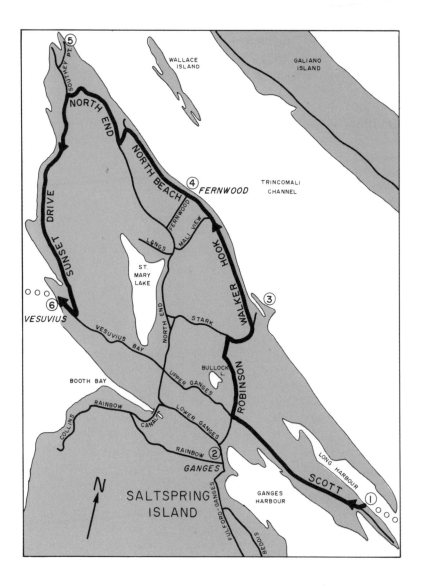

WALLACE ISLAND

GALIANO ISLAND

⑤ SOUTHEY PT.

NORTH END

NORTH BEACH

④ FERNWOOD

TRINCOMALI CHANNEL

SUNSET DRIVE

FERNWOOD

MALI VIEW

LONGS

ST. MARY LAKE

HOOK

○ ○ ○

⑥

VESUVIUS

VESUVIUS BAY

NORTH END

STARK

WALKER

③

BOOTH BAY

UPPER GANGES

BULLOCK L.

ROBINSON

RAINBOW

COLLINS

CANAL

LOWER GANGES

RAINBOW

②

GANGES

N

SALTSPRING ISLAND

FULFORD - GANGES

GANGES HARBOUR

LONG HARBOUR

SCOTT

①

○ ○ ○

BEDDIS

15

2

| VESUVIUS GANGES BEAVER POINT | RATING: Intermediate (2 to 5) DISTANCE: 25.2 km/15.7 mi |

HIGHLIGHTS: Swimming in the many lakes; handicrafts in Ganges; Harbour Park; Peter Arnell Park; camping at Ruckle Provincial Park.
TRAFFIC: Heavy near ferry terminal and in downtown Ganges.
TERRAIN: Rolling hills, some steep sections.
REPAIRS: Bicycle shop in Ganges.
SUPPLIES: Corner store in Vesuvius and Fulford Harbour, supermarkets in Ganges.
CONNECTIONS: Tours 1 & 3. Ferries at Vesuvius and Fulford Harbour.

CHECKPOINTS

km *(mi)*

0.0 *(0.0)* START Vesuvius Ferry Terminal (1). Rolling hills ahead on Vesuvius Bay Road.

3.5 *(2.2)* JUNCTION At the crossroads, go straight ahead on Upper Ganges Road. A left on North End Road Leads to St. Mary Lake (2).

4.4 *(2.8)* CAUTION Sudden descent followed by a sharp corner. Second one ahead.

6.0 *(3.8)* JUNCTION After a right on Robinson Road, remain straight ahead for Ganges. A left on Scott Road leads to Long Harbour Ferry (3).

6.9 *(4.3)* INTEREST Turn left to enter the city of Ganges (4).

7.5 *(4.7)* INTEREST Turn right on the main road out of town. Harbour Park (5) on the left. Large hill ahead on Fulford-Ganges Road.

7.7 *(4.8)* CAMPING At the base of the hill, a right would lead to Mouat Park (6). Heavy-use park. Limited camping space for bicyclists.

7.8 *(4.9)* UPHILL Continue up the steep hill, following Fulford-Ganges Road.

8.9 *(5.6)* JUNCTION Part way up the hill turn left on Beddis Road. Continuing straight on the main road leads to Fulford Harbour Ferry (7).

(continued, p. 18)

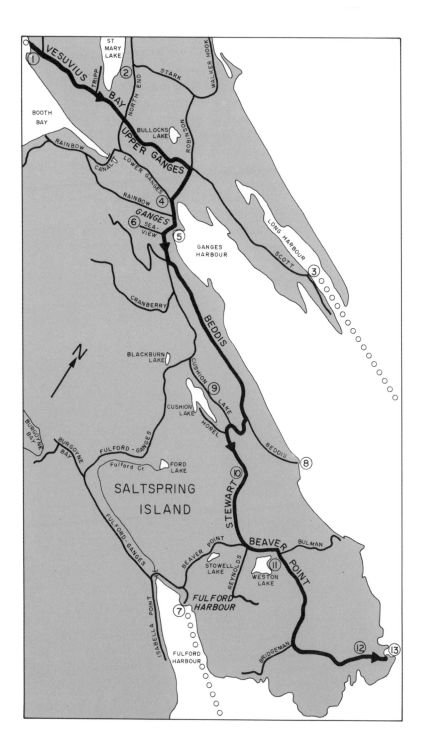

17

13.8 *(8.6)*   JUNCTION   Turn right on Cusheon Lake Road. Straight on leads to Beddis Beach (8) and limited public access.

14.6 *(9.1)*   JUNCTION   Turn left on Stewart Road. Large hill ahead. Straight on leads to swimming hole at Cusheon Lake (9).

16.2 *(10.1)*   INTEREST   After the right bend at the top of the hill, Peter Arnell Park (10) and picnic area is to the right. Good views.

18.1 *(11.3)*   JUNCTION   Turn left on Beaver Point Road for Ruckle Park (12). A right leads to Fulford Harbour Ferry (7).

18.9 *(11.8)*   INTEREST   Swimming hole at Weston Lake (11). Continue on the main road.

22.1 *(13.8)*   UPHILL   Up a steep hill after the community centre and down the other side to enter Ruckle Park (12).

24.6 *(15.4)*   CAMPING   Take the trail right by the water pump to grassy field tenting area overlooking the ocean. Perfect for bicyclists!

25.2 *(15.7)*   FINISH   Beaver Point Light Beacon (13); view of Pender Island.

Relaxing at Beaver Point; the ferry is bound for Swartz Bay.

3

BEAVER POINT FULFORD HARBOUR LONG HARBOUR	RATING: Advanced (5 to 9) DISTANCE: 29.4 km/18.4 mi

HIGHLIGHTS: Swimming in the many lakes; petroglyph at Fulford Harbour; view of Mount Maxwell; handicrafts in Ganges; Harbour Park.

TRAFFIC: Heavy near ferry terminals and in downtown Ganges.

TERRAIN: Steep hill on Fulford-Ganges Road.

REPAIRS: Bicycle shop in Ganges.

SUPPLIES: Corner store in Fulford Harbour, supermarket in Ganges.

CONNECTIONS: Tours 1 & 3. Ferries at Fulford Harbour and Long Harbour.

CHECKPOINTS

km *(mi)*

0.0 *(0.0)* START   Beaver Point in Ruckle Park (1); follow main road out of park back toward Fulford Harbour.

1.0 *(0.7)* UPHILL   Start up a fairly steep hill and down the other side past the community hall. Watch corner on descent.

5.7 *(3.6)* INTEREST   Swimming hole at Weston Lake (2). Continue on main road.

6.5 *(4.1)* JUNCTION   Stay left; following Beaver Point Road to Fulford Harbour. A right on Stewart Road is the short cut to Ganges.

7.5 *(4.7)* INTEREST   Swimming hole at Stowell Lake (3). Continue on main road.

8.2 *(5.1)* DOWNHILL   Steep descent into Fulford Harbour; look for ruin on left.

9.0 *(5.6)* JUNCTION   Turn right on Fulford-Ganges Road. Fulford Harbour and the ferry terminal (4) are a short distance to the left of here.

9.9 *(6.2)* CAUTION   Wooden bridge crossing, shortly after St. Mark's Church (5).

10.0 *(6.3)* JUNCTION   Turn right, remaining on Fulford-Ganges Road. Straight ahead on the left is a small park containing a petroglyph (6).

13.2 *(8.3)* UPHILL   Bend right on the main road, heading uphill steeply for 1.0 km.

18.0 *(11.3)* INTEREST   Swimming hole at Blackburn Lake (7). Continue on main road.

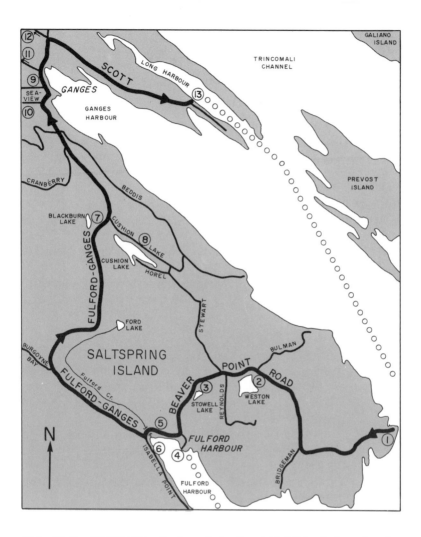

18.5 *(11.6)* INTEREST Cusheon Lake Road (right) leads to swimming at Cusheon Lake (8). Remain on Fulford-Ganges Road with flat section ahead.

20.7 *(12.9)* DOWNHILL Steep descent into Ganges. Control speed!

22.3 *(13.9)* INTEREST At the bottom of the hill enter Ganges (9) with Harbour Park on the right and Mouat Park on the left (10).

24.1 *(15.1)* JUNCTION Turn right for Long Harbour. Straight on Lower Ganges Road leads to St. Mary Lake (11).

25.0 *(15.6)* JUNCTION Turn right on Scott Road; rolling hills ahead. A left just ahead on Upper Ganges Road leads to Vesuvius Ferry (12).

29.4 *(18.4)* FINISH Long Harbour Ferry Terminal and picnic park (13).

4

| STURDIES BAY |
| BLUFF PARK |
| MONTAGUE |
| HARBOUR |

RATING: Beginner (2 to 4)
DISTANCE: 11.0 km/6.9 mi

HIGHLIGHTS:	Bellhouse Park; Bluff Park; views of Active Pass and ferries; camping at Montague Park; shell beach and sandstone formations.
TRAFFIC:	Heavy near ferry terminals.
TERRAIN:	Steep hill before Montague Harbour.
REPAIRS:	No services on Galiano. Bicycle shop in Ganges on Saltspring Island.
SUPPLIES:	Small store at Sturdies Bay, limited store at Montague Harbour.
CONNECTIONS:	Tour 5. Ferries at Sturdies Bay and Montague Harbour.

CHECKPOINTS

km *(mi)*

0.0 *(0.0)* START Sturdies Bay Ferry Terminal (1). Stop by the map of the island and allow traffic to go first. Follow main road.

0.7 *(0.4)* JUNCTION Turn left on Burrill Road. Straight ahead eventually leads to Porlier Pass or Montague Harbour via main roads.

1.2 *(0.8)* JUNCTION Stay right, following Burrill Road straight ahead. A left on Jack Road leads to Bellhouse Park by Active Pass (2).

2.2 *(1.4)* CAUTION Sharp right bend as road becomes Bluff Park Drive, uphill.

3.4 *(2.2)* CAUTION Road narrows upon entering Bluff Park (3), immediately after passing a dirt side road at the top of the hill.

3.8 *(2.4)* INTEREST At the Bluff Park sign, park your bikes and walk left up the road to the Active Pass viewpoint (4). Then continue straight on.

4.1 *(2.6)* CAUTION Descent on Bluff Park Drive is steep with sharp corners.

5.1 *(3.2)* JUNCTION Turn right on Georgeson Bay Road. A left leads to beach access a short distance along Active Pass Drive (5).

5.6 *(3.5)* CAUTION Stay to the right of the tree in the middle of the road.

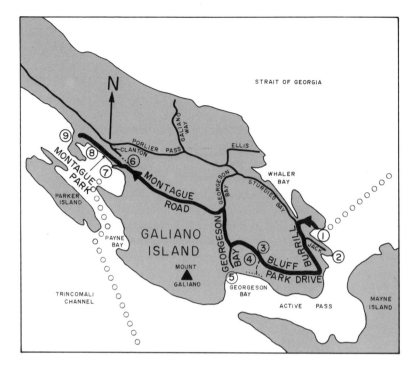

6.2 *(3.9)* JUNCTION   Turn left and start up a steep hill on Montague Road. Straight ahead leads back to Sturdies Bay Ferry.

8.0 *(5.0)* DOWNHILL   Begin steep descent with sharp corners. Slow down at bottom of hill!

9.2 *(5.8)* INTEREST   Old road/trail goes right (6). Good connector to Porlier Pass Road.

9.4 *(5.9)* JUNCTION   Turn right on Montague Harbour Park Road. Straight ahead leads to Montague Harbour Ferry Terminal (7) and beach access.

10.3 *(6.4)* CAMPING   Entering Montague Park (8), stay straight ahead through here.

11.0 *(6.9)* FINISH   Boat launch area and shell beach (9). Excellent sunset viewing.

5

MONTAGUE HARBOUR RETREAT COVE PORLIER PASS	RATING: Intermediate (4) DISTANCE: 21.0 km/13.1 mi

HIGHLIGHTS: Camping at Montague Harbour Park; water access near Retreat Cove, Spotlight Cove and Porlier Pass; Lover's Leap Lookout.

TRAFFIC: Heavy near ferry terminal.

TERRAIN: Rolling hills with some steep grades along Porlier Pass Road.

REPAIRS: Bicycle shop in Ganges on Saltspring Island.

SUPPLIES: Stores in Montague Harbour and North Galiano.

CONNECTIONS: Tour 4. Ferry from Swartz Bay and other Gulf Islands.

CHECKPOINTS

km	(mi)	
0.0	*(0.0)*	START From the Montague Harbour Ferry Terminal (1), follow Montague Harbour Road uphill away from the water.
0.3	*(0.2)*	CAMPING A left on Montague Harbour Park Road leads to camping (2).
0.5	*(0.3)*	CAUTION Locate and follow a dirt road/trail left and uphill. Walk bikes! At top, continue straight on Clanton Road (3).
1.4	*(0.9)*	JUNCTION Turn left on Porlier Pass Road. A right leads to Sturdies Bay (4).
2.5	*(1.6)*	DOWNHILL Rolling hills down, fairly steep. More rolling hills ahead.
10.1	*(6.3)*	INTEREST Retreat Cove Road goes left to Brumhall Park and Retreat Cove (5).
10.8	*(6.7)*	UPHILL Cross Greig Creek and head uphill past Cottage Way.
13.5	*(8.4)*	INTEREST Lover's Leap on the left (6). Cliffs and view to Saltspring Island.
17.4	*(10.8)*	INTEREST Spotlight Cove on the left (7). Better water access ahead.
19.4	*(12.1)*	INTEREST North Galiano townsite (8). Continue straight.
20.2	*(12.6)*	CAUTION At top of abrupt hill, stay left on a dirt road.
20.5	*(12.9)*	INTEREST Entering Indian Reserve Land; water access (9). Land is private.
21.0	*(13.1)*	FINISH Road ends at Porlier Pass (10). Locate a boardwalk trail on the right that leads to Race Point Lighthouse. Respect private property!

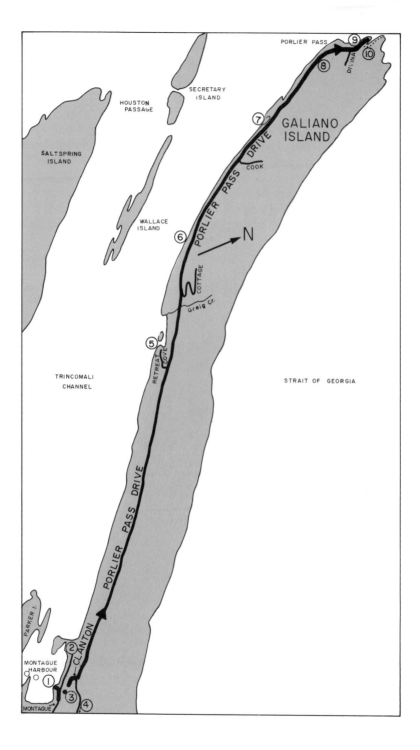

PORLIER PASS

⑨

⑩ DIVINA

⑧

GALIANO
ISLAND

⑦

PORLIER PASS DRIVE

COOK

SECRETARY
ISLAND

HOUSTON
PASSAGE

SALTSPRING
ISLAND

⑥

N

WALLACE
ISLAND

COTTAGE

Greig Cr.

⑤

RETREAT COVE

TRINCOMALI
CHANNEL

STRAIT OF GEORGIA

PORLIER PASS DRIVE

PARKER I.

CLANTON

②

MONTAGUE
HARBOUR

①

③

④

MONTAGUE

25

6

VILLAGE BAY	RATING: Beginner (2)
GEORGINA POINT	DISTANCE: 12.1 km/7.6 mi
BENNETT BAY	

HIGHLIGHTS: Possible hike up Mount Parke from Village Bay Road
               (ask directions); museum in Miners Bay; Georgina Point
               Lighthouse; Campbell Bay Beach.
TRAFFIC: Expect congestion near ferry terminal.
TERRAIN: Rolling hills, especially on Village Bay Road.
REPAIRS: Bicycle shop in Ganges on Saltspring Island.
SUPPLIES: Store in Miners Bay and before Horton Bay Road turn-
               off.
CONNECTIONS: Tour 7. Ferry from Swartz Bay, Tsawwassen and other
               Gulf Islands.

CHECKPOINTS

km   *(mi)*
0.0   *(0.0)*   START   From the ferry terminal in Village Bay (1), take
                    Village Bay Road uphill past Mariners Way toward Mount
                    Parke (2) ahead.
2.4   *(1.5)*   JUNCTION   Turn left into Miners Bay (3) and then right on
                    Georgina Road. A right on Fernhill leads to the Museum/
                    Gaol (4).
3.3   *(2.1)*   UPHILL   Begin a steep hill climb on Georgina Road and
                    then go down again.
5.1   *(3.2)*   JUNCTION   Go straight ahead onto Waughs Road. A left on
                    Georgina Point Road leads to Georgina Point Lighthouse (5)
                    on Active Pass.
6.8   *(4.2)*   CAUTION   Sharp bend right from Waughs Road onto Camp-
                    bell Bay Road.
7.0   *(4.3)*   INTEREST   Trail goes left downhill to Campbell Bay Beach
                    (6).
9.1   *(5.7)*   JUNCTION   Turn left on Fernhill Road. A right returns to
                    Miners Bay.
10.3 *(6.4)*   JUNCTION   Stay straight ahead past Horton Bay Road. A
                    right leads to a small local park by a wishing well and drink-
                    ing water (7).
12.1 *(7.6)*   FINISH   Fernhill Road becomes Bennett Bay Road which
                    ends at Bennett Bay. Beach access here is limited to a small
                    area (8).

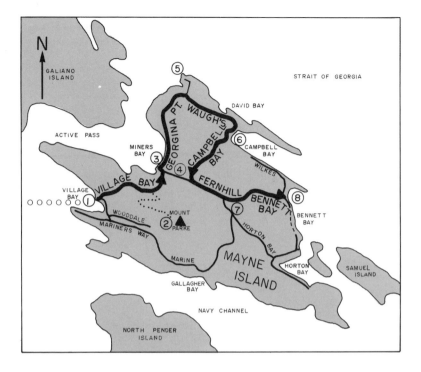

N

GALIANO ISLAND

ACTIVE PASS

STRAIT OF GEORGIA

DAVID BAY

MINERS BAY

CAMPBELL BAY

WILKES

GEORGINA PT.

WAUGH'S

CAMPBELL BAY

FERNHILL

BENNETT BAY

VILLAGE BAY

VILLAGE BAY

WOODDALE

MOUNT PARKE

MARINERS WAY

MARINE

HORTON BAY

MAYNE ISLAND

BENNETT BAY

HORTON BAY

SAMUEL ISLAND

GALLAGHER BAY

NAVY CHANNEL

NORTH PENDER ISLAND

⑤ ⑥ ③ ④ ① ② ⑦ ⑧

7

BENNETT BAY	RATING: Beginner (2 to 4)
GALLAGHER HILL	DISTANCE: 6.4 km/4.0 mi
VILLAGE BAY	

HIGHLIGHTS: Small local park with drinking water, wishing well, wooden swings; excellent views of Pender Island from Gallagher Hill to Village Bay.

TRAFFIC: Expect congestion near ferry terminal.

TERRAIN: Rolling hills with a steep climb over Gallagher Hill.

REPAIRS: Bicycle shop in Ganges on Saltspring Island.

SUPPLIES: One store near park at the start.

CONNECTIONS: Tour 6. Ferry from Swartz Bay, Tsawwassen and other Gulf Islands.

CHECKPOINTS

km   *(mi)*

0.0 *(0.0)* START   From the junction of Horton Bay Road and Fernhill Road (1), take Horton Bay Road to the right if coming from Miners Bay (2).

0.1 *(0.1)* INTEREST   Small local park with wishing well and drinking water (3) left.

0.5 *(0.3)* JUNCTION   Turn right on Gallagher Road. Straight on leads to Horton Bay (4).

0.8 *(0.5)* UPHILL   Begin steep uphill climb over Gallagher hill, staying right.

2.0 *(1.3)* DOWNHILL   Begin winding descent with sharp corners and steepening grade.

2.5 *(1.6)* JUNCTION   Turn right on Marine Drive. Straight on leads down to the water at Gallagher Bay (5). Stay left on Marine Drive ahead.

3.2 *(2.0)* CAUTION   Stay right on Mariner's Way, leaving Marine Drive.

4.6 *(2.9)* DOWNHILL   Gradual descent toward Village Bay. Right on Dalton Way ahead.

5.8 *(3.6)* CAUTION   Sharp bends on Dalton Way. Stay right on Dalton Drive ahead.

6.4 *(4.0)* FINISH   Left enters the Village Bay Ferry Terminal (6).

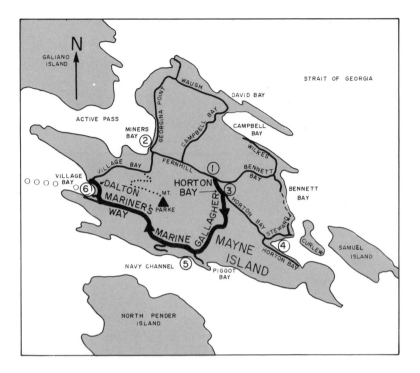

N

GALIANO
ISLAND

STRAIT OF GEORGIA

ACTIVE PASS

WAUGH

DAVID BAY

MINERS
BAY ②

CAMPBELL BAY

CAMPBELL
BAY

GEORGINA POINT

WILKES

VILLAGE BAY

FERNHILL

①

BENNETT
BAY

VILLAGE
BAY ⑥

○ ○ ○ ○ ○

DALTON

MARINER'S
WAY

HORTON
BAY

③

BENNETT
BAY

MT.
PARKE

HORTON BAY

MARINE GALLAGHER

MAYNE
ISLAND

HORTON BAY STEWARD

HORTON BAY

④

CURLEW

SAMUEL
ISLAND

NAVY CHANNEL ⑤

PIGGOT
BAY

NORTH PENDER
ISLAND

**OTTER BAY
NORTH PENDER
CANAL BRIDGE**

RATING: Beginner (2 to 4)
DISTANCE: 12.0 km/7.5 mi

HIGHLIGHTS: Historical markers; water access at Port Washington, Hope Bay, Port Browning and "The Canal"; camping at Prior Park; Pender Island cemetery.

TRAFFIC: Expect congestion near ferry terminal.

TERRAIN: Rolling hills with one large hill after Port Browning.

REPAIRS: Bicycle shop in Ganges on Saltspring Island.

SUPPLIES: Stores in Port Washington, Hope Bay and Port Browning.

CONNECTIONS: Tour 9. Ferry from Swartz Bay and Tsawwassen and other Gulf Islands.

CHECKPOINTS

km *(mi)*

0.0 *(0.0)* START From the ferry terminal in Otter Bay (1), take the main road uphill to connect with MacKinnon Road. Continue right uphill.

0.9 *(0.6)* JUNCTION Turn sharp left on Otter Bay Road. Straight on leads directly to Port Browning. This may be used as a shortcut on the return.

1.7 *(1.1)* INTEREST By the golf course is a historical marker (2) on the right.

2.7 *(1.7)* JUNCTION Turn right on Port Washington Road, going uphill. A left leads downhill steeply into Port Washington (3).

4.4 *(2.8)* DOWNHILL Descend, following Port Washington Road; grade steepens ahead.

5.7 *(3.6)* JUNCTION Turn right on Bedwell Harbour Road. Hope Bay (4) on left.

6.3 *(3.9)* UPHILL Begin uphill on Bedwell Harbour Road, turn sharp left ahead.

6.9 *(4.3)* JUNCTION Go straight on, following Bedwell Harbour Road past the Pender Island cemetery (5). Right on Otter Bay returns to the ferry.

8.4 *(5.2)* DOWNHILL Descend steeply with two sharp bends into Port Browning (6).

9.3 *(5.8)* UPHILL Begin very steep hill past Hamilton Road leading left to beach (7).

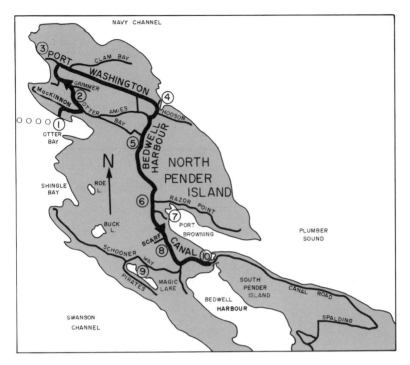

10.0 *(6.3)*   DOWNHILL   By Scarf Road, begin equally steep downhill past Prior Park (8).

11.0 *(6.9)*   JUNCTION   Stay left on Canal Road. A right leads to Magic Lake (9).

11.6 *(7.3)*   CAUTION   Steep descent with wooden plank bridge across "The Canal" ahead.

12.0 *(7.5)*   FINISH   At the hill bottom is a historical marker on the left (10). Cross the wooden bridge ahead for South Pender Island.

9

CANAL BRIDGE	RATING: Beginner (2)
SOUTH PENDER	DISTANCE: 11.8 km/7.4 mi
GOWLLAND POINT	

HIGHLIGHTS: Beach access at Canal Bridge, Bedwell Harbour and Gowlland Point; views and interesting rock formations.
TRAFFIC: Relatively light.
TERRAIN: Rolling hills on Canal and Gowlland Point roads, flat on Spalding Road.
REPAIRS: Bicycle shop in Ganges on Saltspring Island.
SUPPLIES: Store in Bedwell Harbour.
CONNECTIONS: Tour 8.

CHECKPOINTS

km   *(mi)*

0.0   *(0.0)*   START   From the historical marker by Canal Bridge (1), cross the bridge onto South Pender Island and continue along Canal Road.

0.5   *(0.3)*   INTEREST   A dirt road goes left down to picnic area and beach access (2).

2.5   *(1.6)*   INTEREST   Viewpoint to Saturna Island at the top of an abrupt hill (3).

5.4   *(3.4)*   CAUTION   Bend sharply right onto Spalding Road.

8.1   *(5.1)*   CAUTION   Short section of cliffs above Bedwell Harbour ahead.

8.5   *(5.3)*   JUNCTION   Continue straight on, following Gowlland Point Road. A sharp right leads downhill to Bedwell Harbour (4).

9.4   *(5.9)*   INTEREST   Note immense split boulder on right (5). Rolling hills ahead.

10.3   *(6.4)*   DOWNHILL   Begin gradual descent toward Gowlland Point.

11.8   *(7.4)*   FINISH   At the end of the road, stairs lead down to the beach (6).

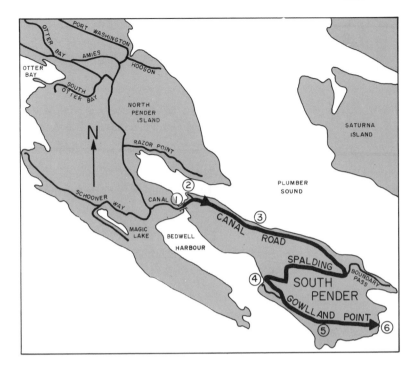

10

LYALL HARBOUR	**RATING:** Intermediate (4 to 5)
ROMAN HILL	
EAST POINT	**DISTANCE:** 14.7 km/9.2 mi

HIGHLIGHTS: Lyall Harbour beach; view from Roman Hill; Winter Cove Park; views of Mount Baker and the U.S.A. from East Point Lighthouse.

TRAFFIC: Heavy only at ferry terminal.

TERRAIN: Two steep hills on either side of Lyall Harbour.

REPAIRS: None on Saturna. Bicycle shop in Ganges on Saltspring Island.

SUPPLIES: Two small stores, one at ferry terminal, other in Lyall Harbour.

CONNECTIONS: Ferry service to Saturna is infrequent; check the schedule carefully.

CHECKPOINTS

km	*(mi)*	
0.0	*(0.0)*	**START** From Saturna Ferry Terminal (1) head uphill on the main road.
1.6	*(1.0)*	**JUNCTION** After the uphill, turn left on East Point Road into Lyall harbour (2). Narvaez Bay Road goes right to a nice viewpoint.
1.8	*(1.1)*	**DOWNHILL** Steep descent to valley and Lyall Harbour.
2.6	*(1.6)*	**JUNCTION** Continue straight on East Point Road. A left on Sunset Boulevard leads to a pebble beach on the harbour.
2.8	*(1.8)*	**UPHILL** Begin steep ascent up Roman Hill. Excellent views of harbour.
3.7	*(2.3)*	**CAUTION** Deceptively safe descent ends with a sharp corner right ahead.
4.8	*(3.0)*	**JUNCTION** Turn right on East Point Road. A left here leads to Winter Cove Park (3) and picnic area.
5.9	*(3.7)*	**INTEREST** East Point Road follows the shore line with many places for gaining beach access. Good views across the water.
14.7	*(9.2)*	**FINISH** East Point Lighthouse (4). Dirt road goes left to beach, but take trail right to sandstone cliffs. Use care around cliffs.

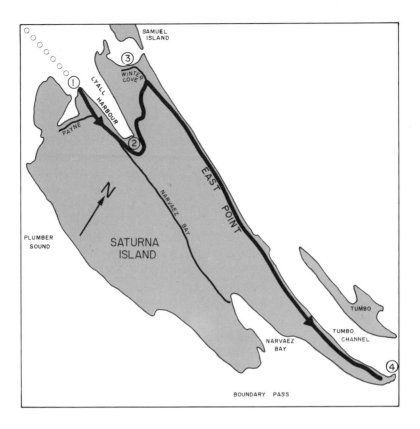

SAMUEL ISLAND

③

WINTER COVE

①

LYALL HARBOUR

PAYNE

②

N

EAST POINT

NARVAEZ BAY

PLUMBER SOUND

SATURNA ISLAND

TUMBO

TUMBO CHANNEL

NARVAEZ BAY

④

BOUNDARY PASS

REGION B   VICTORIA/SAANICH

The Saanich Peninsula is Vancouver Island's most densely populated area. It consists of farmlands, small towns, a major international airport, and the province's capital city of Victoria, located at the peninsula's southernmost tip. The town of Sidney is the site of an American ferry terminal which gives access to the San Juan Islands in Washington State. Many parks, lakes, the world-famous Butchart gardens and a national astronomical observatory are highlights of this area.

Key points of interest in the downtown core are the Parliament buildings and the provincial museum. Victoria's rich history can be discovered by visits to the many historical sites and buildings, including a castle, fort and military college. A naval base and several defence stations are found west of Victoria toward Sooke Basin.

The Trans-Canada Highway, which terminates at St. John's, Newfoundland, originates in Victoria near Beacon Hill Park. From the city it is possible to make a ferry connection to Port Angeles, Washington, and the Olympic Peninsula.

Tour Ratings
All Intermediate except 20, Advanced

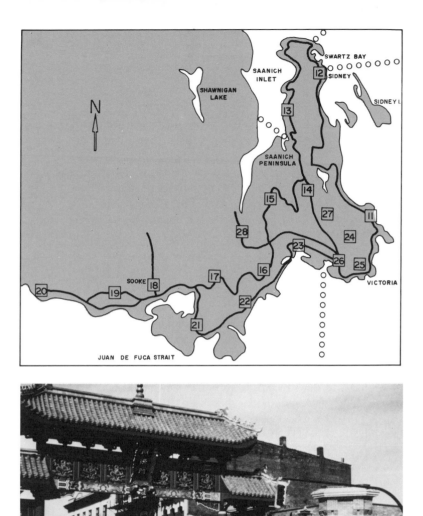

Victoria: Passing through Chinatown in downtown Victoria

11

BEACON HILL PARK	RATING: Intermediate (5)
TELEGRAPH BAY	DISTANCE: 29.3 km/18.3 mi
ELK LAKE	

HIGHLIGHTS: Beacon Hill Park; waterfront parks and viewpoints along scenic shoreline; Sealand Aquarium; Fable Cottage; Douglas and Elk Lake parks.
TRAFFIC: Heavy and slow; route follows well-known scenic drive.
TERRAIN: Rolling hills with a couple of steep spots.
REPAIRS: Many bicycle shops in the Victoria area.
SUPPLIES: Many corner stores and supermarkets along the route.
CONNECTIONS: Tours 12, 14, 24, 25, 26, 27.

CHECKPOINTS

km *(mi)*

0.0 *(0.0)* START From the junction of Douglas, Superior and Southgate streets near the Provincial Museum, continue on Douglas past Beacon Hill Park (1).

1.1 *(0.7)* JUNCTION Turn left on Dallas Road at Mile 0 of the Trans-Canada Highway (2). A right leads to Coast Guard docks (3).

4.0 *(2.5)* CAUTION After Ross Bay stay on the main road along the shoreline. Dallas becomes Hollywood, Cresent and then King George Terrace ahead.

5.4 *(3.4)* UPHILL Head up short steep hill; views of King George.

6.1 *(3.8)* JUNCTION Turn right on Beach Drive. A left leads back toward Victoria.

9.0 *(5.6)* INTEREST Sealand Aquarium on the right (4). Continue into Uplands ahead.

15.5 *(9.7)* JUNCTION After bending onto Telegraph Bay Road, turn left on Arbutus Road. Straight leads to Telegraph Bay (5).

18.2 *(11.4)* JUNCTION Turn right on Gordon Head Road and left on Ferndale to Grandview, which becomes Ash. A left on Gordon Head leads to the University of Victoria (6).

21.6 *(13.5)* INTEREST Douglas Park on the right (7). Continue straight on right, following Cordova Bay Road to Cordova Bay.

26.1 *(16.3)* INTEREST Fable Cottage on the right (8), in Cordova Bay.

26.7 *(16.7)* UPHILL Stay right on Fowler Road and then left on Sayward Road going uphill.

28.6 *(17.9)* CAUTION Go straight across Highway 17 (Swartz Bay Highway) on Sayward. Turn immediate left on Hamsterly and then right on Brookleigh.

29.3 *(18.3)* FINISH Hamsterly Beach at Elk Lake Park (9).

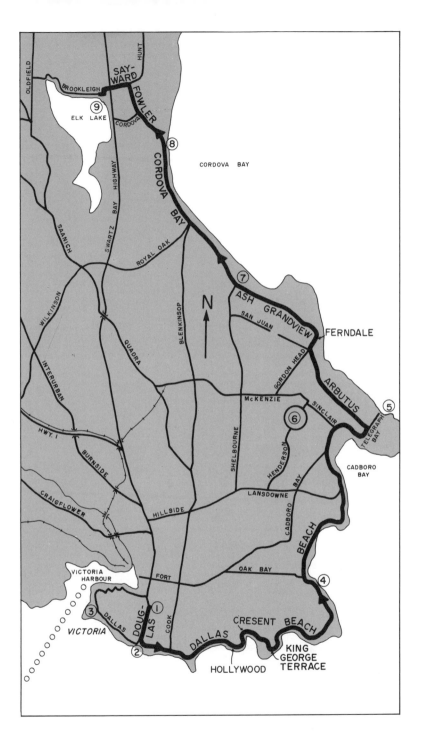

39

12

ELK LAKE SIDNEY SWARTZ BAY

RATING: Intermediate (5)
DISTANCE: 27.7 km/17.3 mi

HIGHLIGHTS: Elk Lake Park; Bazan Bay Park; Butchart Gardens; Maritime Museum; camping at McDonald Park; ferry to San Juan Islands and Anacortes, U.S.A.
TRAFFIC: Heavy on Highway 17 and in Sidney.
TERRAIN: Rolling hills.
REPAIRS: Bicycle shop in Sidney.
SUPPLIES: Stores in Saanichton and Sidney.
CONNECTIONS: Tours 11 & 13. Ferries to Vancouver, Gulf Islands and United States.

CHECKPOINTS

km *(mi)*
0.0 *(0.0)* START   From the entrance to Elk Lake Park (1), continue on Brookleigh Road away from Highway 17 and past the boat launch area.

Mount Baker, seen from southern Vancouver Island

1.6 *(1.0)* CAUTION After a creek crossing, bend sharply left across Bear Hill Road.

1.9 *(1.2)* JUNCTION Turn right on Oldfield Road. A left leads to West Saanich Road (2).

4.7 *(2.9)* JUNCTION Turn right on Keating Cross Road. A left leads to Butchart Gardens (3).

5.7 *(3.6)* JUNCTION Turn left on Central Saanich Road. Straight ahead leads to Highway 17.

6.7 *(4.2)* CAUTION Straight across East Saanich Road, going downhill.

9.1 *(5.7)* JUNCTION Turn right on Mount Newton Cross Road. A left leads to Saanichton Centre (4).

9.6 *(6.0)* CAUTION Cross Highway 17. Turn left on Lochside Drive ahead.

13.9 *(8.7)* INTEREST Bazan Bay Park and beach access on right (5).

17.0 *(10.6)* JUNCTION Turn right on First (Ocean) Avenue past the San Juan Island and Anacortes, U.S.A. Ferry Terminal (6).

17.9 *(11.2)* INTEREST Maritime Museum on Bevan Street (7). Turn left on Beacon ahead.

20.0 *(12.5)* INTEREST Roberts Bay Park (8) on the right, leaving Sidney on Resthaven Road.

25.4 *(15.9)* CAMPING McDonald Park Campground on left (9). Turn right on Swartz Bay Road (Highway 17) ahead.

27.2 *(17.0)* DOWNHILL Over the hill and down to Swartz Bay past Canoe Cove (10).

27.7 *(17.3)* FINISH Swartz Bay Ferry Terminal (11). Catch ferry to Vancouver or any one of five Gulf Islands.

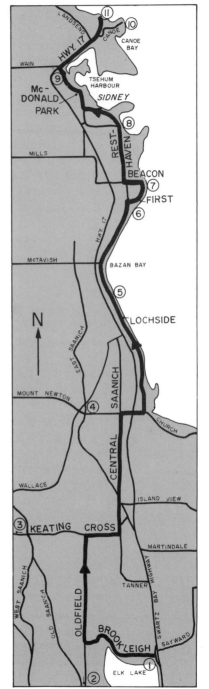

13

SWARTZ BAY	RATING: Intermediate (5)
PATRICIA BAY	DISTANCE: 30.3 km/18.9 mi
BRENTWOOD BAY	

HIGHLIGHTS: Beach access at Landsend, Patricia, Deep and Ardmore beaches; Institute of Oceanographic Sciences; old church and cemeteries.
TRAFFIC: Heavy on West Saanich Road (Highway 17A).
TERRAIN: Rolling hills.
REPAIRS: Bicycle shop in Sidney.
SUPPLIES: Stores in Deep Cove, Patricia Bay and Brentwood.
CONNECTIONS: Tours 12, 14 & 15. Ferry to Mill Bay (Tours 29, 30 & 33).

CHECKPOINTS

km *(mi)*

0.0 *(0.0)* START From the Swartz Bay Ferry Terminal (1), take Highway 17 uphill.

0.9 *(0.6)* JUNCTION After the hilltop, turn right on Landsend Road. Straight ahead on Highway 17 takes you directly to Victoria (2).

5.1 *(3.2)* JUNCTION Go straight on past West Saanich Road. A left leads directly to Patricia Bay and a right gives water access (3).

9.2 *(5.7)* INTEREST Town of Deep Cove (4). Turn right on Madrona Drive, left on Downey.

14.7 *(9.2)* INTEREST Patricia Bay Beach on the right (5), following West Saanich Road.

15.3 *(9.6)* INTEREST Holy Trinity Church on the left by Mills Road (6).

15.9 *(9.9)* INTEREST Airport, left (7) and Oceanography Institute, right (8).

17.2 *(10.7)* JUNCTION Turn right onto Ardmore Drive. Straight ahead on West Saanich Road shortcuts this by-pass.

19.4 *(12.1)* INTEREST Beach access right on Braemar Avenue (9).

28.8 *(18.0)* JUNCTION Turn right on Verdier Avenue after passing Stelly's Cross Road. Continuing straight on West Saanich Road leads to Prospect Lake (10).

30.3 *(18.9)* FINISH At the foot of Verdier is the Brentwood Bay Ferry Terminal (11). Catch the ferry from here to Mill Bay, avoiding Malahat Summit.

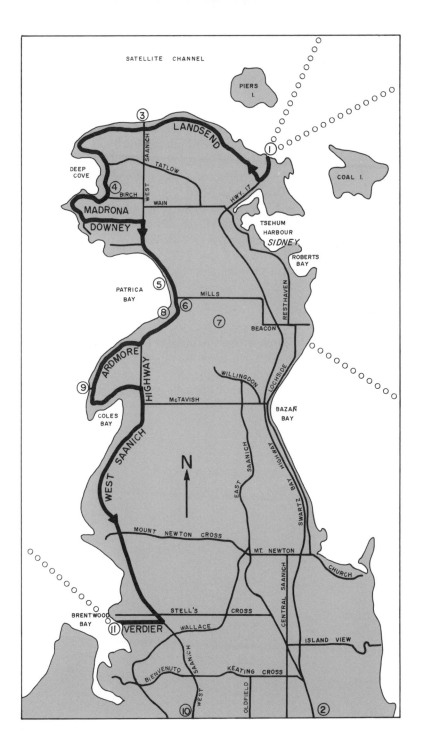

SATELLITE CHANNEL

PIERS I.

COAL I.

③

LANDSEND

SAANICH
TATLOW

DEEP
COVE

④ BIRCH

WEST

WAIN

HWY. 17

MADRONA

DOWNEY

TSEHUM
HARBOUR
SIDNEY

ROBERTS
BAY

RESTHAVEN

PATRICA
BAY

⑤

MILLS

⑧ ⑥

⑦

BEACON

ARDMORE

HIGHWAY

WILLINGDON

LOCHSIDE

⑨

McTAVISH

BAZAN
BAY

COLES
BAY

WEST SAANICH

N

EAST SAANICH

HIGHWAY

SWARTZ BAY

MOUNT NEWTON CROSS

MT. NEWTON

CHURCH

CENTRAL SAANICH

STELL'S CROSS

BRENTWOOD
BAY

⑪ VERDIER

WALLACE

ISLAND VIEW

BIENVENUTO

WEST SAANICH

KEATING CROSS

OLDFIELD

⑩

②

14 BRENTWOOD BAY OBSERVATORY HILL BEACON HILL PARK

RATING: Intermediate (5 to 6)
DISTANCE: 23.0 km/14.4 mi

HIGHLIGHTS: Butchart Gardens; Astrophysical Observatory; Colquitz River Park; Provincial Museum and Thunderbird Park; Beacon Hill Park.

TRAFFIC: Heavy on West Saanich Road, Burnside Avenue and especially Douglas Street.

TERRAIN: Rolling hills, flat on Wallace and Interurban.

REPAIRS: Many bicycle shops in the Victoria area.

SUPPLIES: Many stores along the city route.

CONNECTIONS: Tours 11, 13, 15, 24, 25, 26, 27 & 28. U.S.A. ferry docks in Victoria.

CHECKPOINTS

km *(mi)*

0.0 *(0.0)* START From the ferry terminal at Brentwood Bay (1), take Verdier Road uphill away from the water and turn right on Brentwood (Beach).

1.8 *(1.1)* JUNCTION Turn right on Wallace from Hagan. A left leads to Bazan Bay (2).

2.7 *(1.7)* INTEREST Benvenuto goes right to Butchart Gardens (3). Continue straight on Wallace.

6.7 *(4.2)* CAUTION Wallace merges right into West Saanich Road (Highway 17A).

9.3 *(5.8)* INTEREST A left leads steeply uphill to the top of Observatory Hill (4).

10.4 *(6.5)* JUNCTION Turn right on Goward Road, then left on Interurban Road. Straight ahead on West Saanich Road leads to Royal Oak (5).

11.8 *(7.4)* CAUTION Cross small creek bridge at the bottom of a hill dip.

12.8 *(8.0)* INTEREST Camosun College on the left (6). Rolling hills ahead.

16.2 *(10.1)* INTEREST Cross Marigold Road. Interurban crosses and follows the Colquitz River on the right. Nice local park with trails (7).

17.3 *(10.8)* CAUTION Pass underneath Highway 1. Continue on Burnside Road.

19.2 *(12.0)* CAUTION Pass over railway bridge with park on the right (8).

20.1 *(12.6)* CAUTION Merge into Douglas Street (Highway 1). Avoid Government Steet ahead.

23.0 *(14.4)* FINISH Provincial Museum on the right (9). Beacon Hill Park left (10).

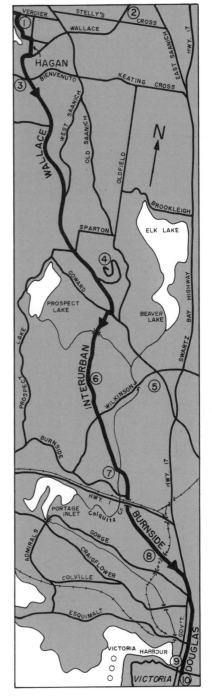

15

BRENTWOOD **PROSPECT LAKE** **MILLSTREAM**	**RATING:** Intermediate (4 to 5) **DISTANCE:** 26.1 km/16.3 mi

HIGHLIGHTS: Several parks and water access at Prospect Lake; parks with hiking trails on Munns Road.
TRAFFIC: Generally light except heavy on West Saanich Road.
TERRAIN: Rolling hills, some steep gravel sections on Munns Road.
REPAIRS: Many bicycle shops in the Victoria area.
SUPPLIES: Stores in Brentwood and Prospect Lake.
CONNECTIONS: Tours 13, 14 & 16.

CHECKPOINTS

km *(mi)*

0.0 *(0.0)* START   From the junction of West Saanich Road and Verdier Avenue (1) in Brentwood, continue on West Saanich Road toward Victoria.

2.3 *(1.4)* JUNCTION   Veer left onto Old Saanich Road into rolling hills. Straight on West Saanich (Highway 17A) goes to Victoria (2).

6.4 *(4.0)* JUNCTION   At the bottom of the hill, turn sharp right onto Sparton Road. Straight on Old Saanich eventually rejoins West Saanich Road.

8.0 *(5.0)* CAUTION   In Prospect Lake (3) go straight on across West Saanich Road following Prospect Lake Road downhill.

8.9 *(5.6)* INTEREST   Lakeside Park on Prospect Lake (4). Stay right.

9.2 *(5.8)* CAUTION   Prospect Lake Road is narrow and hilly for the next 5.3 km.

14.5 *(9.1)* JUNCTION   Turn sharp right on Munns Road by Francis/King Park (5). Straight on Prospect Lake Road leads to Langford and Colwood (6).

19.0 *(11.9)* UPHILL   Begin fairly steep uphill grade for the next 2.3 km.

21.9 *(13.7)* CAUTION   Switchback hills ahead on short uphill section.

22.6 *(14.1)* DOWNHILL   Begin fairly steep downhill grade with some sharp corners.

24.3 *(15.2)* CAUTION   Merge into Millstream Lake Road. Rolling hills ahead.

25.3 *(15.8)* CAUTION   Merge into Millstream Road. Relatively flat through here.

26.1 *(16.3)* FINISH   At the junction with Finlayson Arm Road (7). Millstream Road continues to Langford/Colwood area.

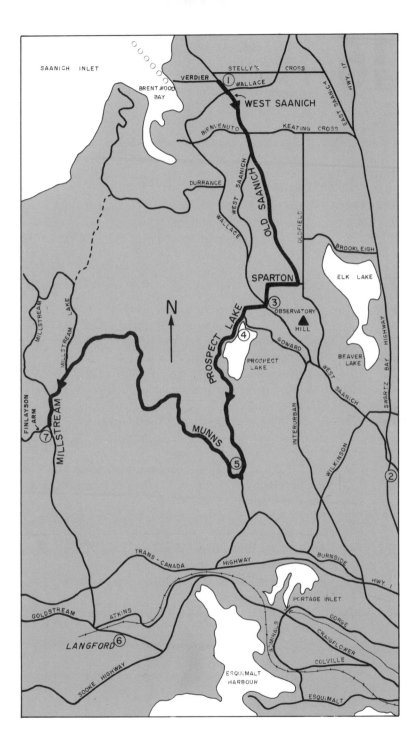

SAANICH INLET

BRENTWOOD
BAY

VERDIER
STELLY'S   CROSS

① WALLACE

WEST SAANICH

BIENVENUTO   KEATING CROSS

DURRANCE

WEST SAANICH

WALLACE

OLD SAANICH

OLDFIELD

BROOKLEIGH

SPARTON

ELK LAKE

③ OBSERVATORY

N

HILL

PROSPECT LAKE

④

GOWARD

PROSPECT
LAKE

BEAVER
LAKE

MILLSTREAM

MILLSTREAM LAKE

MILLSTREAM

WEST SAANICH

SWARTZ BAY HIGHWAY

MUNNS

INTERURBAN

FINLAYSON
ARM

⑦

⑤

WILKINSON

②

TRANS - CANADA   HIGHWAY

BURNSIDE

HWY. I

GOLDSTREAM

ATKINS

PORTAGE INLET

GORGE

ADMIRALS

CRAIGFLOWER

LANGFORD ⑥

COLVILLE

SOOKE HIGHWAY

ESQUIMALT
HARBOUR

ESQUIMALT

47

16

MILLSTREAM LANGFORD/ COLWOOD HAPPY VALLEY

RATING: Intermediate (5 to 6)
DISTANCE: 16.4 km/10.3 mi

HIGHLIGHTS:	Royal Roads Military College in Hatley Park; farmlands along Latoria and in Happy Valley.
TRAFFIC:	Heavy on Millstream, Goldstream and Sooke roads (Highways 1A and 14).
TERRAIN:	Rolling hills.
REPAIRS:	Many bicycle shops in the Victoria area.
SUPPLIES:	Stores in Langford, Colwood and Happy Valley.
CONNECTIONS:	Tours 15, 17, 23 & 28.

CHECKPOINTS

km *(mi)*

0.0 *(0.0)* START From the junction of Millstream Road and Finlayson Arm Road (1) in Millstream, take Millstream Road straight toward Highway 1.

2.8 *(1.7)* CAUTION Small creek bridge over Mill Stream.

4.9 *(3.0)* CAUTION Continue straight across Highway 1, following Millstream Road.

6.1 *(3.8)* CAUTION Cross railway tracks and then stay left, following Goldstream Avenue through Langford and Colwood area (2).

8.0 *(5.0)* JUNCTION Turn right on Sooke Road (Highway 14). A left on Island Highway (Highway 1A) leads to Esquimalt (3) and then into Victoria.

8.7 *(5.4)* INTEREST Cross railway tracks; Royal Roads College is on the left (4).

10.2 *(6.4)* JUNCTION Turn left on Metchosin Road. Straight ahead leads to Sooke (5).

11.1 *(6.9)* JUNCTION Turn right on Wishart Road. Straight ahead leads to Metchosin (6).

13.3 *(8.3)* DOWNHILL Drop down on Wishart and then turn right on Latoria Road.

16.4 *(10.3)* FINISH At Happy Valley Road and Latoria Road in Happy Valley (7).

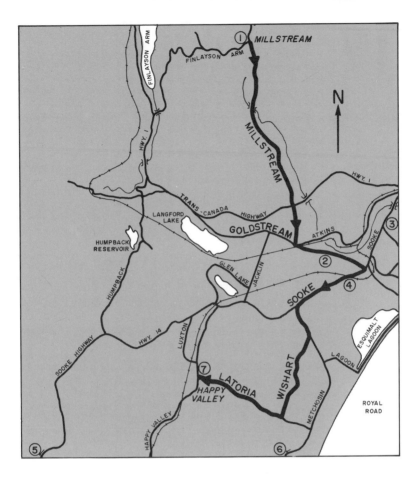

17

HAPPY VALLEY	RATING: Intermediate (5)
METCHOSIN	DISTANCE: 13.9 km/8.7 mi
HUTCHINSON COVE	

HIGHLIGHTS: Farmlands through Happy Valley; views from Mount Blinkhorn.
TRAFFIC: Heavy on Highway 14.
TERRAIN: Rolling hills.
REPAIRS: Many bicycle shops in the Victoria area.
SUPPLIES: Stores in Happy Valley and Metchosin.
CONNECTIONS: Tours 16, 18, 21 & 22.

CHECKPOINTS

km *(mi)*

0.0 *(0.0)* START From the junction of Happy Valley Road and Latoria Road (1) in Happy Valley, take Happy Valley Road left away from Highway 14.

0.5 *(0.3)* CAUTION Veer right across wooden bridge over Bilston Creek.

0.9 *(0.6)* CAUTION Cross railway tracks; second set further ahead.

4.7 *(2.9)* JUNCTION Turn right on Rocky Point Road. Metchosin is straight ahead (2).

5.8 *(3.6)* JUNCTION Turn right on Kangaroo Road. Straight ahead leads to Matheson Lake Park (3) near Rocky Point and Becher Bay.

8.0 *(5.0)* UPHILL Begin gradual ascent for 1.0 km over Mount Blinkhorn.

9.6 *(6.0)* INTEREST Blinkhorn Lake on the right (4), not easily reached.

11.0 *(6.9)* JUNCTION Cross bridge over Veitch Creek and turn left on Highway 14. A right leads to Glen Lake (5) near Langford/Colwood.

12.4 *(7.7)* CAUTION Cross bridge over Impala Creek. Rolling hills down ahead.

13.9 *(8.7)* FINISH At the corner of Gillespie Road and Highway 14 (6). A left leads to East Sooke Regional Park and Sooke lies straight on.

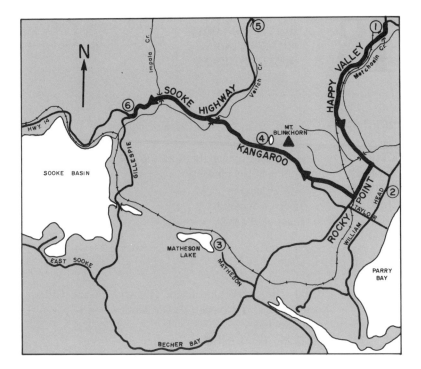

N

HWY. 14
SOOKE BASIN
EAST SOOKE
BECHER BAY

SOOKE HIGHWAY
Impala Cr.
Veitch Cr.
GILLESPIE
MATHESON LAKE
MATHESON
KANGAROO
MT. BLINKHORN
ROCKY POINT
TAYLOR HEAD
WILLIAM
PARRY BAY
HAPPY VALLEY
Merchosin Cr.

① ② ③ ④ ⑤ ⑥

18

HUTCHINSON COVE MILNE'S LANDING SOOKE POTHOLES PARK	RATING: Intermediate (5) DISTANCE: 12.7 km/7.9 mi

HIGHLIGHTS: Views of Sooke Basin along Highway 14; swimming at Potholes Park.

TRAFFIC: Heavy on Highway 14 (Sooke Road).

TERRAIN: Rolling hills with some flat sections.

REPAIRS: Bicycle shop in Sooke.

SUPPLIES: Stores in Sooke.

CONNECTIONS: Tours 17, 19 & 21.

CHECKPOINTS

km *(mi)*

0.0 *(0.0)* START From the junction of Highway 14 and Gillespie Road (1) near Hutchinson Cove, continue on Highway 14 toward Sooke.

3.1 *(1.9)* CAUTION Cross railway tracks and enter Cooper Cove and Saseenos (2).

4.0 *(2.5)* CAUTION Bridge over Ayum Creek. Relatively flat ahead.

6.1 *(3.8)* UPHILL Begin a fairly steep uphill stretch for next 1.0 km.

7.1 *(4.4)* JUNCTION At the hilltop, turn right on Sooke River Road. Straight on leads to Sooke (3) and eventually to Port Renfrew.

9.4 *(5.9)* DOWNHILL Descend gently, past two old railway crossings.

10.6 *(6.6)* CAUTION Cross bridge over Charters River.

11.9 *(7.4)* INTEREST Entering Sooke Potholes Park (4), continue straight ahead.

12.6 *(7.8)* CAUTION Cross bridge over Todd Creek.

12.7 *(7.9)* FINISH Road ends at a gated dirt road. The potholes and falls are a short hike along the road (5).

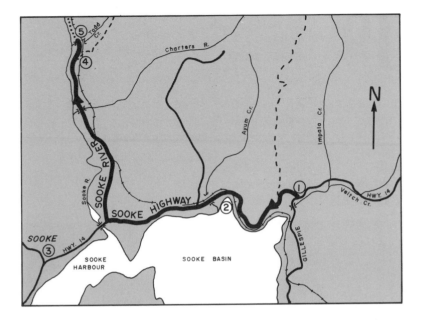

N

Charters R.

Ayum Cr.

Impala Cr.

Todd Cr.

Sooke R.

SOOKE RIVER

SOOKE HIGHWAY

Veitch Cr.

HWY. 14

GILLESPIE

SOOKE

HWY. 14

SOOKE
HARBOUR

SOOKE BASIN

⑤ ④ ① ② ③

19

| MILNE'S LANDING SOOKE OTTER POINT | **RATING:** Intermediate (2 to 5) **DISTANCE:** 14.6 km/9.1 mi |

HIGHLIGHTS: Water access at Sooke and Orveas Bay near Otter Point; good views from Otter Point Road.

TRAFFIC: Heavy on Highway 14 and near Sooke.

TERRAIN: Rolling hills with some fairly steep uphill sections.

REPAIRS: Bicycle shop in Sooke.

SUPPLIES: Stores in Sooke.

CONNECTIONS: Tours 18 & 20.

A great blue heron suns on a log boom near the Sooke Basin.

CHECKPOINTS

km *(mi)*

0.0 *(0.0)* START From the junction of Sooke River Road and Highway 14 (1), take Highway 14 across the Sooke River Bridge away from Milne's Landing.

0.6 *(0.4)* UPHILL Begin steady and steep ascent into Sooke (2) for next 1.0 km.

2.1 *(1.3)* JUNCTION Turn right on Otter Point Road in the centre of Sooke. Straight on Highway 14 also leads to Otter Point.

2.3 *(1.4)* UPHILL Begin long and steady rise out of Sooke into rolling hills.

7.3 *(4.6)* CAUTION Cross private industrial road near Young Lake (3).

9.3 *(5.8)* INTEREST Otter Point townsite (4) at Kemp Lake Road. Go straight on.

9.7 *(6.1)* DOWNHILL Descent for 1.6 km becomes steep near the end.

11.9 *(7.4)* DOWNHILL After a small rise, begin downhill again. Good views.

14.6 *(9.1)* FINISH At the hill bottom, you reach Highway 14 on Orveas Bay with good beach access (5). Right for Port Renfrew; left for return to Sooke.

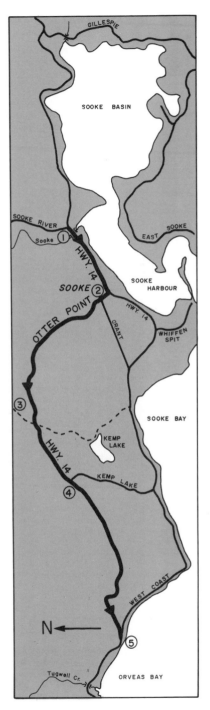

20

SOOKE	RATING: Advanced (8)
OTTER POINT	DISTANCE: 22.4 km/14.0 mi
FRENCH BEACH	

HIGHLIGHTS: Beach access at Whiffin Spit, Otter Point, Orveas Bay and French Beach; good views across Juan de Fuca Strait to U.S.A.

TRAFFIC: Heavy on Highway 14 (West Coast Road) between Sooke and Otter Point.

TERRAIN: Steep hills and sharp corners after Otter Point.

REPAIRS: Bicycle shop in Sooke.

SUPPLIES: Stores in Sooke.

CONNECTIONS: Tour 19.

Whitetail deer frequent logged-off areas near the road.

CHECKPOINTS

km *(mi)*

0.0 *(0.0)* START From the junction of Otter Point Road and Sooke Road (Highway 14) in Sooke (1), take Highway 14 (West Coast Road) downhill.

1.2 *(0.7)* UPHILL Begin uphill climb past Whiffin Spit Road. A left leads down to Whiffin Spit (2).

3.2 *(2.0)* DOWNHILL Pass Grant and Ella roads going downhill to follow the shoreline.

4.2 *(2.6)* CAUTION Cross private industrial road by a camp. Beach access (3) ahead.

6.9 *(4.3)* JUNCTION Stay left, avoiding Kemp Lake Road going uphill to Kemp Lake (4).

9.2 *(5.7)* INTEREST Road bends right past Otter Point on the left (5).

12.1 *(7.6)* INTEREST Pass Otter Point Road; plenty of beach access on left (6).

12.4 *(7.8)* CAUTION Bridge over Tugwell Creek; uphill on the other side.

13.8 *(8.6)* CAUTION Bridge over Muir Creek; uphill on far side with a sharp bend.

17.5 *(10.9)* DOWNHILL Steep descent with some twisting corners.

18.3 *(11.4)* CAUTION Bridge over Kirby Creek; uphill ahead, steep at beginning.

22.1 *(13.8)* JUNCTION Turn left on Woodhaven Road. Straight ahead leads to Port Renfrew (7).

22.4 *(14.0)* FINISH French Beach Park (8). Camping and trail to beach access.

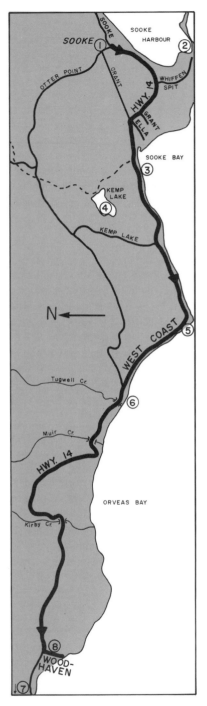

21

HUTCHINSON COVE	RATING: Intermediate (5)
ANDERSON COVE	DISTANCE: 10.0 km/6.3 mi
BECHER BAY	

HIGHLIGHTS: Veitch Falls; Roche Cove; Anderson Cove Picnic Area; Old Faultless, historical farm and petroglyphs at East Sooke Park and Becher Bay.

TRAFFIC: Heavy in summer.

TERRAIN: Rolling hills and relatively flat.

REPAIRS: Bicycle shop in Sooke and in the Victoria area.

SUPPLIES: Stores in Sooke and Metchosin.

CONNECTIONS: Tour 17, 18 & 22.

CHECKPOINTS

km *(mi)*

0.0 *(0.0)* START   From the junction of Gillespie Road and Highway 14 (1) near Hutchinson Cove, take Gillespie Road downhill.

0.5 *(0.3)* CAUTION   Cross bridge over Veitch Creek with waterfall on left (2).

1.2 *(0.7)* UPHILL   Bend sharp left and go up a short steep hill.

2.1 *(1.3)* DOWNHILL   Bend right going downhill past the "Grouse Nest" (private home).

2.9 *(1.8)* CAUTION   Pass underneath a railway trestle. More downhill ahead.

3.3 *(2.1)* INTEREST   Cross wooden bridge over Roche Cove. Water access here (3).

6.0 *(3.8)* JUNCTION   After rolling hills, turn left on East Sooke Road. A right leads to Anderson Cove picnic area (4).

8.0 *(5.0)* JUNCTION   Turn right on Becher Bay Road. Straight ahead leads to Matheson Lake Park (5) near Rocky Point.

9.7 *(6.1)* INTEREST   Enter East Sooke Park (6). Many hiking trails, no camping.

10.0 *(6.3)* FINISH   Historical farm and old shipwreck (7) at end of trail that leaves from the parking lot. Explore for petroglyphs.

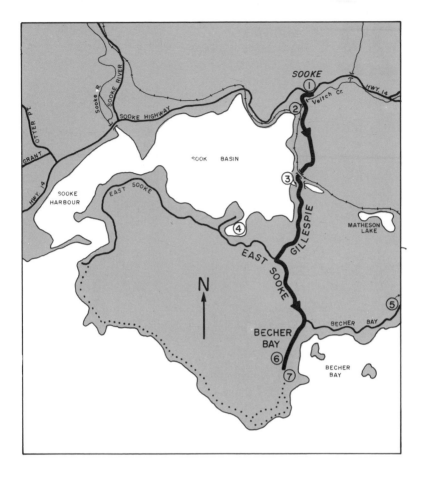

22

BECHER BAY	RATING: Intermediate (5)
MATHESON LAKE	DISTANCE: 12.4 km/7.8 mi
METCHOSIN	
LAGOON	

HIGHLIGHTS:	Many viewpoints on East Sooke Road; camping at Matheson Lake; beach access at the foot of Taylor Road and at Witty's (Metchosin) Lagoon Park.
TRAFFIC:	Heavy in summer.
TERRAIN:	Rolling hills.
REPAIRS:	Bicycle shops in the Victoria area.
SUPPLIES:	Stores in Metchosin.
CONNECTIONS:	Tours 17, 21 & 23.

CHECKPOINTS

km	(mi)	
0.0	*(0.0)*	START From the junction of East Sooke Road and Becher Bay Road (1), continue on East Sooke Road toward Metchosin.
1.6	*(1.0)*	INTEREST Viewpoint on the right (2). Rolling hills ahead.
2.3	*(1.4)*	INTEREST Entering Becher Bay Indian Reserve (3).
2.6	*(1.6)*	INTEREST Hilltop viewpoint on right (4). Rolling hills ahead.
4.9	*(3.1)*	JUNCTION Turn left on Rocky Point Road. A right leads to a naval base (5).
5.2	*(3.3)*	CAMPING Matheson Lake Road goes left to Matheson Park (6). Limited camping available. Cross old railway ahead on Rocky Point Road.
9.0	*(5.6)*	JUNCTION Turn right on Taylor Road. Straight ahead leads to Happy Valley Road (7).
9.7	*(6.1)*	JUNCTION Turn left on William Head Road. Continue straight ahead for beach access (8).
11.1	*(6.9)*	INTEREST Go straight on, following Metchosin Road, past Happy Valley Road. This intersection is the centre of Metchosin (9).
12.0	*(7.5)*	CAUTION Bridge over Metchosin Creek.
12.4	*(7.8)*	FINISH Witty's Lagoon Park and Metchosin Lagoon on right (10).

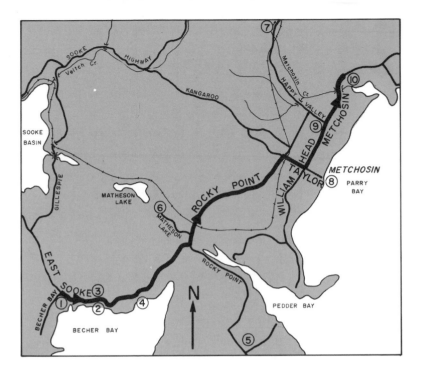

23

| METCHOSIN LAGOON ESQUIMALT LAGOON ESQUIMALT HARBOUR | RATING: Intermediate (4 to 5) DISTANCE: 14.8 km/9.3 mi |

HIGHLIGHTS: Esquimalt Lagoon and Coburg Peninsula; Royal Roads Military College; Fort Rodd Hill Historical Park; Craigflower Manor.
TRAFFIC: Heavy on Highway 1A (Island Highway).
TERRAIN: Rolling hills with steep hill down to the lagoon and up again.
REPAIRS: Many bicycle shops in the Victoria area.
SUPPLIES: Many stores along this city route.
CONNECTIONS: Tours 16, 22, 24, 26 & 28.

CHECKPOINTS

km *(mi)*

0.0 *(0.0)* START From Witty's Lagoon Park by Metchosin Lagoon (1), continue on Metchosin Road toward Victoria. Rolling hills ahead.

2.6 *(1.6)* UPHILL Pass Duke Road and go uphill steeply for 0.6 km.

5.4 *(3.4)* JUNCTION Turn right on Lagoon Road and go downhill steeply. Straight ahead on Metchosin Road leads into Langford/Colwood area (2).

6.4 *(4.0)* INTEREST Turn left at hill bottom and follow Lagoon Road along Coburg Peninsula, past Esquimalt Lagoon (3).

8.2 *(5.1)* CAUTION Cross bridge over the lagoon heading uphill past Royal Roads (4).

8.9 *(5.6)* INTEREST Fort Rodd Hill National Historical Site on the right (5).

11.0 *(6.9)* JUNCTION At the hilltop, turn right on Old Island Highway for Victoria. A left leads back through Langford/Colwood toward Sooke (6).

12.5 *(7.8)* CAUTION Bridge over Mill Stream and Parson's Inlet.

13.2 *(8.3)* CAUTION Stay right on Highway 1A (Island Highway). Do not enter Highway 1.

14.2 *(8.9)* CAUTION After rolling hills, pass under railway trestle in View Royal (7).

14.8 *(9.3)* FINISH At the junction of Island Highway and Admirals Road. Craigflower Manor on corner (8). Straight ahead leads into Victoria.

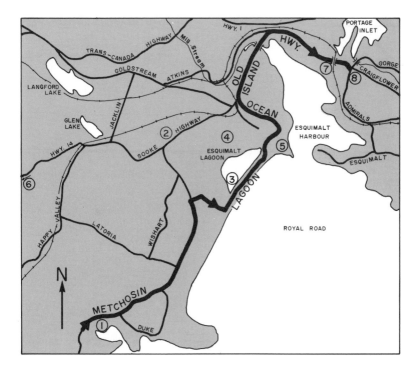

63

24

ESQUIMALT HARBOUR GOVERNMENT HOUSE MOUNT DOUGLAS PARK

RATING: Intermediate (4 to 5)
DISTANCE: 20.5 km/12.8 mi

HIGHLIGHTS: Esquimalt Harbour shipyards; many points of interest in the core of Victoria; Government House; Craigdarroch Castle; Mount Douglas Park.
TRAFFIC: Heavy in Victoria and on Cedar Hill Road.
TERRAIN: Rolling hills, final steep hill up to Mount Douglas.
REPAIRS: Many bicycle shops in the Victoria area.
SUPPLIES: Many stores along the city route.
CONNECTIONS: Tours 11, 14, 23, 25 & 26.

CHECKPOINTS

km	(mi)	
0.0	*(0.0)*	START From the junction of Admirals Road and Craigflower Road (1), take Admirals toward Esquimalt. Craigflower Manor on corner.
1.9	*(1.2)*	CAUTION Cross railway tracks. Navy shipyards on the right (2).
3.1	*(1.9)*	INTEREST Cross Fraser Street following Lyall Street. A right leads to Saxe Point (3).
4.4	*(2.8)*	INTEREST Work Point Barracks (4). Turn left on Head Road, uphill ahead.
5.3	*(3.3)*	CAUTION Turn sharp right on Old Esquimalt Road. Railway tracks ahead.
7.7	*(4.8)*	CAUTION Continue on Esquimalt Road; pass beneath a railway trestle. Cross Johnson Street Bridge and turn right on Wharf Street.
8.3	*(5.2)*	INTEREST Bastion Square on the left (5). Turn left on Courtney Street.
9.3	*(5.8)*	INTEREST Christ Church Cathedral (6). Follow Rockland Avenue.
10.6	*(6.6)*	INTEREST Government House on the right (7). Turn left on Joan Crescent.
10.8	*(6.7)*	INTEREST Craigdarroch Castle on the left (8). Follow Joan Crescent to Fort Street. Walk bikes across and continue on Fernwood Road.

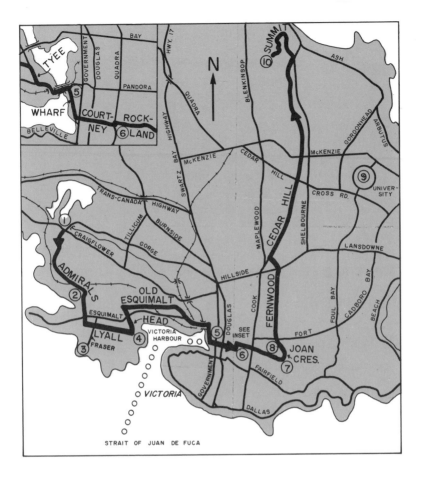

12.8 *(8.0)*   CAUTION   Fernwood Road merges into Cedar Hill Road and crosses Hillside Avenue.

13.3 *(8.3)*   CAUTION   Bend right with Cedar Hill. Rolling hills ahead.

18.9 *(11.8)*   JUNCTION   Cedar Hill Road ends at Shelbourne Street; turn left. A right leads back to Victoria Centre or to University of Victoria (9).

19.0 *(11.9)*   UPHILL   Turn left to enter Mount Douglas Park and begin a steep hill climb.

20.5 *(12.8)*   FINISH   At top of hill is Mount Douglas Lookout (10) and view of Victoria.

25

MOUNT DOUGLAS PARK **MOUNT TOLMIE LOOKOUT** **DENNISON LOOKOUT**	**RATING:** Intermediate (4 to 5) **DISTANCE:** 13.0 km/8.1 mi

HIGHLIGHTS: Mount Douglas Park; University of Victoria; Mount Tolmie Lookout; weather station and observatory; Dennison Lookout (Gonzales Hill).

TRAFFIC: Heavy on Richmond Avenue.

TERRAIN: Rolling hills with steep hill climbs up Mount Tolmie and Gonzales Hill.

REPAIRS: Many bicycle shops in the Victoria area.

SUPPLIES: Many stores along the city route.

CONNECTIONS: Tours 11, 14, 24 & 26.

CHECKPOINTS

km *(mi)*

0.0 *(0.0)* **START** From the junction of Cordova Bay Road and Ash Road in Mount Douglas Park (1), take Shelbourne Road uphill away from the park.

1.4 *(0.9)* **JUNCTION** Turn left on San Juan Avenue. Straight ahead leads to Victoria (2).

2.4 *(1.5)* **CAUTION** After crossing Torquay, continue on a footpath to San Juan again.

3.7 *(2.3)* **JUNCTION** Turn right on Gordon Head Road. A left returns to Mount Douglas.

5.2 *(3.2)* **INTEREST** Cross McKenzie Avenue with the University of Victoria on left (3).

6.1 *(3.8)* **JUNCTION** Turn right on Cedar Hill Cross Road and then left on Mayfair Road going uphill steeply. A left leads to the University of Victoria.

6.9 *(4.3)* **INTEREST** Mount Tolmie Lookout at the top of the hill (4).

7.0 *(4.4)* **DOWNHILL** Descend steeply from Mount Tolmie. Turn left on Richmond Avenue.

11.8 *(7.4)* **JUNCTION** Turn left on Fairfield Road. A right leads to Beacon Hill Park (5).

12.4 *(7.7)* **JUNCTION** Turn right on Dennison Road. Straight ahead leads to Beach Drive.

12.6 *(7.9)* **INTEREST** Weather Station on the right (6). Continue on Dennison.

13.0 *(8.1)* **FINISH** Dennison Lookout (7). Park, views and historical marker.

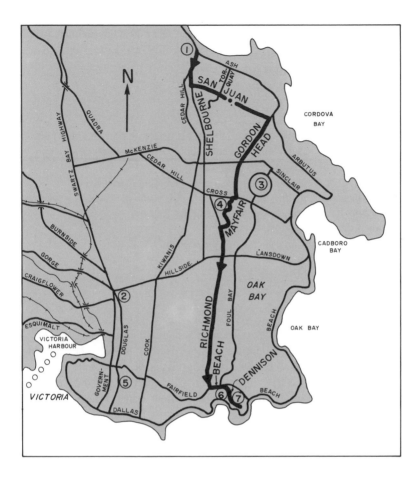

N

① ASH
TOR-
QUAY
SAN JUAN
CEDAR HILL
SHELBOURNE
GORDON HEAD
CORDOVA
BAY
SWARTZ BAY HIGHWAY
QUADRA
McKENZIE
CEDAR HILL
ARBUTUS
SINCLAIR
③
CROSS
④
MAYFAIR
CADBORO
BAY
BURNSIDE
KIWANIS
HILLSIDE
LANSDOWN
GORGE
OAK BAY
CRAIGFLOWER
②
RICHMOND BEACH
FOUL BAY
BEACH
OAK BAY
ESQUIMALT
DOUGLAS
COOK
VICTORIA HARBOUR
DENNISON
GOVERN-MENT
⑤
FAIRFIELD
BEACH
VICTORIA
DALLAS
⑥ ⑦

26

DENNISON LOOKOUT	RATING: Intermediate (5)
PARLIAMENT	DISTANCE: 15.3 km/9.6 mi
BUILDINGS	
THE GORGE	

HIGHLIGHTS: Weather station tours, historical marker and viewpoint at Dennison Lookout; many points of interest in the core of Victoria; Craigflower Manor.
TRAFFIC: Heavy on Government Street and Gorge Road.
TERRAIN: Rolling hills.
REPAIRS: Many bicycle shops in the Victoria area.
SUPPLIES: Many stores along the city route.
CONNECTIONS: Tours 11, 14, 24, 25 & 27.

CHECKPOINTS

km	(mi)		
0.0	*(0.0)*	START	From the junction of Beach Drive and King George Terrace (1), take Beach left and uphill away from the water.
0.7	*(0.4)*	INTEREST	Dennison Lookout on the left (2). Continue straight on Fairfield Road past Foul Bay Road.
3.5	*(2.2)*	JUNCTION	Turn left on Cook Street and then right on Southgate Street. A right on Cook leads to the Victoria Art Gallery (3).
4.4	*(2.7)*	INTEREST	Go straight across Douglas and Government streets, following Superior Road past Beacon Hill Park (4) and "The Bird Cages" (5).
7.8	*(4.9)*	JUNCTION	Turn left on Government Street. Continuing straight on Dallas Road returns you to the starting point at Beach Drive.
8.5	*(5.3)*	INTEREST	Follow Government across Belville Street past the Provincial Museum (6), Wax Museum and Undersea Gardens (7), and the Empress Hotel (8).
8.7	*(5.4)*	INTEREST	Tourist Information on left (9). Continue on Government through Victoria and past Bastion Square (10) and Chinatown (11).
10.5	*(6.6)*	JUNCTION	Veer left onto Gorge Road at a major intersection. Highway 1 continues straight ahead as Douglas Road.
13.2	*(8.3)*	INTEREST	Go straight on Gorge Road. Anne Hathaway's Cottage is left on Tillicum Road across the bridge (12).
14.9	*(9.3)*	CAUTION	Turn left on Admirals Road across the bridge.
15.3	*(9.6)*	FINISH	At the junction of Admirals and Craigflower roads. Craigflower Manor and historical site on the right (13).

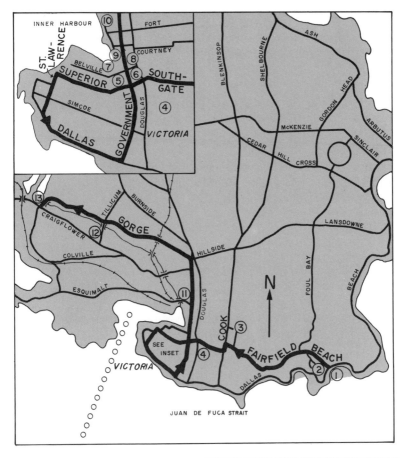

Cycling past the Parliament Buildings in Victoria

27

THE GORGE	RATING: Intermediate (5)
ROYAL OAK	DISTANCE: 18.7 km/11.7 mi
SWAN LAKE	

HIGHLIGHTS: Farmlands along Blenkinsop Road; Swan Lake Nature House and trails.
TRAFFIC: Heavy on Saanich Road and near Highway 17.
TERRAIN: Rolling hills.
REPAIRS: Many bicycle shops in the Victoria area.
SUPPLIES: Many stores along the city route.
CONNECTIONS: Tours 11, 14, 26 & 28.

CHECKPOINTS

km *(mi)*

0.0 *(0.0)* START From the junction of Harriet Road and Gorge Road near The Gorge (1), follow Harriet Road right and uphill away from the water.

1.4 *(0.9)* CAUTION Cross bridge over railway and cross Douglas Street onto Saanich Road.

1.7 *(1.1)* CAUTION Cross Highway 17 in two parts: Blanshard Street and Vernon Road, uphill.

1.9 *(1.2)* JUNCTION Stay right on Tattersall Drive. A left leads to Swan Lake (2).

3.7 *(2.2)* JUNCTION Turn left on Blenkinsop Road. A right leads back to Victoria (3).

8.5 *(5.3)* JUNCTION Turn sharp left onto Royal Oak Drive. A right on Cordova Bay Road leads to Mount Douglas Park (4); straight to Cordova Bay (5).

11.0 *(6.9)* CAUTION Cross overpass above Swartz Bay Highway (Highway 17).

11.7 *(7.3)* JUNCTION Cross West Saanich Road onto Wilkinson Road. A right leads to Brentwood (6) and a left leads to Victoria.

12.5 *(7.8)* CAUTION Cross bridge over Colquitz River. Rolling hills.

13.2 *(8.2)* JUNCTION Turn left on Carey Road and cross bridge over Colquitz River. Straight ahead leads to Portage Inlet (7).

16.0 *(10.0)* CAUTION At a confusing intersection merging with Glanford Road, turn left, across traffic, onto Ralph Road. Downhill to Swan Creek.

16.7 *(10.4)* CAUTION Straight on across Swartz Bay Highway (Highway 17) once more.

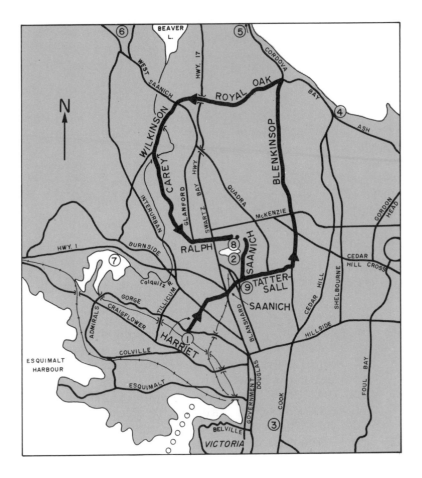

17.0 *(10.6)* INTEREST   Swan Lake Nature House on the right (8). Take the trail ahead.

17.5 *(10.9)* CAUTION   Trail ends at Saanich Road. Turn right to return to start.

17.9 *(11.2)* CAUTION   Cross railway tracks at the bottom of a small hill.

18.7 *(11.7)* FINISH   Back at the corner of Tattersall Drive and Saanich Road (9). Stay right to retrace steps to the starting point.

28

**PORTAGE INLET
GLEN LAKE
GOLDSTREAM**

RATING: Intermediate (4 to 6)
DISTANCE: 23.8 km/14.9 mi

HIGHLIGHTS: Water access at Glen Lake; water pipeline from Humpback Reservoir; camping at Goldstream Park.
TRAFFIC: Heavy near Highway 1 and on Highway 14.
TERRAIN: Rolling hills, fairly steep around Humpback Reservoir.
REPAIRS: Many bicycle shops in the Victoria area.
SUPPLIES: Stores in Langford/Colwood and at Goldstream.
CONNECTIONS: Tours 14, 16, 23, 27 & 29.

CHECKPOINTS

km *(mi)*

0.0 *(0.0)* START   From the junction of Wilkinson Road and Carey Road (1), go straight on Wilkinson and cross Interurban Road ahead.

2.5 *(1.6)* JUNCTION   Turn right on Burnside Road. A left leads into Victoria (2).

4.8 *(3.0)* JUNCTION   Go straight, past Prospect Lake Road. A right leads toward Brentwood Bay (3).

6.7 *(4.2)* CAUTION   After crossing a bridge over a railway, merge right onto Highway 1 and then take the immediate exit right toward Colwood.

7.1 *(4.4)* JUNCTION   Turn right on Atkins Avenue after passing underneath Highway 1 and a railway trestle. Straight ahead leads to Colwood (4).

7.2 *(4.5)* CAUTION   Cross railroad tracks and turn left, following Atkins.

8.0 *(5.0)* CAUTION   At Chilco, cross the railway again and continue on Atkins. Cross two more separate sets of railroad tracks ahead.

11.3 *(7.1)* CAUTION   At Millstream Road, turn left across the railway and immediately turn right on Station Avenue to parallel the tracks.

13.0 *(8.1)* INTEREST   Turn right onto Jenkins Avenue from Jacklin Road to circle around Glen Lake (5) on Glen Lake Road.

15.5 *(9.7)* JUNCTION   Turn right on Highway 14 (Sooke Road). A left leads to Colwood.

19.0 *(11.9)* JUNCTION   Turn right on Humpback Road. Straight ahead leads to Sooke (6).

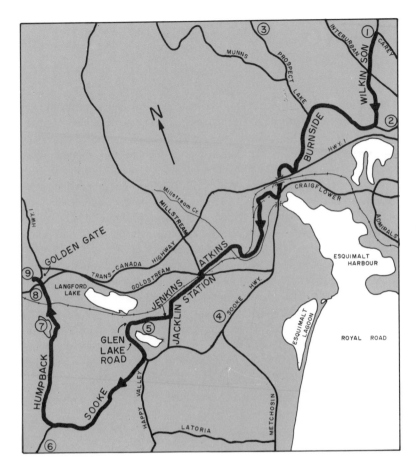

22.0 *(13.8)* INTEREST   Dam at Humpback Reservoir (7). Stay left ahead.

23.0 *(14.4)* CAUTION   Cross railway to enter Goldstream (8). Straight ahead leads to Goldengate.

23.8 *(14.9)* FINISH   Entrance to Goldstream Park (9). Camping is available here.

This region stretches from an area known as the Malahat on the south flank of Victoria to the town of Chemainus to the north. Chemainus is the jumping-off point for a ferry ride to Thetis Island, one of the lesser travelled Gulf Islands. The Malahat is a mountainous section which requires an obligatory hill climb along the Trans-Canada Highway in order to reach the Cowichan Valley. Many cyclists bypass this lengthy and steep ascent by taking the ferry from Brentwood Bay on the Saanich Peninsula to Mill Bay near Duncan. Another ferry connects Crofton with Vesuvius on Saltspring Island, and a fine weekend trip may be made by circling back to Victoria via Saltspring and Swartz Bay.

West of Duncan lies Cowichan Lake, which is comfortably reached since construction of a new super-highway has left the old highway with very little traffic. The area includes a demonstration forest, many access points to the Cowichan River, and camp sites at the lake.

To the northeast of Duncan are many lakes and three interesting churches. One, the "Butter Church," is now being restored. Interesting tourist stops include a forestry museum north of Duncan and Whippletree Junction, a fully restored pioneer town to the south.

Tour Ratings
All Intermediate except 29, Advanced

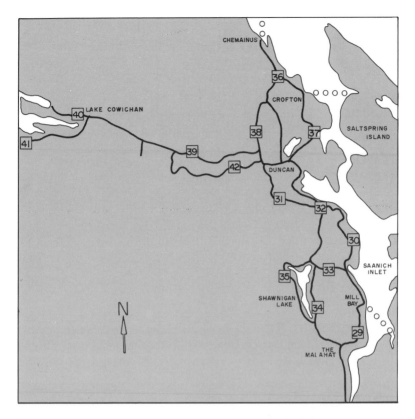

Duncan: The ferry from Swartz Bay connects Vancouver Island with the mainland.

29	GOLDSTREAM MALAHAT SUMMIT MILL BAY	RATING: Advanced (9) DISTANCE: 21.9 km/13.7 mi

HIGHLIGHTS:	Camping at Goldstream Park; picnic area at Spectacle Lake Park; fabulous views from Malahat Summit; camping at Bamberton Park.
TRAFFIC:	Heavy on Highway 1 (Malahat Scenic Highway).
TERRAIN:	Steep hill climbs from sea level to 500 m and down again.
REPAIRS:	Bicycle shops in Victoria.
SUPPLIES:	Stores in Goldstream and Malahat townsite.
CONNECTIONS:	Tours 28, 30 & 34. Ferry to Brentwood Bay (Tours 13, 14 & 15).

CHECKPOINTS

km *(mi)*

0.0 *(0.0)* START From the entrance to Goldstream Park Campground (1), continue on Golden Gate Road downhill toward Highway 1.

Crimson columbine, a spring wildflower

0.7 *(0.4)* JUNCTION Turn left on Highway 1. A right leads to Victoria (2).

1.0 *(0.6)* CAUTION Cross bridge over Goldstream River. Begin Malahat Highway.

2.2 *(1.4)* INTEREST Entrance to Goldstream Park picnic area (3).

2.7 *(1.7)* UPHILL Pass rest area (4) and begin long steady hill for next 8.0 km.

9.6 *(6.0)* INTEREST Pass through Malahat townsite more than halfway up the hill. (5).

11.8 *(7.4)* JUNCTION Stay right on Highway 1. A left leads to Shawnigan Lake (6).

12.8 *(8.0)* INTEREST Spectacle Lake Park (7), turnoff left. Malahat Summit ahead.

13.9 *(8.7)* INTEREST Malahat Lookout on the right (8). Excellent views.

16.0 *(10.0)* INTEREST Rest area on the right (9). Other viewpoints ahead.

16.7 *(10.4)* DOWNHILL Begin steep descent for next 4.0 km. Use care and attention!

19.8 *(12.4)* JUNCTION Cross Northgate industrial road and turn right on Mill Bay Road. Straight on Highway 1 leads to town of Mill Bay (10).

20.0 *(12.5)* CAMPING A right leads down to Bamberton Park (11); continue straight.

21.6 *(13.5)* CAUTION At the bottom of a steep hill turn sharp right on Ferry Road.

21.9 *(13.7)* FINISH Mill Bay Ferry Terminal (12). Catch ferry to Brentwood Bay.

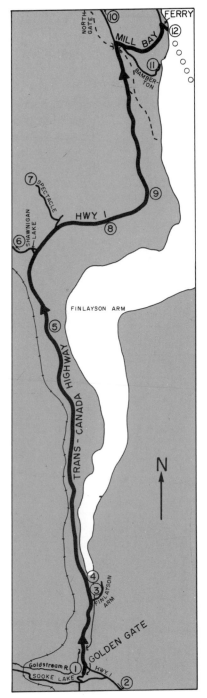

30

| BRENTWOOD FERRY |
| MILL BAY |
| CHERRY POINT |

RATING: Intermediate (5 to 6)
DISTANCE: 19.4 km/12.1 mi

HIGHLIGHTS: Indian cemetery at Mill Bay; plenty of beach access on Saanich Inlet; Boatswain Beach near Garnet Bay.
TRAFFIC: Heavy on Highway 1.
TERRAIN: Rolling hills after Mill Bay.
REPAIRS: Bicycle shop in Duncan or Victoria.
SUPPLIES: Store in Mill Bay near Highway 1.
CONNECTIONS: Tours 29, 31, 32 & 33. Ferry from Brentwood Bay (Tours 13, 14 & 15).

A cyclist on his way to school crosses the suspension bridge at Bright Angel Park. (Tour 31)

CHECKPOINTS

km *(mi)*

0.0 *(0.0)* START From the Mill Bay Ferry Terminal (1), take Ferry Road uphill.

0.3 *(0.2)* INTEREST On the right is an Indian cemetery (2). Right on Mill Bay Road.

0.8 *(0.5)* INTEREST Beach access on the right (3) at the bottom of a small hill.

1.8 *(1.1)* INTEREST More beach access on the right (4). Small hill ahead.

2.7 *(1.7)* INTEREST Third and final beach access point on the right (5). Uphill ahead.

5.6 *(3.5)* JUNCTION Turn right on Highway 1 and cross Shawnigan Creek Bridge. A left leads to Victoria via the Malahat Summit (6).

7.0 *(4.4)* JUNCTION Turn right on Kilmalu Road. Straight on leads to Duncan (7).

7.5 *(4.7)* UPHILL Turn left on Telegraph Road. Begin uphill into rolling hills.

13.6 *(8.5)* JUNCTION Turn right on Cherry Point Road after merging with Fisher Road. Straight ahead on Telegraph Road leads to Cowichan Bay (8).

15.0 *(9.4)* UPHILL After passing Garnet Road to Boatswain Beach (9), begin ascent.

19.4 *(12.1)* FINISH Go straight on across Cowichan Bay Road, following Koksilah Road (10). A right leads downhill steeply to Cowichan Bay.

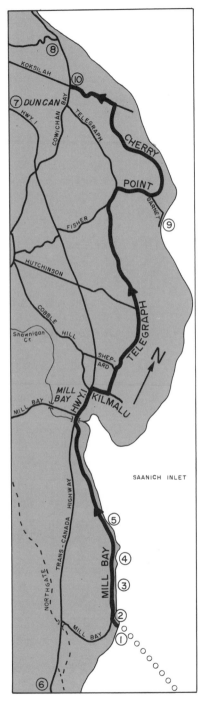

31

CHERRY POINT
COWICHAN STATION
QUAMICHAN LAKE

RATING: Intermediate (5)
DISTANCE: 15.8 km/9.9 mi

HIGHLIGHTS: Museum and historic town of Whippletree; Cowichan Station; Bright Angel Falls Park; Fairbridge Church and Old Koksilah School; Art Mann Park.
TRAFFIC: Heavy through Duncan.
TERRAIN: Rolling hills, steep around Cowichan Station.
REPAIRS: Bicycle shop in Duncan.
SUPPLIES: Supermarkets in Duncan.
CONNECTIONS: Tours 30, 32, 36, 37, 38 & 42.

CHECKPOINTS

km	*(mi)*		
0.0	*(0.0)*	START	From the junction of Cherry Point Road and Cowichan Bay Road (1) take Koksilah Road away from Cowichan Bay.
2.4	*(1.5)*	CAUTION	Go straight across Highway 1. Whippletree is to the right (2).
3.3	*(2.1)*	DOWNHILL	Begin descent past school. Stay left; pass Bench Road.
4.5	*(2.8)*	CAUTION	Pass under narrow railway trestle at Cowichan Station (3).
4.6	*(2.9)*	CAUTION	Cross narrow one-lane bridge over Koksilah River, uphill.
5.4	*(3.4)*	INTEREST	Bright Angel Falls Park and suspension bridge on right (4).
7.7	*(4.8)*	INTEREST	Fairbridge Church and Old Koksilah School on right (5).
8.2	*(5.1)*	CAUTION	Cross bridge over Kelvin (Glenora) Creek.
9.1	*(5.7)*	CAUTION	Cross logging road and railway. Go straight across Miller.
11.7	*(7.3)*	CAUTION	Turn right across Cowichan River Bridge, following Allenby Road.
12.5	*(7.8)*	CAUTION	After a right on Underwood, follow Trunk across railroad tracks.
13.0	*(8.1)*	CAUTION	Go straight across Highway 1. Stay on Trunk, bending left.
14.4	*(9.0)*	CAUTION	Bridge over Somenos Creek by the Sewage Plant (6).

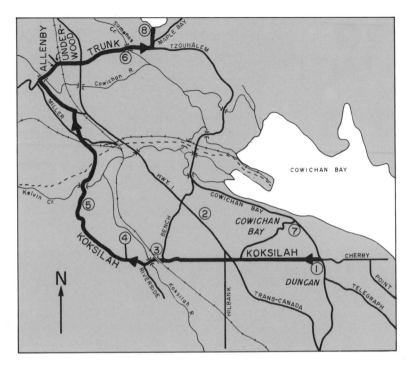

15.0 *(9.4)* JUNCTION   Turn left on Maple Bay Road and go straight ahead on Indian Road. Straight on Tzouhalem leads to Cowichan Bay (7).

15.8 *(9.9)* FINISH   Art Mann Park on Quamichan Lake (8). Picnic and swim area.

32

| QUAMICHAN LAKE
COWICHAN BAY
COBBLE HILL | RATING: Intermediate (5 to 7)
DISTANCE: 13.9 km/8.7 mi |

HIGHLIGHTS: Three historic churches on Tzouhalem Road; historical site near Cowichan Bay; water access at Cowichan Bay; rest area beside Highway 1.

TRAFFIC: Heavy around Cowichan Bay. Watch for logging trucks.

TERRAIN: Rolling hills, steep hill out of Cowichan Bay.

REPAIRS: Bicycle shop in Duncan.

SUPPLIES: Stores in Duncan, Cowichan Bay and Cobble Hill.

CONNECTIONS: Tours 30, 31, 33, 37 & 38.

One of three historical churches near Quamichan Lake

CHECKPOINTS

km *(mi)*

0.0 *(0.0)* START From the junction of Trunk Road and Maple Bay Road (1) near Quamichan Lake, turn left on Tzouhalem Road away from Duncan area.

0.3 *(0.2)* INTEREST On the hill to the left is St. Peter's Church (2).

1.5 *(0.9)* INTEREST On the left is St. Anne's Church and minister's house (3).

2.7 *(1.7)* INTEREST On the hilltop right is the Old Stone (Butter) Church (4). Please respect the Indian Reserve Land on which it is located.

3.0 *(1.9)* CAUTION Cross six creek bridges over Chemainus River for next 1.5 km.

5.1 *(3.2)* CAUTION Cross railway, logging road and the last of the six bridges.

5.3 *(3.3)* JUNCTION Go straight ahead on Cowichan Bay Road. A right leads to Duncan.

5.9 *(3.7)* INTEREST Historical site on the right (5). Stay left ahead, into hills.

7.4 *(4.6)* UPHILL After Cowichan Bay (6), go up a very steep hill for 0.7 km.

8.8 *(5.5)* JUNCTION Cross Koksilah and Cherry Point roads.

11.5 *(7.2)* CAUTION Go straight on across Highway 1 onto Cobble Hill Road. Rest area (7).

13.9 *(8.7)* FINISH By Fisher Road in the centre of Cobble Hill (8).

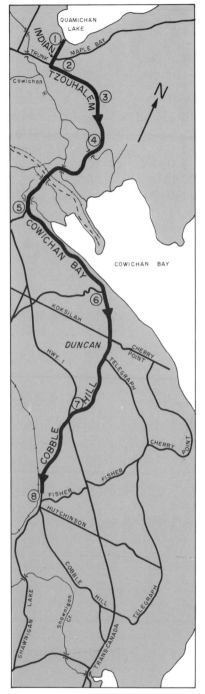

33 COBBLE HILL SHAWNIGAN VILLAGE MILL BAY

RATING: Intermediate (5 to 6)
DISTANCE: 16.0 km/10.0 mi

HIGHLIGHTS: Lime Kiln historical site near Northgate Road; beach access at Mill Bay and Shawnigan Lake; Indian cemetery at Mill Bay ferry terminal.
TRAFFIC: May be heavy on Shawnigan Lake–Mill Bay Highway.
TERRAIN: Rolling hills.
REPAIRS: Bicycle shops in Duncan and Victoria.
SUPPLIES: Stores in Cobble Hill, Shawnigan Village and Mill Bay.
CONNECTIONS: Tours 29, 30, 32, 34 & 35. Ferry to Brentwood Bay (Tours 13, 14 & 15).

CHECKPOINTS

km	(mi)	
0.0	*(0.0)*	**START** From the corner of Cobble Hill Road and Fisher Road (1) in Cobble Hill, take Cobble Hill Road toward Shawnigan Lake.
0.2	*(0.1)*	**JUNCTION** Turn right on Shawnigan Lake Road. Straight leads to Mill Bay.
2.6	*(1.6)*	**CAUTION** Cross Northgate industrial road beside a railway trestle.
2.9	*(1.8)*	**INTEREST** Lime Kiln Historical Site on the right (2).
3.2	*(2.0)*	**CAUTION** Bridge over Shawnigan Creek. Uphill ahead.
4.6	*(2.9)*	**INTEREST** Beach access beside Shawnigan Lake on the right (3).
5.1	*(3.2)*	**JUNCTION** Turn left on Shawnigan Lake–Mill Bay Highway at Shawnigan Village (4). A right takes you on a trip around the lake area.
5.6	*(3.5)*	**INTEREST** Historical site on the right (5). Continue on the highway.
7.2	*(4.5)*	**CAUTION** Cross Northgate industrial road leading to Bamberton (6).
9.4	*(5.9)*	**CAUTION** Cross bridge over Shawnigan Creek, entering Mill Bay (7).
10.1	*(6.3)*	**JUNCTION** Turn right on Highway 1 across the bridge and then left on Deloume Road. A left on Highway 1 leads to Duncan (8).

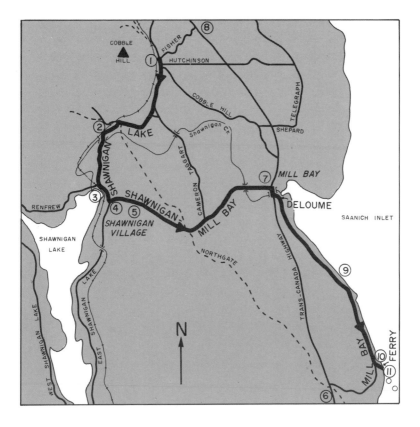

13.3 *(8.3)*   INTEREST   Beach access (9); two more beaches ahead. Rolling hills.

15.7 *(9.8)*   INTEREST   Indian cemetery on the left (10). Turn left on Ferry Road.

16.0 *(10.0)*   FINISH   Mill Bay Ferry Terminal (11) and ferry to Brentwood Bay.

34

| SHAWNIGAN VILLAGE SHAWNIGAN LAKE MALAHAT JUNCTION | RATING: Intermediate (5) DISTANCE: 13.4 km/8.4 mi |

HIGHLIGHTS: Winding road past lakeshore cottages; limited water access; Memory Island Park offshore about 2.5 km after Strathcona Lodge.

TRAFFIC: Heavy in summer.

TERRAIN: Rolling hills, uphill to Malahat Junction.

REPAIRS: Bicycle shops in Duncan and Victoria.

SUPPLIES: Store in Shawnigan Village.

CONNECTIONS: Tours 29, 33 & 35.

Cyclists aboard the Brentwood ferry at Mill Bay (Tour 33)

CHECKPOINTS

km *(mi)*

0.0 *(0.0)* START From the junction of Shawnigan Lake Road and Shawnigan Lake–Mill Bay Highway (1), go straight on East Shawnigan Lake Road.

0.7 *(0.4)* DOWNHILL Pass Elford Road, going downhill past cemetery (2).

1.3 *(0.8)* CAUTION Pass beneath a railway trestle. Rolling hills ahead.

6.2 *(3.9)* INTEREST Lake access down a small lane on the right (3).

7.5 *(4.7)* JUNCTION Continue straight on East Shawnigan Lake Road and pass Sooke Lake Road. A right on West Shawnigan Lake Road circles the lake.

12.1 *(7.6)* CAUTION Cross railroad tracks after considerable rolling hills.

13.4 *(8.4)* FINISH Malahat Junction on Highway 1 (4). Right to Victoria; left for Mill Bay and Duncan.

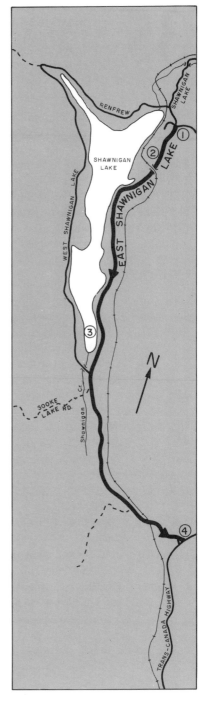

35

| SHAWNIGAN CREEK WEST SHAWNIGAN PARK SHAWNIGAN VILLAGE | RATING: Intermediate (5) DISTANCE: 13.8 km/8.6 mi |

HIGHLIGHTS: View of Memory Island Park; beach access at West Shawnigan Lake Park and in Shawnigan Village.
TRAFFIC: Heavy in summer.
TERRAIN: Rolling hills.
REPAIRS: Bicycle shops in Duncan and Victoria.
SUPPLIES: Store in Shawnigan Village.
CONNECTIONS: Tour 34. Dirt and gravel road to Port Renfrew. Not recommended.

CHECKPOINTS

km *(mi)*

0.0 *(0.0)* START   From the junction of East and West Shawnigan Lake roads (1) at the south end of the lake, go left on West Shawnigan Lake Road.

0.5 *(0.3)* CAUTION   Cross a pair of bridges over Shawnigan Creek. Rolling hills ahead.

2.2 *(1.4)* INTEREST   Viewpoint to Memory Island and Shawnigan Lake (2).

6.6 *(4.1)* INTEREST   West Shawnigan Lake Park on the right (3).

9.1 *(5.7)* JUNCTION   After a right bend, turn right on Renfrew Road. A left leads 65 km to Port Renfrew and Highway 14 on the west coast.

13.0 *(8.1)* INTEREST   Small beach and swimming area by a park on the right (4).

13.1 *(8.2)* CAUTION   Cross bridge over Shawnigan Creek and railroad tracks.

13.3 *(8.3)* JUNCTION   Turn right on Shawnigan Lake Road. A left leads to Cobble Hill (5).

13.8 *(8.6)* FINISH   Shawnigan Village centre (6). Junction of Shawnigan Lake Road and Shawnigan Lake–Mill Bay Highway.

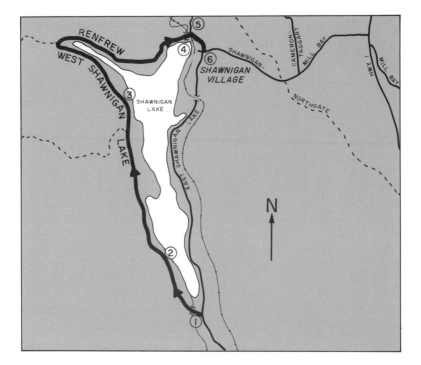

RENFREW

WEST SHAWNIGAN LAKE

SHAWNIGAN LAKE

EAST SHAWNIGAN LAKE

⑤

④

⑥

SHAWNIGAN VILLAGE

SHAWNIGAN-

CAMERON-TAGGART

MILL BAY

HWY. 1

MILL BAY

NORTHGATE

③

②

①

N

36

| DUNCAN
WESTHOLME
CHEMAINUS | RATING: Intermediate (5)
DISTANCE: 20.5 km/12.8 mi |

HIGHLIGHTS: B.C. Forest Museum on Somenos Lake; cemeteries near Chemainus; route follows the old Trans-Canada Highway, now Highway 1A.

TRAFFIC: Heavy near Duncan.

TERRAIN: Rolling hills.

REPAIRS: Bicycle shops in Duncan or Chemainus.

SUPPLIES: Supermarkets in Duncan, stores in Chemainus.

CONNECTIONS: Tours 37, 38, 42 & 44. Ferry to Thetis Island (Tour 43).

CHECKPOINTS

km *(mi)*

0.0 *(0.0)* START From the intersection of Highway 1 and Trunk Road in the centre of Duncan (1), take Highway 1 toward Nanaimo.

The Forestry Museum north of Duncan is worth a visit.

3.2 *(2.0)* INTEREST Forest Museum Park on the right (2). Turn right on Drinkwater Road and then left on Bell-McKinnon Road parallel to Highway 1.

8.6 *(5.4)* JUNCTION Turn right on Westholme Road, going uphill past Richards Trail. A left leads to Stratfords Crossing at Highway 1 (3).

10.9 *(6.8)* CAUTION Cross creek bridge and railway and pass through Westholme (4).

12.5 *(7.8)* CAUTION Cross second railway and creek bridge.

13.3 *(8.3)* JUNCTION Turn left on Chemainus. A right leads to Crofton (5).

13.8 *(8.6)* CAUTION Cross Chemainus River Bridge. Cemetery on left (6).

14.4 *(9.4)* CAUTION Cross railroad tracks. Rolling hills ahead on Highway 1A.

17.0 *(10.6)* CAUTION Cross railway again. Cemetery ahead on the right (7).

17.9 *(11.2)* CAUTION Cross Henry Road and railroad side track into Chemainus (8).

19.7 *(12.3)* JUNCTION Turn right on Oak Street. Straight ahead leads to Ladysmith (9).

20.5 *(12.8)* FINISH At the foot of Oak Street is the Chemainus Ferry Terminal (10). Catch the boat to Thetis Island.

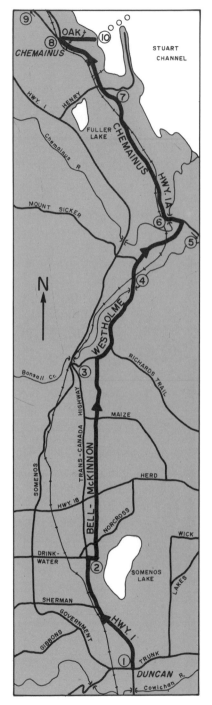

37

CROFTON	RATING: Intermediate (5)
MAPLE BAY	DISTANCE: 17.9 km/11.2 mi
QUAMICHAN LAKE	

HIGHLIGHTS: Crofton Pulp Mill; Maple Mountain Park; Art Mann Park at Quamichan Lake; Crofton Ferry to Vesuvius Bay on Saltspring Island.
TRAFFIC: Heavy around Crofton and the mill.
TERRAIN: Rolling hills with a large climb over Maple Mountain.
REPAIRS: Bicycle shop in Duncan.
SUPPLIES: Stores in Crofton and Maple Bay.
CONNECTIONS: Tours 36 & 38. Ferry to Saltspring (Tours 1 & 2).

CHECKPOINTS

km *(mi)*

0.0 *(0.0)* START   From the corner of Westholme and Chemainus roads (Highway 1A) near the Chemainus River Bridge (1), follow Crofton Road.

0.5 *(0.3)* CAUTION   Pair of creek bridges to cross, followed by a railway.

2.2 *(1.4)* INTEREST   Crofton Pulp Mill on the left (2). Rolling hills ahead.

3.7 *(2.3)* JUNCTION   In Crofton turn left on Chaplain Street and then right on York Avenue (Osborne Bay Road) uphill. Straight ahead on Chaplain Street for Saltspring ferry (3).

5.9 *(3.7)* INTEREST   At the hilltop, dirt roads lead to Maple Mountain Park (4).

8.6 *(5.4)* JUNCTION   Turn left on Herd Road. A right leads to Somenos (5).

11.4 *(7.1)* JUNCTION   Turn right on Maple Bay Road. A left drops down to Maple Bay (6).

17.1 *(10.7)* JUNCTION   Turn sharp right on Indian Road. Left leads to Tzouhalem Road and a right from there to Duncan (7).

17.9 *(11.2)* FINISH   At the end of Indian Road is Art Mann Park on Quamichan Lake (8).

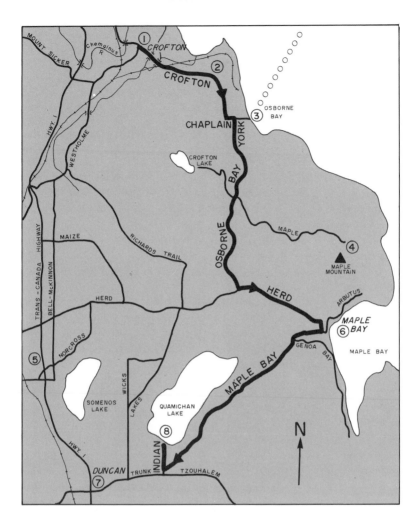

38

QUAMICHAN LAKE	**RATING:** Intermediate (5)
STRATFORDS	**DISTANCE:** 19.8 km/12.4 mi
CROSSING	
HAYWARD	

HIGHLIGHTS: Farmlands along Richards Trail; good views of Somenos and Quamichan valleys; a good circle tour from Duncan.
TRAFFIC: Heavy near Duncan.
TERRAIN: Rolling hills.
REPAIRS: Bicycle shop in Duncan.
SUPPLIES: Stores in Hayward and Duncan.
CONNECTIONS: Tours 36, 37 & 39.

CHECKPOINTS

km *(mi)*

0.0 *(0.0)* START   Just past the junction of Indian Road and Maple Bay Road (1) near Quamichan Lake, turn right on Tzouhalem Road.

1.1 *(0.7)* CAUTION   Cross Somenos Creek Bridge and turn right on Lakes Road ahead.

1.6 *(1.0)* UPHILL   Cross a second bridge over Somenos Creek, going uphill ahead.

6.1 *(3.8)* JUNCTION   Turn right on Herd Road and immediately left on Richards Trail. Continuing right on Herd Road leads to Maple Bay (2), left leads to Somenos (3).

7.4 *(4.6)* CAUTION   Bend left at the hill bottom and continue on gravel road.

11.8 *(7.4)* JUNCTION   Turn left on Westholme Road. A right leads to Westholme (4).

13.1 *(8.2)* CAUTION   Cross Highway 1 at Stratfords Crossing (5); follow Somenos Road.

14.4 *(9.0)* UPHILL   Cross railway, bend left and go uphill into rolling hills.

17.4 *(10.9)* CAUTION   Cross Highway 18 (New Cowichan Lake Highway).

18.6 *(11.6)* INTEREST   Pass cemetery on the left (6).

19.8 *(12.4)* FINISH   At the junction of Somenos Road and Sherman Road (7) in Hayward. A right on Cowichan Lake Road leads to Skutz Falls.

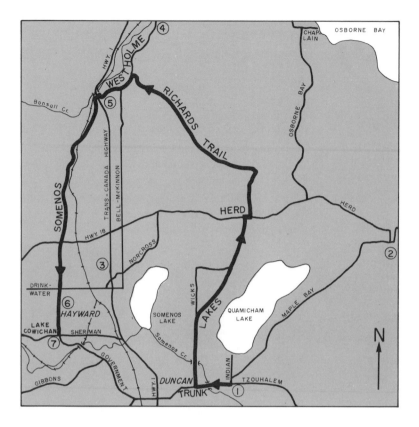

39 | HAYWARD
PALDI
SKUTZ FALLS

RATING: Intermediate (5)
DISTANCE: 20.3 km/12.7 mi

HIGHLIGHTS: Rest area on Highway 18 near viewpoint for Cowichan Valley Demonstration Forest; camping at Skutz Falls.
TRAFFIC: Heavy near Hayward and on Highway 18.
TERRAIN: Rolling hills, some steep sections.
REPAIRS: Bicycle shop in Duncan.
SUPPLIES: Stores in Hayward and Paldi, supermarket in Lake Cowichan.
CONNECTIONS: Tours 38, 40 & 42.

Fish ladders near Skutz Falls

CHECKPOINTS

km *(mi)*

0.0 *(0.0)* START From the junction of Somenos Road and Sherman Road in Hayward (1), take Lake Cowichan Road uphill away from Duncan area.

1.9 *(1.2)* CAUTION Turn left following Lake Cowichan Road across rough railroad.

5.8 *(3.6)* JUNCTION Stay right on Lake Cowichan Road. A left leads to Riverbottom Road (2).

8.6 *(5.4)* JUNCTION Stay left on Lake Cowichan Road. A right leads to Paldi (3).

12.0 *(7.5)* JUNCTION Go straight and cross railway. A left on Stolz Road leads downhill steeply to the Cowichan River (4) and back to Duncan.

13.9 *(8.7)* JUNCTION Stay left. A right connects to Highway 18 (Cowichan Valley Highway) and a rest area (5).

17.1 *(10.7)* JUNCTION Turn left on Mayo Road, across the railway and downhill. Straight ahead leads to Lake Cowichan (6).

19.8 *(12.4)* CAUTION Cross railroad tracks and turn right on dirt road.

20.3 *(12.7)* FINISH Skutz Falls and fish ladder on the left (7). Primitive camping available in this area.

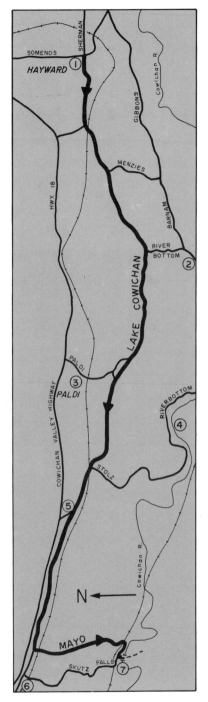

40

| SKUTZ FALLS |
| LAKE COWICHAN |
| VILLAGE |
| SUNSET BAY |

RATING: Intermediate (5)
DISTANCE: 14.9 km/9.3 mi

HIGHLIGHTS: Park and water access in Lake Cowichan Village; satellite tracking station; arboretum; excellent sunset views from Sunset Bay.
TRAFFIC: Heavy in Lake Cowichan Village and on Highway 18.
TERRAIN: Rolling hills.
REPAIRS: Bicycle shop in Duncan.
SUPPLIES: Stores and supermarket in Lake Cowichan Village.
CONNECTIONS: Tours 39 & 41.

Cyclist out for a short day trip

CHECKPOINTS

km *(mi)*

0.0 *(0.0)* START From the Mayo Road turnoff to Skutz Falls (1), continue on Lake Cowichan Road toward the village of Lake Cowichan.

0.8 *(0.5)* INTEREST Pass Skutz Falls Road. A left here also leads down to Skutz Falls (2), but on a less desirable road.

7.8 *(4.9)* CAUTION Merge with Highway 18 to enter Lake Cowichan Village (3).

8.5 *(5.3)* JUNCTION Turn right on North Road opposite Central Park (4). Straight ahead on South Road across the bridge leads to Gordon Bay (5).

9.6 *(6.0)* INTEREST Water access to Lake Cowichan on left (6). Leaving Lake Cowichan Village.

11.5 *(7.2)* JUNCTION Turn left on Meads Creek Road. Straight ahead on North Road leads to Highway 18 and a satellite tracking station on the hill (7).

11.7 *(7.3)* CAUTION Pass logging road and go downhill.

13.1 *(8.2)* CAUTION Pair of bridges over Meads Creek; good water access here.

13.6 *(8.5)* CAUTION Creek bridge and arboretum on the right (8).

14.7 *(9.2)* JUNCTION Turn left on Sunset Drive just before the railway. Highway 18 just ahead continues to Youbou (9).

14.9 *(9.3)* FINISH At water access on Lake Cowichan (10) at Sunset Bay.

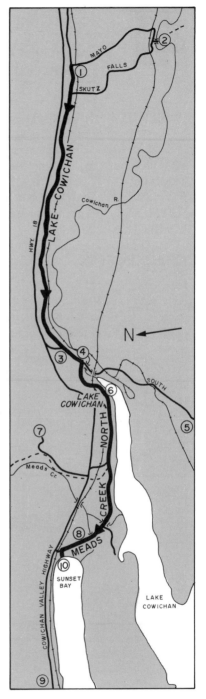

41

| LAKE COWICHAN VILLAGE MESACHIE LAKE GORDON BAY | RATING: Intermediate (5) DISTANCE: 14.0 km/8.7 mi |

HIGHLIGHTS: Several parks and a museum in Lake Cowichan Village; Forestry Research Station and park; camping, picnicking and swimming at Gordon Bay.

TRAFFIC: Watch for logging trucks on South Road.

TERRAIN: Rolling hills.

REPAIRS: Bicycle shop in Duncan.

SUPPLIES: Supermarket in Lake Cowichan Village.

CONNECTIONS: Tour 40.

CHECKPOINTS

km *(mi)*

0.0 *(0.0)* START From the junction of North Road and Lake Cowichan Road (1) in Lake Cowichan Village, take South Road across the bridge.

Harbour seal swimming off the coast

0.5 *(0.3)* CAUTION Pass beneath railway trestle. Footbridge across Cowichan River, right.

0.8 *(0.5)* INTEREST Museum on the right (2) in old train station. Cross railway.

1.3 *(0.8)* CAUTION Cross railroad tracks heading uphill on South Road.

2.4 *(1.5)* CAUTION Cross logging road and railway. Right on logging road leads to Lakeview Park (3).

5.8 *(3.6)* INTEREST Rest area above Mesachie Lake on the right (4). Railroad ahead.

6.6 *(4.1)* JUNCTION Continue straight ahead. A right leads to Forestry Research Station (5). Pass through town of Mesachie Lake (6).

7.1 *(4.4)* CAUTION Cross logging road. A left leads 64 km to Port Renfrew.

7.9 *(4.9)* CAUTION Cross creek bridge, railway and bridge over Robertson River.

10.2 *(6.4)* CAUTION Cross major logging road entering Honeymoon Bay (7).

11.0 *(6.9)* CAUTION Cross bridge over Ashburnham Creek after passing the mill (8).

12.1 *(7.6)* CAUTION Cross bridge over Sutton Creek after leaving Honeymoon Bay.

12.4 *(7.8)* JUNCTION Turn right on Walton Road. Straight ahead is wildflower reserve (9).

14.0 *(8.7)* FINISH Gordon Bay Park (10). Camping and beach access.

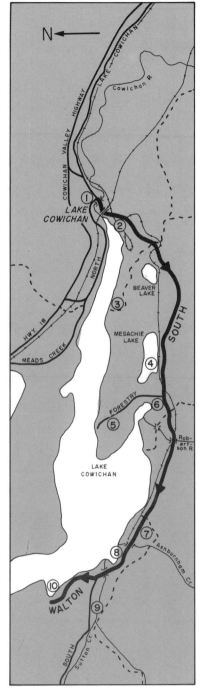

42

| PALDI |
| RIVERBOTTOM |
| DUNCAN |

RATING: Intermediate (4)
DISTANCE: 19.7 km/12.3 mi

HIGHLIGHTS: Many points of water access on the Cowichan River; farmlands outside Duncan; optional return route from Lake Cowichan.

TRAFFIC: Usually light.

TERRAIN: Rolling hills with a steep downhill section near the beginning.

REPAIRS: Bicycle shop in Duncan.

SUPPLIES: Supermarkets in Duncan.

CONNECTIONS: Tours 36 & 39.

CHECKPOINTS

km *(mi)*

0.0 *(0.0)* START From the intersection of Stolz Road and Lake Cowichan Road (1) near Paldi, take Stolz Road away from the railway tracks.

The stone "Butter Church" on the Indian Reserve east of Duncan (Tour 32)

1.0 *(0.6)* DOWNHILL Begin extremely steep descent with several sharp corners.

4.8 *(3.0)* INTEREST Water access on the right beside the Cowichan River (2).

5.8 *(3.6)* INTEREST After a short hill, more water access to the right (3).

6.9 *(4.3)* INTEREST Last opportunity for water access on the right (4).

10.7 *(6.7)* JUNCTION Turn right on Barnam Road. Straight on leads to Sahtlam (5).

14.2 *(8.9)* CAUTION Cross small creek bridge, continuing on Gibbons Road.

17.6 *(11.0)* JUNCTION Turn right on Lake Cowichan Road and then stay right following Government Street. A left on Lake Cowichan Road leads to Hayward (6).

19.0 *(11.9)* CAUTION Merge into Trunk Road and continue across the railroad tracks.

19.7 *(12.3)* FINISH In the centre of Duncan at the crossroads of Highway 1 and Trunk (7).

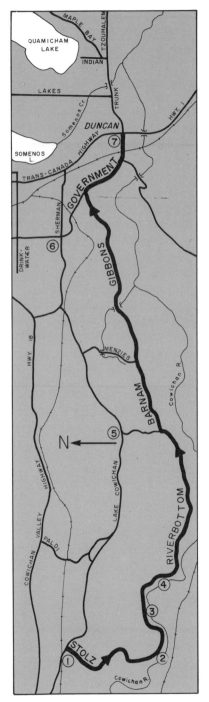

The small town of Ladysmith was a major forestry centre in the 1860s, and a visit to its forestry museum is recommended. A major provincial campground is located just north of Ladysmith, and the rolling hills around Yellow Point and Cedar make for excellent touring through gentle farming country.

Of interest are the Nanaimo coal mines which for many years extended underground beneath the Strait of Georgia. Today visitors can see the mine ruins and browse in the town's museum with its reconstructed mining scenes and artifacts.

Nanaimo is also the site of a major ferry terminal connecting to Horseshoe Bay near Vancouver on the mainland. A second ferry services Gabriola Island, which is fast becoming a "bedroom community" of Nanaimo. Among Gabriola's attractions is the massive sandstone formation called the "Malaspina Galleries."

Nanaimo has many small lakes and beaches, each having at least one small local park with swimming facilities. These parks make excellent lunch stops.

Tour Ratings
All Intermediate except 52, Advanced

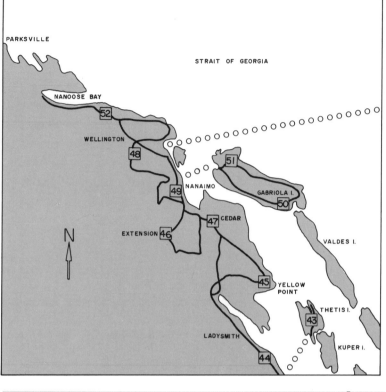

Nanaimo: Pedalling along the Jingle Pot bicycle route outside Nanaimo

43

| THETIS ISLAND |
| MOORE HILL |
| PILKEY POINT |

RATING: Intermediate (4)
DISTANCE: 7.5 km/4.7 mi

HIGHLIGHTS: Water access at Telegraph Harbour, "The Gut" and Pilkey Point; excellent views from the road on Moore Hill.
TRAFFIC: Minimal.
TERRAIN: Steep hill up and down Moore Hill.
REPAIRS: Bicycle shop in Chemainus.
SUPPLIES: Stores in Chemainus.
CONNECTIONS: Tours 36 & 44. Ferry from Chemainus and Kuper Island. See note below.

CHECKPOINTS

km *(mi)*

0.0 *(0.0)* START   Disembark from the ferry at Preedy Harbour (1); stay left on Telegraph Harbour Road.

0.5 *(0.3)* JUNCTION   Stay right on Pilkey Point Road. A left leads to North Cove. (2).

0.8 *(0.5)* JUNCTION   Stay left on the main road. A right on Marina Road leads to water access at "The Gut" (3) beside Kuper Island.

3.7 *(2.3)* UPHILL   Begin extremely steep hill climb after Sunrise Point Road.

4.8 *(3.0)* INTEREST   Moore Hill (4) at the hilltop. Good views during descent.

5.5 *(3.4)* CAUTION   Sharp left bend during descent. Slow down!

6.4 *(4.0)* JUNCTION   Turn left for Pilkey Point. A right leads to Ivy's Gift Shop (5).

7.5 *(4.7)* FINISH   At the end of the paved road is beach access at Pilkey Point (6).

NOTE: Kuper Island is an Indian Reserve and permission must be obtained from the Band Office in Chemainus to travel on the island. "The Gut" was once spanned by a bridge that connected Thetis and Kuper islands.

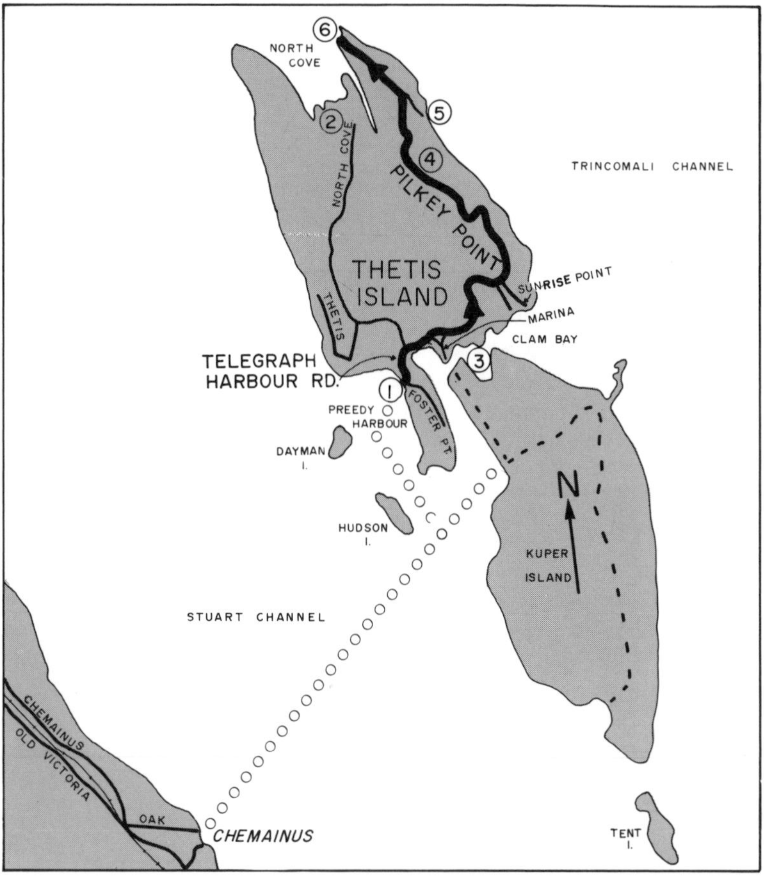
NORTH COVE
NORTH COVE
TRINCOMALI CHANNEL
PILKEY POINT
THETIS ISLAND
THETIS
SUNRISE POINT
MARINA
CLAM BAY
TELEGRAPH HARBOUR RD.
PREEDY HARBOUR
FOSTER PT.
DAYMAN I.
HUDSON I.
N
KUPER ISLAND
STUART CHANNEL
CHEMAINUS
OLD VICTORIA
OAK
CHEMAINUS
TENT I.

44

| CHEMAINUS LADYSMITH IVY GREEN PARK | RATING: Intermediate (5 to 6)
DISTANCE: 15.8 km/9.9 mi |

HIGHLIGHTS: Water access at Davis Lagoon, Crown Zellerbach Park and Ivy Green Park; museum in Ladysmith; camping at Ivy Green Park.

TRAFFIC: Heavy around Ladysmith and on the Trans-Canada Highway.

TERRAIN: Rolling hills.

REPAIRS: Bicycle shop in Ladysmith or Chemainus.

SUPPLIES: Supermarkets in Ladysmith, store in Chemainus.

CONNECTIONS: Tours 36, 45 & 47. Ferry from Thetis Island (Tour 43).

Be a sensible and responsible bicyclist. Always wear an approved helmet.

CHECKPOINTS

km *(mi)*

0.0 *(0.0)* START From the Thetis Island Ferry (1), take Oak Street through town.

1.0 *(0.6)* JUNCTION Turn right on Chemainus Road (Highway 1A). A left leads toward Duncan and Crofton (2). Rolling hills ahead along railway.

5.6 *(3.5)* DOWNHILL Begin descent through town of Saltair (3).

7.2 *(4.5)* CAUTION Cross bridge over Davis Lagoon (4). Uphill ahead.

9.6 *(6.0)* CAUTION Cross railway, turn right on Highway 1 into Ladysmith (5).

11.5 *(7.2)* INTEREST Crown Zellerbach Park on the right (6); Black Nugget Museum on the left (7). Cross the 49th parallel ahead.

13.6 *(8.5)* CAUTION Narrow bridge over the railroad tracks.

15.4 *(9.6)* JUNCTION Cross bridge over Bush Creek and turn right into Ivy Green Park (8). Straight on Highway 1 leads toward Nanaimo.

15.8 *(9.9)* FINISH Beach area on Ladysmith Harbour (9). Camping available.

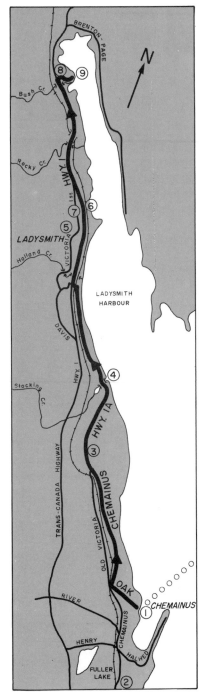

45 | IVY GREEN PARK
YELLOW POINT
CEDAR | **RATING:** Intermediate (5)
DISTANCE: 19.7 km/12.3 mi

HIGHLIGHTS: Camping at Ivy Green Park; rest area and drinking water; beach access at Roberts Memorial Park near Yellow Point.

TRAFFIC: Heavy near Ladysmith on Highway 1.

TERRAIN: Rolling hills near Yellow Point.

REPAIRS: Bicycle shop in Ladysmith or Nanaimo.

SUPPLIES: Stores in Cedar, supermarkets in Ladysmith.

CONNECTIONS: Tours 44, 46 & 47.

CHECKPOINTS

km *(mi)*

0.0 *(0.0)*   START   From Ivy Green Park (1), continue on Highway 1 toward Nanaimo.

0.8 *(0.5)*   INTEREST   Rest area and drinking water on the left (2); spring ahead.

1.6 *(1.0)*   JUNCTION   Continue straight on Highway 1. Right leads to Shell Beach (3). Turn right on Cedar Road ahead.

5.3 *(3.3)*   JUNCTION   Turn right on Yellow Point Road. Straight ahead leads to Cedar.

6.1 *(3.8)*   UPHILL   Cross a small creek and begin ascent through rolling hills.

8.8 *(5.5)*   DOWNHILL   Rolling hill descent toward Yellow Point.

11.3 *(7.1)*   CAUTION   Bend sharply left; private road goes right to Yellow Point (4).

13.0 *(8.1)*   INTEREST   Roberts Memorial Park on the right (5); hiking trail to beach.

16.5 *(10.3)*   INTEREST   Quennell Lake on the left (6). Relatively flat ahead.

19.7 *(12.3)*   FINISH   Junction of Yellow Point Road with Cedar Road near Cedar (7).

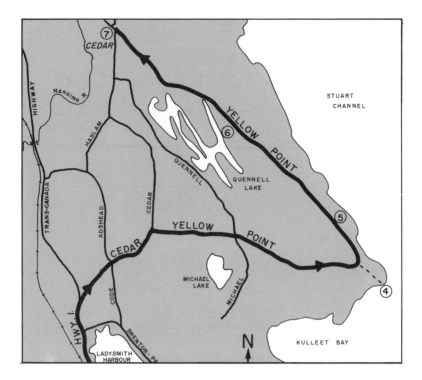

46

| CEDAR EXTENSION CHASE RIVER | **RATING:** Intermediate (5) **DISTANCE:** 23.4 km/14.6 mi |

HIGHLIGHTS: Harmac Pulp Mill tours; coal mine ruins; water access on the Nanaimo River; old mining town of Extension; petroglyphs near Nanaimo.

TRAFFIC: Heavy on Highway 1 at the end.

TERRAIN: Rolling hills, some steep parts near Nanaimo River.

REPAIRS: Bicycle shop in Nanaimo.

SUPPLIES: Stores in Cedar, Extension, Chase River and South Wellington.

CONNECTIONS: Tours 45, 47 & 48.

CHECKPOINTS

km *(mi)*

0.0 *(0.0)* START   From the junction of Yellow Point and Cedar roads (1), take Cedar Road toward Cedar and turn right on Wobank Road.

0.8 *(0.5)* INTEREST   Pass Humer Road with Humer Park to the right (2).

3.2 *(2.0)* JUNCTION   Turn left on Harmac Road. Straight ahead is Harmac Pulp Mill (3).

4.3 *(2.7)* CAUTION   Cross Nanaimo River Bridge. Water access from Raines Road (4).

4.5 *(2.8)* JUNCTION   Turn left on Wilkinson and then left on Akenhead Road. Straight ahead on Cedar Road leads directly to Chase River.

7.0 *(4.4)* INTEREST   Turn right on Morden Road. A left leads to Morden Colliery Historical Park and coal mine ruins (5).

7.7 *(4.8)* CAUTION   Cross Highway 1 and turn left on South Wellington.

9.6 *(6.0)* CAUTION   Turn right on Nanaimo Lakes Road, uphill across rough railway.

12.2 *(7.6)* INTEREST   River Terrace leads right to Gold Pan Trail and water access (6).

12.5 *(7.8)* UPHILL   Continue uphill away from the river. Turn right at the top.

14.4 *(9.0)* JUNCTION   Turn left on Godfrey Road across small creek bridge. Continuing straight on White Rapids Road bypasses the town of Extension.

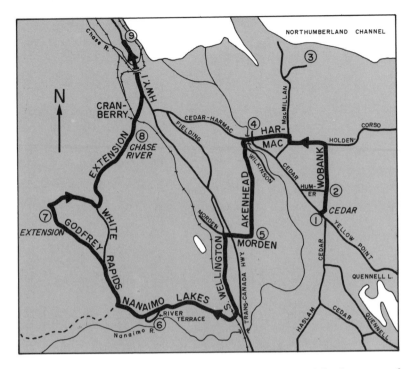

16.6 *(10.4)* INTEREST Turn right on Extension Road in the town of Extension (7).

20.6 *(12.9)* INTEREST Local park on the right (8). Enter Chase River.

21.0 *(13.1)* CAUTION Cross the railroad tracks and turn left on Cranberry Street.

22.4 *(14.0)* CAUTION Follow Highway 1 uphill; pass beneath railway trestle.

23.4 *(14.6)* FINISH Petroglyph Park on the right (9). Trails to rock carvings.

47 | CHASE RIVER
CEDAR
IVY GREEN PARK

RATING: Intermediate (5)
DISTANCE: 18.6 km/11.6 mi

HIGHLIGHTS: Petroglyph Park; Humer Park; Cedar Cemetery; camping at Ivy Green Park; water access at Nanaimo River bridge.

TRAFFIC: Heavy around Chase River and Cedar.

TERRAIN: Rolling hills.

REPAIRS: Bicycle shop in Nanaimo.

SUPPLIES: Stores in Chase River and Cedar, supermarkets in Ladysmith.

CONNECTIONS: Tours 44, 45, 46 & 48.

Coal mine ruins at Morden Colliery Historical Park near Cedar (Tour 46)

CHECKPOINTS

km *(mi)*

0.0 *(0.0)* START From Petro-glyph Park (1), take Highway 1 toward Chase River.

1.0 *(0.6)* CAUTION Pass beneath railway trestle and enter Chase River (2).

2.1 *(1.3)* JUNCTION Turn left on Cedar-Harmac Road. Straight ahead on Highway 1 leads to South Wellington (3) and eventually to Ladysmith.

4.8 *(3.0)* CAUTION Cross bridge over Nanaimo River and then turn right, uphill.

6.7 *(4.2)* INTEREST A left on Humer Road leads to Humer Park (4).

7.7 *(4.8)* JUNCTION Stay right on Cedar Road. Straight leads to Yellow Point (5).

8.6 *(5.4)* INTEREST Cedar Cemetery on the right (6).

10.6 *(6.6)* DOWNHILL After turning right on Haslam Road, go downhill fairly steeply.

11.5 *(7.2)* JUNCTION Turn left on Adshead Road. A right leads to Cassidy (7).

14.1 *(8.8)* CAUTION Cross Cedar Road, following Code Road downhill.

15.8 *(9.9)* JUNCTION Turn right on Brenton-Page Road. A left leads to Shell Beach (8).

17.0 *(10.6)* JUNCTION Turn left on Highway 1. A right leads back to Chase River.

17.8 *(11.1)* INTEREST Rest area and drinking water on the right (9).

18.6 *(11.6)* FINISH Ivy Green Park (10). Ladysmith is farther ahead on Highway 1.

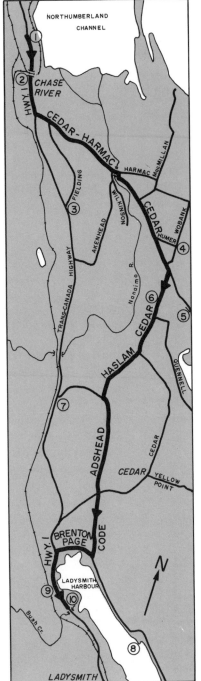

| | CHASE RIVER
JINGLE POT ROAD
HAMMOND BAY | RATING: Intermediate (5)
DISTANCE: 28.8 km/18.0 mi |

HIGHLIGHTS: Swimming at Nanaimo Lakes Colliery Dam, Westwood and Long lakes; beach access at Departure Bay and Page's Lagoon; Planta Park and Marine Station.

TRAFFIC: Heavy around Nanaimo.

TERRAIN: Rolling hills.

REPAIRS: Bicycle shop in Nanaimo.

SUPPLIES: Supermarkets in Nanaimo.

CONNECTIONS: Tours 46 & 49.

CHECKPOINTS

km *(mi)*

0.0 *(0.0)* START From the railway trestle underpass in Chase River (1), take Highway 1 toward Nanaimo and turn left on Victoria Drive.

2.2 *(1.4)* CAUTION Turn left on Seventh Street, across the railway and downhill.

2.7 *(1.7)* CAUTION Bridge over the Chase River at bottom of hill.

3.5 *(2.2)* UPHILL Cross Howard Avenue and begin ascent on Harewood Mines Road.

6.2 *(3.9)* DOWNHILL Turn right on Nanaimo Lakes Road and descend past reservoir (2).

9.0 *(5.6)* INTEREST Turn left on Wakesiah Avenue. A right leads to Colliery Dam and Nanaimo Lakes Park (3). Good swimming.

10.6 *(6.6)* JUNCTION Turn left on Jingle Pot Road past the bird sanctuary (4) and go uphill. Straight ahead leads to Bowen Park at Comox Road (5).

12.6 *(7.9)* JUNCTION Continue uphill and straight on Jingle Pot Road. A left on Westwood Road leads to Westwood Lake Park and swimming area (6).

17.9 *(11.2)* CAUTION Bend sharp left and go downhill steeply to cross a creek bridge.

21.4 *(13.4)* CAUTION Cross railway and Highway 19 onto Norwell.

21.9 *(13.7)* INTEREST Loudon Walkway goes left to water access on Long Lake (7).

22.7 *(14.2)* DOWNHILL Turn left on Departure Bay Road. Steep descent on main road.

25.3 *(15.8)* JUNCTION Turn left on Hammond Bay Road. Straight on Departure Bay Road leads past Kinsmen Park (8) to ferry (9).

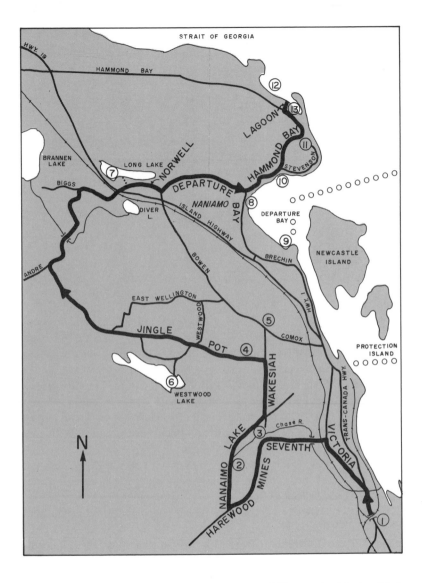

26.6 *(16.6)* UPHILL   Go up and over a steep hill past the Marine Biology Station (10) and the turnoff on Stevenson Point Road to Planta Park (11).

27.7 *(17.3)* CAUTION   Sharp left bend coming down the hill toward Hammond Bay (12).

28.5 *(17.8)* JUNCTION   Turn right on Lagoon Road at the hill bottom. Straight ahead leads back uphill on Hammond Bay Road to Highway 19.

28.8 *(18.0)* FINISH   Page's Lagoon (13); water access and good views.

49

HAMMOND BAY	RATING: Intermediate (5)
NANAIMO CENTRE	DISTANCE: 24.3 km/15.3 mi
CHASE RIVER	

HIGHLIGHTS: Beach access at Page's Lagoon; Hammond Bay; Maffeo Sutton and Georgia parks; Petroglyph, Comox and Diver Lake parks; museum and Bastion.

TRAFFIC: Heavy on Highway 1 and in Nanaimo.

TERRAIN: Rolling hills, relatively flat in places.

REPAIRS: Bicycle shop in Nanaimo.

SUPPLIES: Supermarkets in Nanaimo.

CONNECTIONS: Tours 46, 47, 48, 52. Ferry to Gabriola Island (Tours 50 & 51). Ferries to Vancouver and Newcastle Island.

CHECKPOINTS

km *(mi)*

0.0 *(0.0)* START   From Page's Lagoon turnoff (1), continue on Hammond Bay Road.

0.3 *(0.2)* INTEREST   Boat launch on right (2) gives water access to Hammond Bay.

0.8 *(0.5)* UPHILL   Rolling hills up for the next 6.0 km along Hammond Bay Road.

6.7 *(4.2)* CAUTION   Cross Highway 19 and turn left on Metral Drive.

9.6 *(6.0)* CAUTION   Cross railroad tracks and follow Wellington Road.

12.0 *(7.5)* JUNCTION   Shenton Road ends at Labieux Road. Turn left and cross Bowen Road. A right on Labieux leads to Diver Lake Park (3).

13.8 *(8.6)* CAUTION   Cross railway and Highway 19; turn right onto Highland.

15.5 *(9.7)* DOWNHILL   Merge with Brechin Road and follow it downhill steeply.

16.6 *(10.4)* JUNCTION   Turn right on Stewart Avenue (Trans-Canada Highway). A left leads to Departure Bay Ferry Terminal (4).

18.6 *(11.6)* CAUTION   Turn left on Island Highway (Terminal Avenue) across bridge over Millstone River. Maffeo Sutton Park on left (5).

18.9 *(11.8)* JUNCTION   Turn left on Front Street and bend right past Georgia Park (6). A right on Comox (Bowen) Road leads to Comox Park (7).

19.4 *(12.1)* INTEREST   The Bastion (8) is on the left; just ahead on the hill are Tourist Information Centre and mining museum (9).

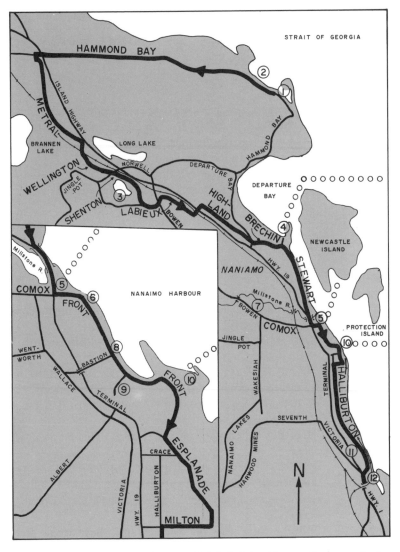

19.7 *(12.3)* INTEREST Ferry to Gabriola Island leaves from terminal at left (10).

23.8 *(14.9)* JUNCTION Turn left on Highway 1 from Haliburton Road. A right leads uphill to Petroglyph Park (11), with trails to rock carvings.

24.3 *(15.3)* FINISH Pass underneath the railway trestle, entering Chase River (12).

50

DESCANSO BAY	RATING: Intermediate (5)
SOUTH ROAD	DISTANCE: 15.0 km/9.4 mi
SILVA BAY	

HIGHLIGHTS: Water access at False Narrows, Degnen Bay, Drumbeg Park and Silva Bay; Hoggan Lake; cemetery; farmlands and cottages by the water.

TRAFFIC: Congested around ferry terminal.

TERRAIN: Rolling hills, steep hill at start.

REPAIRS: Bicycle shop in Nanaimo; local minor repairs available.

SUPPLIES: Stores in Silva Bay and Taylor Bay.

CONNECTIONS: Tour 51. Ferry from Nanaimo (Tour 49).

CHECKPOINTS

km   *(mi)*

0.0   *(0.0)*   START   Disembark from the ferry at Descanso Bay (1), letting traffic go first. Follow the main road straight ahead and uphill steeply.

0.5   *(0.3)*   JUNCTION   Take the right fork onto South Road. Left is North Road.

3.4   *(2.1)*   INTEREST   Hoggan Lake on the right (2). Rolling hills.

3.9   *(2.4)*   DOWNHILL   Begin steep descent toward False Narrows.

7.0   *(4.4)*   INTEREST   Water access at the hill bottom (3); view to Harmac Mill (4).

8.8   *(5.5)*   INTEREST   Cemetery on the right (5). Fairly steep hill ahead.

12.5   *(7.8)*   INTEREST   Degnen Bay on the right (6). Steep hill ahead.

13.6   *(8.5)*   JUNCTION   Continue straight on South Road. A right on Coast Road and then right on Stalker Road leads to Drumbeg Park (7).

15.0   *(9.4)*   FINISH   Silva Bay on the right (8). Best access from marina.

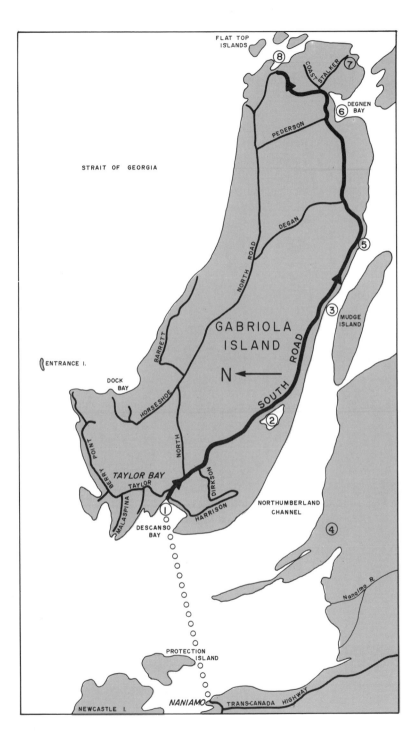

FLAT TOP
ISLANDS

⑧

COAST STALKER

⑦

DEGNEN
BAY

⑥

PEDERSON

STRAIT OF GEORGIA

DEGAN

⑤

NORTH ROAD

③

MUDGE
ISLAND

GABRIOLA
ISLAND

N ←

SOUTH ROAD

BARRETT

②

ENTRANCE I.

DOCK
BAY

HORSESHOE

NORTH

BERRY POINT

TAYLOR BAY

TAYLOR

DIRKSON

NORTHUMBERLAND
CHANNEL

MALASPINA

①

HARRISON

DESCANSO
BAY

④

Nanaimo R.

PROTECTION
ISLAND

NANIAMO   TRANS-CANADA HIGHWAY

NEWCASTLE I.

121

51

SILVA BAY	**RATING:** Intermediate (5)	
NORTH ROAD	**DISTANCE:** 17.2 km/10.8 mi	
ORLEBAR POINT		

HIGHLIGHTS: Tree tunnel on North Road; Galiano Gallery; sandstone formations at Orlebar Point; Twin Beaches at Gabriola Sands near Taylor Bay.

TRAFFIC: Congested around ferry terminal.

TERRAIN: Gradual hill on North Road, rolling hills to Taylor Bay.

REPAIRS: Bicycle shop in Nanaimo, local minor repairs available.

SUPPLIES: Stores in Silva Bay and Taylor Bay.

CONNECTIONS: Tour 50. Ferry from Nanaimo (Tour 49).

CHECKPOINTS

km   *(mi)*

0.0   *(0.0)*   START   From Silva Bay (1) continue on South Road, which becomes North Road at the bottom of a short, unexpected hill. Uphill ahead.

2.6   *(1.6)*   JUNCTION   Continue straight ahead on North Road into a tunnel of trees. A left on Pederson Road leads back to Degnen Bay (2).

7.6   *(4.8)*   DOWNHILL   At the end of the gradual uphill, begin a rolling hill descent.

9.5   *(5.9)*   JUNCTION   Turn left following North Road. Straight ahead is Lock Bay (3).

9.6   *(6.0)*   UPHILL   Steep hill, followed by rolling hill descent.

11.9   *(7.4)*   DOWNHILL   Merge with South Road and descend steeply toward the ferry terminal (4).

12.3   *(7.7)*   JUNCTION   Turn right on Taylor Bay Road, just before the ferry terminal.

13.9   *(8.7)*   INTEREST   At the end of Malaspina Road is Galiano Gallery, a massive sandstone ''wave'' formation (5). Bend right ahead.

14.3   *(8.9)*   INTEREST   A left on Ricardo Road leads to Gabriola Sands Park (6) and beach access at Twin Beaches. Continue on Berry Point Road.

15.9   *(9.9)*   INTEREST   Beach access on the left (7). Stay left ahead.

17.2   *(10.8)*   FINISH   Orlebar Point (8) with beach access and view of Entrance Island (9).

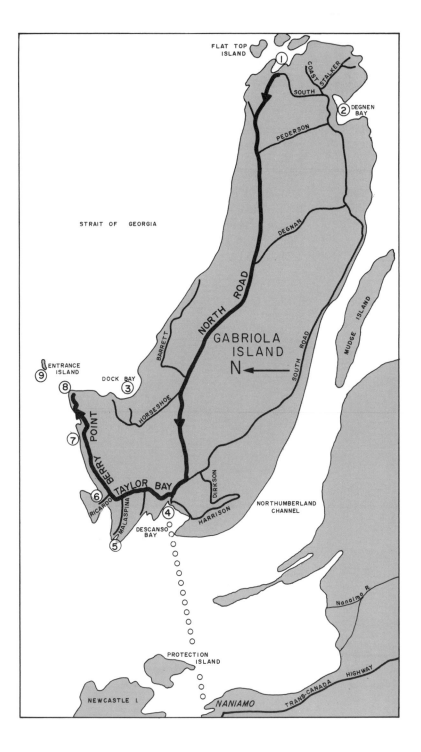

FLAT TOP
ISLAND

COAST STALKER

SOUTH

DEGNEN
BAY

PEDERSON

STRAIT OF GEORGIA

DEGNAN

NORTH ROAD

GABRIOLA
ISLAND

N

SOUTH ROAD

MUDGE ISLAND

BARRETT

ENTRANCE
ISLAND

DOCK BAY

HORSESHOE

BERRY POINT

DIRKSON

TAYLOR BAY

NORTHUMBERLAND
CHANNEL

RICARDO

MALASPINA

HARRISON

DESCANSO
BAY

PROTECTION
ISLAND

NEWCASTLE L

NANIAMO

Nanaimo R.

TRANS-CANADA HIGHWAY

123

52 | WELLINGTON LANTZVILLE NANOOSE BAY

RATING: Advanced (5 to 8)
DISTANCE: 14.1 km/8.8 mi

HIGHLIGHTS:	Water access at several points in Lantzville and opposite rest area near Nanoose Bay; stay on the Island Highway to avoid Lantzville.
TRAFFIC:	Heavy on Island Highway 19.
TERRAIN:	Rolling hills.
REPAIRS:	Bicycle store in Nanaimo.
SUPPLIES:	Supermarkets in Wellington (Nanaimo), stores in Lantzville.
CONNECTIONS:	Tours 49, 53 & 63.

Canadian Armed Forces warship anchored in Nanoose Harbour.

CHECKPOINTS

km *(mi)*

0.0 *(0.0)* START From the junction of Highway 19 and Hammond Bay Road (1) near Wellington, take Aulds Road past Metral Drive and shopping mall.

1.1 *(0.7)* CAUTION Cross railroad tracks and go uphill leaving Nanaimo district.

3.4 *(2.1)* CAUTION Turn right onto Ware Road. Cross railway and Highway 19, heading downhill.

4.6 *(2.9)* INTEREST Centre of Lantzville at Dickenson Road (2); continue straight ahead on Lantzville Road into rolling hills.

8.3 *(5.2)* JUNCTION Turn right on Highway 19. A left returns to Wellington (3).

9.1 *(5.7)* CAUTION Bridge over railway. Downhill ahead.

11.8 *(7.4)* INTEREST Rest area on the left (4). Views of Nanoose Bay.

13.9 *(8.7)* CAUTION Bridge over Bonell Creek. Enter Nanoose Bay.

14.1 *(8.8)* FINISH Junction of Northwest Bay Road and Highway 19 in Nanoose Bay (5). Both lead to Parksville and points north.

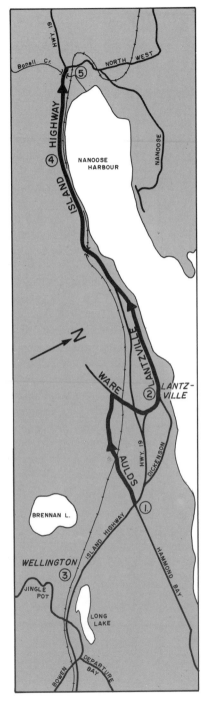

Nanoose Bay, north of Nanaimo, is a place where paths diverge. Cyclists may continue north up-island toward Courtenay and Campbell River or turn west toward the Alberni Valley and Pacific Rim National Park.

At the tip of Alberni Inlet lies the city of Port Alberni, the site of a gigantic pulp and paper operation, and the centre of much of the island's present-day forestry business. Branching away from the city are many back roads that lead through farmlands to salmon-filled rivers.

To reach Port Alberni, the cyclist must conquer Arrowsmith Summit. This requires a fairly steep hill climb, but the views along the way are most rewarding. Several campgrounds near waterfalls are a highlight of this trip, and a virgin stand of timber just past Cameron Lake makes a good rest stop before the summit climb.

Beyond Port Alberni, cyclists follow a highway alongside Sproat Lake and the Kennedy River. To bypass a difficult piece of this highway, it is possible once a week to take a passenger ferry from Port Alberni to Ucluelet and on to Pacific Rim National Park.

The park, with its magnificent, broad, sandy beaches, brings you to the sea and its diversified marine life, including, if you are fortunate, the sight of whales. You will also be rewarded by a magnificent view from an old sea radar station atop a small hill. The two towns at either end of the park, Tofino and Ucluelet, are approximately forty km apart, and have few facilities; and summer camping in the park is by reservation only. If campgrounds are full, try camping outside the park boundaries. Chesterman Beach near Tofino has open camping on an island which can be reached by wading at low tide.

Tour Ratings
Intermediate: 55, 57, 61, 62
Advanced: 53, 54, 56, 58, 59, 60

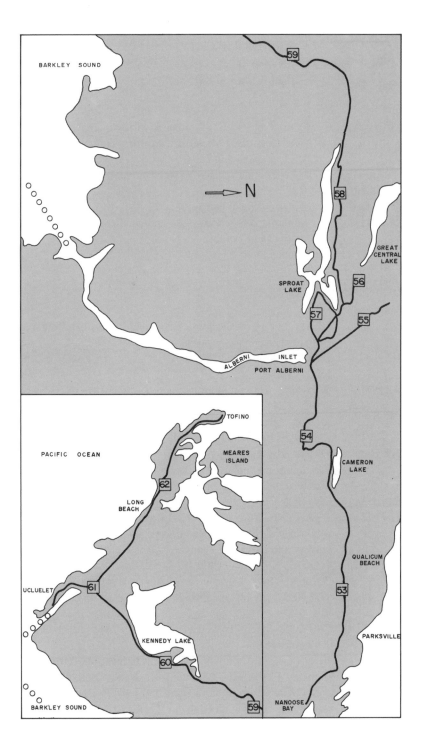

53

NANOOSE BAY	RATING: Advanced (8)
COOMBS	DISTANCE: 30.7 km/19.2 mi
QUALICUM FALLS	

HIGHLIGHTS: Petroglyphs at Englishman River; camping at English-man Falls and Little Qualicum Falls parks; hiking trails at Little Qualicum Falls.

TRAFFIC: Heaviest entering and leaving Coombs.

TERRAIN: Rolling hills.

REPAIRS: Bicycle shop in Parksville.

SUPPLIES: Supermarkets in Parksville and Qualicum, stores in Err-ington and Coombs.

CONNECTIONS: Tours 52, 54, 63, 65 & 66.

CHECKPOINTS

km	*(mi)*	
0.0	*(0.0)*	START From the Nanoose Bay Road turnoff (1), continue straight ahead on Highway 19 toward Parksville.
0.5	*(0.3)*	UPHILL After Nanoose Creek Bridge, begin a steep ascent for 2.4 km.
4.4	*(2.7)*	CAUTION Cross major logging road. Steep downhill ahead.
6.4	*(4.0)*	JUNCTION Turn left on Highway 4B (Parksville Bypass) for Port Alberni. Straight ahead across the railway leads to Rathtrevor Beach and Parksville (2).
6.9	*(4.2)*	INTEREST Left on Allsbrook Road leads to Petroglyph Park and some Indian rock carvings at Englishman River (3). Continue on highway.
8.0	*(5.0)*	CAUTION Bridge over Englishman River at the hill bottom.
12.1	*(7.6)*	JUNCTION Turn left on Highway 4 (Port Alberni High-way); bend right uphill. Right on Highway 4 leads across the railway into Parksville centre.
12.6	*(7.9)*	INTEREST At top of hill Allsbrook Road leads left back to Petroglyph Park. Continue on Highway 4; rolling hills.
15.7	*(9.8)*	INTEREST A left on Errington Road leads to Englishman Falls (4).
19.8	*(12.4)*	CAUTION Highway 4 crosses the bridge over French Creek in Coombs (5).
24.6	*(15.4)*	JUNCTION Go straight ahead on Highway 4. A right on Highway 4A leads to Qualicum Village and beach (6).
29.3	*(18.3)*	JUNCTION Turn right on Qualicum Falls Road. Cross rail-way tracks. Straight on Highway 4 leads to Port Alberni.
30.7	*(19.2)*	FINISH Parking lot and trails to Little Qualicum Falls (7). Camping is available in the park.

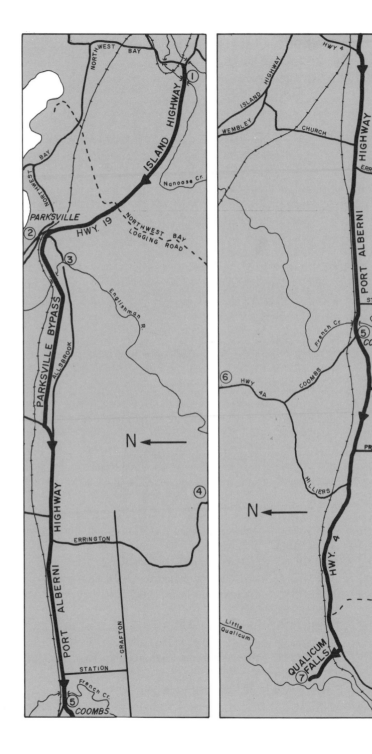

129

54

QUALICUM FALLS	RATING: Advanced (8 to 9)
ARROWSMITH SUMMIT PORT ALBERNI	DISTANCE: 32.0 km/20.0 mi

HIGHLIGHTS: Two picnic areas on Cameron Lake; views of railway trestles and Mount Arrowsmith; Cathedral Grove virgin forest; Port Alberni Pulp Mill.

TRAFFIC: Heavy around Port Alberni.

TERRAIN: Large hill up from Cameron Lake to Arrowsmith Pass and down to Port Alberni.

REPAIRS: Bicycle shop in Port Alberni.

SUPPLIES: Supermarkets in Port Alberni.

CONNECTIONS: Tours 53, 55 & 56. Passenger ferry to Ucluelet (Tour 61). See note below.

CHECKPOINTS

km	(mi)	
0.0	*(0.0)*	START From the Little Qualicum Falls Park turnoff (1), continue on Highway 4 (Port Alberni Highway), straight ahead and over a small hill.
3.5	*(2.2)*	CAUTION Two bridges over Lockwood and McBey creeks.
4.3	*(2.7)*	INTEREST Cameron Lake Picnic Area on the right (2).
7.2	*(4.5)*	INTEREST Beaufort Picnic Area on the right (3) by Cameron Lake.
10.2	*(6.4)*	CAUTION Pair of bridges over Cameron River.
10.7	*(6.7)*	INTEREST Cathedral Grove Nature Trails (4) in MacMillan Park.
15.4	*(9.6)*	UPHILL Pass close to Cameron River; start up steep hill.
18.4	*(11.5)*	INTEREST At the top of the hill is Arrowsmith Summit (5).
19.5	*(12.2)*	DOWNHILL Begin descent which steepens toward the end.
20.0	*(12.5)*	CAUTION Cross Arrowsmith Logging Road.
21.9	*(13.7)*	CAUTION Sharp left bend in middle of descending hill.
24.8	*(15.5)*	INTEREST Tourist information on the right, entering Alberni Valley (6).
25.6	*(16.0)*	JUNCTION Turn left for Port Alberni centre. A right leads to Pacific Rim. The left goes to the Lady Rose ferry.
30.4	*(19.0)*	JUNCTION Turn left from Redford onto Third Avenue. Turn right on Kingsway and then right on Argyle Street. A right from Argyle leads to the mill (7).
32.0	*(20.0)*	FINISH At foot of Argyle Street is Lady Rose passenger ferry dock (8); ferry to Ucluelet and Tofino.

NOTE: The Lady Rose ferry trip enables cyclists to avoid the unpleasant road conditions to be found on Tour 60, by taking them directly to Ucluelet near Pacific Rim Park.

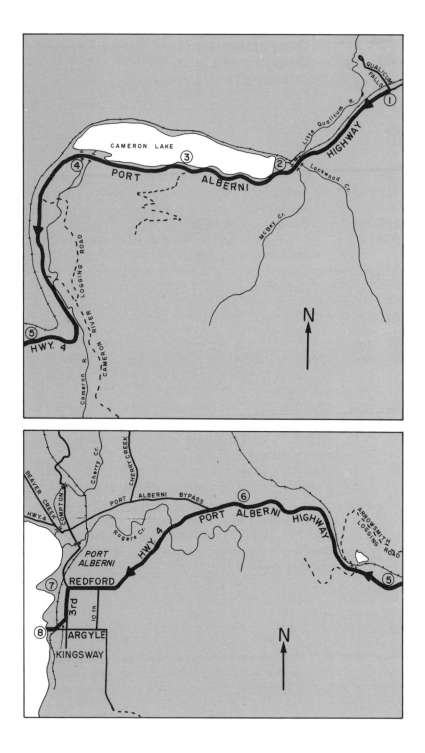

55

PORT ALBERNI	RATING: Intermediate (5)
CHERRY CREEK	DISTANCE: 31.4 km/19.6 mi
STAMP FALLS	

HIGHLIGHTS: Port Alberni Pulp Mill; views of Mount Arrowsmith from Cherry Creek; salmon run at Stamp Falls; camping in the park and good fishing.

TRAFFIC: Heavy around Port Alberni city centre.

TERRAIN: Rolling hills, steep descent on Highway 4 (Johnston Road).

REPAIRS: Bicycle shop in Port Alberni.

SUPPLIES: Supermarkets in Port Alberni, small stores in Beaver Creek and Cherry Creek.

CONNECTIONS: Tours 54 and 56. Passenger ferry from Ucluelet docks in Port Alberni.

CHECKPOINTS

km   *(mi)*

0.0   *(0.0)*   START   From the Lady Rose passenger ferry dock (1), follow Argyle Street and turn left on Kingsway before Argyle goes uphill.

1.0   *(0.6)*   CAUTION   Just after Fisherman's Harbour, merge left into 3rd Avenue.

2.1   *(1.3)*   INTEREST   Pass Redford Road and follow Stamp Road past the pulp mill (2).

2.9   *(1.8)*   CAUTION   Cross bridge over Roger's Creek. Continue straight on Gertrude Street through the centre of town.

3.4   *(2.1)*   JUNCTION   Cross Johnston Road (Highway 4). A left leads to the Somass River (3) and eventually to Pacific Rim Park.

4.5   *(2.8)*   CAUTION   Cross bridge over Kitsuksis Creek, bend left ahead and then turn right from Compton onto Kitsuksis Road near the school.

5.3 *(3.3)* CAUTION Cross railway tracks, heading uphill for next 1.0 km.

8.4 *(5.2)* JUNCTION Turn right on Batty Road, cross creek bridge and head uphill. A left leads to Beaver Creek (4).

11.8 *(7.4)* INTEREST Cherry Creek townsite (5); turn right onto Cherry Creek Road.

13.0 *(8.1)* CAUTION Bridge over Cherry Creek. Rolling hills ahead.

13.8 *(8.6)* JUNCTION Turn right on Highway 4 (Alberni Bypass). A left goes to Parksville.

15.1 *(9.4)* CAUTION Extremely rough railroad crossing during steep descent. STOP BEFORE CROSSING!

15.6 *(9.7)* JUNCTION Cross Gertrude Street and turn right on Victoria Quay ahead. A left here leads back to the pulp mill.

16.0 *(10.0)* JUNCTION After crossing the bridge over Kitsuksis Creek, veer right onto Beaver Creek Road. A left on River Road follows the Somass River.

21.3 *(13.3)* INTEREST Evergreen Park on the right (6). Rolling hills through here.

25.6 *(16.0)* INTEREST After crossing Beaver Creek, bend left into town of Beaver Creek.

29.3 *(18.3)* INTEREST After crossing Deer Creek, turn left into Stamp Falls Park (7).

31.4 *(19.6)* FINISH Dirt road ends at the hill bottom near the river. Follow the short trail downstream to reach the waterfall viewpoints (8).

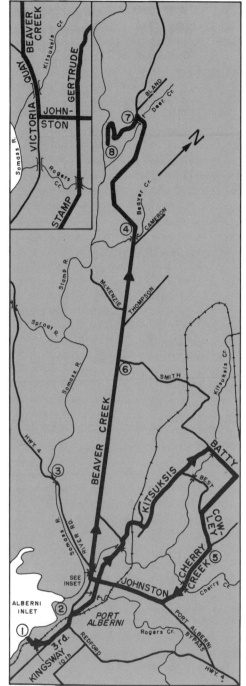

56

| PORT ALBERNI SPROAT FALLS GREAT CENTRAL LAKE | RATING: Advanced (5 to 8) DISTANCE: 23.2 km/14.5 mi |

HIGHLIGHTS: Port Alberni Pulp Mill; Somass River parks; Sproat Falls and fish ladder; camping at Sproat Lake Park; Robertson Creek Hatchery.

TRAFFIC: Heavy near Port Alberni and on Highway 4.

TERRAIN: Rolling hills with some steep parts before Sproat Falls.

REPAIRS: Bicycle shop in Port Alberni.

SUPPLIES: Supermarkets in Port Alberni.

CONNECTIONS: Tours 54, 55, 57 & 58.

CHECKPOINTS

km   *(mi)*

0.0   *(0.0)*   START   From the Port Alberni city centre turnoff (1) on Highway 4, stay right on the Alberni Bypass through Cherry Creek.

2.4   *(1.5)*   DOWNHILL   Pass Cherry Creek Road and begin steepening descent into town.

3.7 *(2.3)* CAUTION Extremely rough railway crossing. Slow down and Stop!

4.5 *(2.8)* JUNCTION Turn right on Victoria Quay, cross Kitsuksis Creek and stay left on River Road. A left on Victoria leads to the pulp mill (2).

5.9 *(3.7)* INTEREST Small park on left (3); views of seaplanes and local airport.

7.5 *(4.7)* CAUTION Bend sharp left across Somass River Bridge.

8.2 *(5.1)* CAUTION Cross bridge over McCoy Creek near McCoy Lake Road. Uphill ahead.

12.8 *(8.0)* CAUTION Narrow bridge over Sproat River. *Do not stop on the bridge.*

13.0 *(8.1)* INTEREST Sproat Falls are a short distance downstream on road right (4).

15.0 *(9.4)* JUNCTION Turn right on Great Central Road. Straight leads to Sproat Lake (5).

15.2 *(9.5)* CAMPING Sproat Lake Park Campground on the left (6). Continue straight.

19.2 *(12.0)* CAUTION Logging road crossing, bumpy road with sharp dips ahead.

21.3 *(13.3)* CAUTION Logging road crossing and bridge over Robertson Creek ahead.

21.8 *(13.6)* JUNCTION Great Central Lake (7) is just ahead, but turn right to hatchery.

22.7 *(14.2)* CAUTION Narrow bridge over Robertson Creek. Hatcheries nearby.

23.2 *(14.5)* FINISH Robertson Creek Hatchery (8) by Stamp Lagoon.

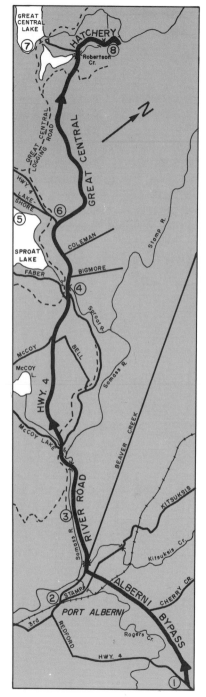

57

| McCOY LAKE |
| SPROAT LAKE |
| SOMASS RIVER |

RATING: Intermediate (5)
DISTANCE: 21.8 km/13.6 mi

HIGHLIGHTS:	Water Pipeline; McCoy Lake views; water access to Sterling Arm of Sproat Lake; look for water bombers on lake; this is a round-trip tour.
TRAFFIC:	Very light.
TERRAIN:	Rolling hills to Sproat Lake, mostly flat along Somass River Road.
REPAIRS:	Bicycle shop in Port Alberni.
SUPPLIES:	Supermarkets in Port Alberni.
CONNECTIONS:	Tour 56.

CHECKPOINTS

km	*(mi)*	
0.0	*(0.0)*	START From Highway 4, shortly after the Somass River Bridge, turn left on McCoy Lake Road, just before McCoy Creek bridge (1).
0.2	*(0.1)*	CAUTION Cross small logging road. Uphill fairly steeply ahead.
1.8	*(1.1)*	INTEREST Water supply pipeline for Port Alberni on left (2).
3.5	*(2.2)*	JUNCTION Turn left on Sterling Arm Drive, uphill. Straight on McCoy Lake Road leads past McCoy Lake (3) back to Highway 4.
5.4	*(3.4)*	CAUTION Cross major logging road; sharp right bend ahead.
9.0	*(5.6)*	JUNCTION Stay left past Faber Road. (You join it later.)
11.2	*(7.0)*	JUNCTION Merge left onto Faber Road, continuing past the firehall (4).
15.8	*(9.9)*	CAUTION Cross major logging road.
16.0	*(10.0)*	CAUTION Cross Highway 4, locate dirt road on the far side, and follow it right downhill to Somass River (Hector) Road.
21.6	*(13.5)*	JUNCTION Somass River (Hector) Road ends at Highway 4. Cross McCoy Creek Bridge to McCoy Lake Road.
21.8	*(13.6)*	FINISH Back at the start by McCoy Lake Road.

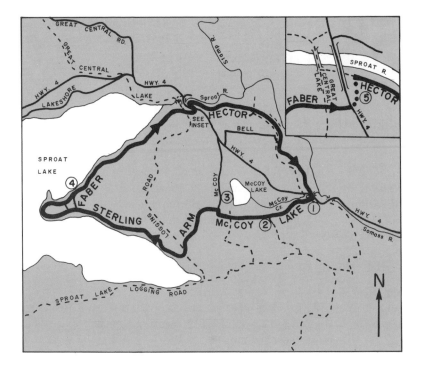

58

| GREAT CENTRAL LAKE TAYLOR ARM TAYLOR RIVER | **RATING:** Advanced (8)
DISTANCE: 29.8 km/18.6 mi |

HIGHLIGHTS: Camping, picnic area and swimming at Sproat Lake Park; views of Sproat Lake and Klitsa Mountain; rest areas on Taylor Arm and at Taylor River.
TRAFFIC: Heavy in summer months.
TERRAIN: Many rolling hills along Sproat Lake.
REPAIRS: Bicycle shop in Port Alberni.
SUPPLIES: Supermarkets in Port Alberni.
CONNECTIONS: Tours 57 & 59.

CHECKPOINTS

km *(mi)*

0.0 *(0.0)* START   From the intersection of Great Central Road and Highway 4 near Sproat Lake Park Campground (1), continue on the main highway.

0.3 *(0.2)* CAUTION   Cross major logging road from Great Central Lake.

0.6 *(0.4)* INTEREST   A left leads to Sproat Lake Park and Picnic Area (2).

4.5 *(2.8)* UPHILL   Pass Lakeshore Drive and start uphill into rolling hills.

9.0 *(5.6)* INTEREST   Taylor Arm Provincial Park Group Campsite on right (3).

9.1 *(5.7)* CAUTION   Bridge over Clutesi Creek. Cliff section ahead.

10.6 *(6.6)* CAUTION   Bridge over Freisen Creek. Logging road crossing ahead.

14.4 *(9.0)* INTEREST   Viewpoint and stop of interest on the left (4). Uphill ahead.

21.0 *(13.1)* CAUTION   Logging road crossing. Pass the end of Taylor Arm (5).

23.5 *(14.7)* CAUTION   Logging road crossing. Relatively flat ahead.

25.0 *(15.6)* CAUTION   Bridge over Porter Creek. Plenty of water access ahead.

29.8 *(18.6)* FINISH   Taylor River Rest Area (6) on right, just before the bridge.

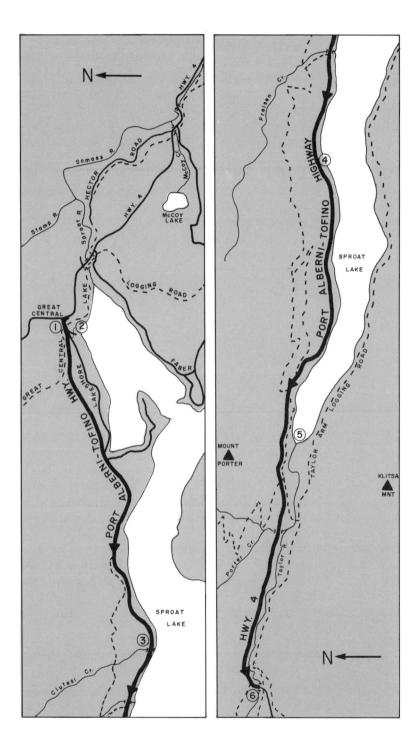

59

TAYLOR RIVER	**RATING:** Advanced (8)
SUTTON PASS	**DISTANCE:** 20.2 km/12.6 mi
KENNEDY RIVER	

HIGHLIGHTS:	Views of Taylor River and Kennedy River canyons and cataracts; many stop areas; Kennedy Falls; Kennedy River Rest Area.
TRAFFIC:	Heavy in summer months.
TERRAIN:	Steep up to Sutton Pass, then rolling hills along Kennedy River.
REPAIRS:	Bicycle shop in Port Alberni.
SUPPLIES:	Supermarkets in Port Alberni.
CONNECTIONS:	Tours 58 & 60.

CHECKPOINTS

km *(mi)*

0.0 *(0.0)* START From the Taylor River Rest Area (1), cross the bridge over Taylor River and continue straight ahead on the highway.

0.2 *(0.1)* CAUTION Cross Taylor River Logging Road. Uphill gently ahead.

1.1 *(0.7)* CAUTION Bridge over Sutton #1 (south) Creek. More uphill ahead.

3.5 *(2.2)* CAUTION Bridge over Sutton #2 (north) Creek. Steeply uphill ahead.

5.3 *(3.3)* INTEREST Cross major logging road at Sutton Pass (2).

7.0 *(4.4)* CAUTION Cross small creek bridge. Highway 4 (Port Alberni–Tofino Highway) follows Kennedy River.

8.2 *(5.1)* CAMPING Wilderness campsite to right of road before creek bridge (3).

8.8 *(5.5)* CAUTION Bridge over Foster Creek.

10.6 *(6.6)* INTEREST Stop area on the right (4). Creek bridge ahead.

12.3 *(7.7)* INTEREST Just after a small creek bridge, Kennedy Falls on the right (5).

14.1 *(8.8)* CAUTION Bridge over Canoe Creek with logging road intersection.

15.8 *(9.9)* INTEREST Stop area on the right (6).

17.0 *(10.6)* CAUTION Bridge over Braydon Creek. Pullover area on far right side.

18.4 *(11.5)* CAUTION Bridge over a small creek. River access and pullover areas ahead.

20.2 *(12.6)* FINISH Kennedy River Rest Area on the right (7).

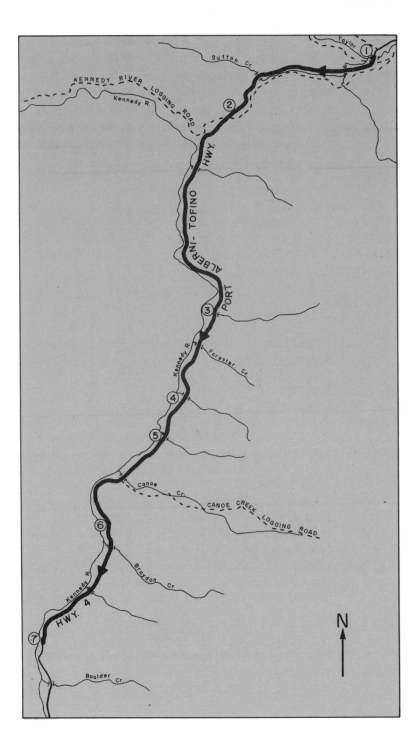

141

60

| KENNEDY RIVER |
| KENNEDY LAKE |
| PACIFIC RIM PARK |

RATING: Advanced (9 to 10)
DISTANCE: 29.6 km/18.5 mi

HIGHLIGHTS: Plenty of water access to Kennedy Lake and other small lakes; great views from hilltop corners; camping on Kennedy Lake.

TRAFFIC: Heavy in summer months (best to travel this route in early morning).

TERRAIN: Rolling hills with many sharp corners, three large hills by the lake.

REPAIRS: Bicycle shop in Port Alberni.

SUPPLIES: Grocery stores in Ucluelet.

CONNECTIONS: Tours 59 & 61.

CHECKPOINTS

km	*(mi)*	
0.0	*(0.0)*	START From the Kennedy River Rest Area (1), continue on Highway 4. Sharp corner and narrow section of road ahead.
1.4	*(0.9)*	CAUTION Bridge over a small creek. Cross logging roads.
2.9	*(1.8)*	CAUTION Hynes Creek Bridge. Sharp left bend 1.0 km ahead.
4.2	*(2.6)*	INTEREST Boat launch on Kennedy Lake (2), right. Uphill ahead.
5.6	*(3.5)*	CAUTION Sharp bend left near hilltop; pass Larry Lake (3).
6.1	*(3.8)*	CAUTION After Larry Lake, begin steep, winding descent. Sharp curves!
7.4	*(4.6)*	UPHILL Go uphill again away from Kennedy Lake. Watch for sharp corners.
9.0	*(5.6)*	DOWNHILL Part way down the descent, bend sharp left; more downhill.
10.2	*(6.4)*	UPHILL Climb uphill again into rolling hills with many sharp corners.
11.4	*(7.1)*	CAUTION Very sharp left bend, just after a sharp right bend.
12.2	*(7.6)*	INTEREST Small lake, right; pullover area, left (4). Good place for a break.

(continued, p. 144)

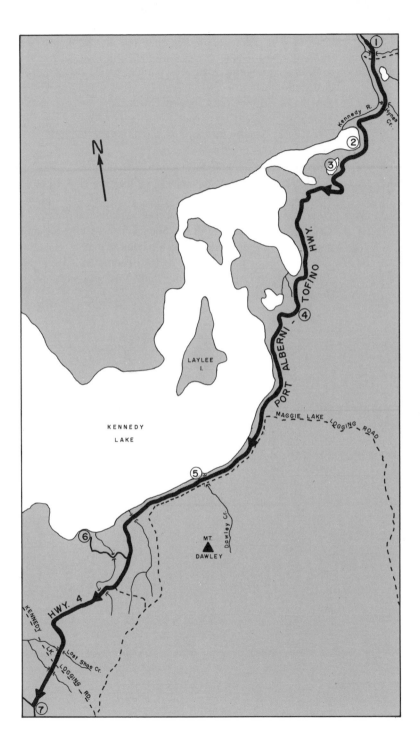

KENNEDY
LAKE

LAYLEE
I.

N

①
②
③
Kennedy R.
Hynes Cr.

PORT ALBERNI - TOFINO HWY.

④

MAGGIE LAKE LOGGING ROAD

⑤
Dawley Cr.

MT.
DAWLEY

⑥

HWY. 4

KENNEDY
LK.
Lost Shoe Cr.
LOGGING RD.

⑦

13.9 *(8.7)*   DOWNHILL   Bend sharp left and drop down to the flats along the lake.

16.7 *(10.4)*   CAUTION   Logging road runs parallel to the highway for 5.0 km.

18.9 *(11.8)*   CAUTION   Bridge over Dawley Creek. Water access on the right (5).

22.1 *(13.8)*   CAUTION   Small creek bridge just after the logging road bends away.

22.4 *(14.0)*   UPHILL   Bend left and start uphill, fairly steep.

23.4 *(14.6)*   CAMPING   Just after the hilltop a dirt road goes right to camping (6).

24.3 *(15.2)*   CAUTION   Logging road intersection. Small bridge ahead.

27.4 *(17.1)*   CAUTION   Bridge over Lost Shoe Creek. Major logging road crossing ahead followed by a second bridge.

29.6 *(18.5)*   FINISH   Major junction (7): right to Pacific Rim Park and Tofino; left to Ucluelet and the Lady Rose passenger ferry dock.

Florencia (Shipwreck) Bay at Pacific Rim Park

61

| UCLUELET |
| WICKANINNISH BAY |
| GREEN POINT |

RATING: Intermediate (5 to 6)
DISTANCE: 22.4 km/14.0 mi

HIGHLIGHTS:	Amphitrite Lighthouse; Ucluelet Cemetery; hiking trails and beach access at Florencia, Wickaninnish, Combers, and Green Point; camping at Green Point.
TRAFFIC:	Very heavy in summer months.
TERRAIN:	Mostly flat in Pacific Rim Park, rolling hills near Ucluelet.
REPAIRS:	Bicycle shop in Port Alberni.
SUPPLIES:	Stores in Ucluelet.
CONNECTIONS:	Tours 60 & 61. Passenger ferry from Port Alberni (Tour 54).

CHECKPOINTS

km	*(mi)*		
0.0	*(0.0)*	START	From the Lady Rose passenger ferry dock (1) in Ucluelet, follow Main Road uphill and left into town.
0.3	*(0.2)*	JUNCTION	Turn sharp right on Ucluth Peninsula Road. A left leads to Coast Guard Road and the Amphitrite Point Lighthouse (2).
7.0	*(4.4)*	JUNCTION	Continue straight ahead on Peninsula Road past Thornton Road, which goes right to Port Albion (3).
7.4	*(4.6)*	INTEREST	Ucluelet Cemetery on the right (4).
8.5	*(5.3)*	JUNCTION	Stay left for Pacific Rim Park. A right on Highway 4 returns to possible camping on Kennedy Lake (5).
9.9	*(6.2)*	INTEREST	Enter Pacific Rim Park and cross the 49th Parallel (6).
11.2	*(7.0)*	CAUTION	Bridge over Lost Shoe Creek. Park Information on right (7).
12.3	*(7.7)*	INTEREST	Gold Mine Hiking Trail on left (8) leads to Florencia Bay.
13.4	*(8.4)*	JUNCTION	Go straight ahead on Highway 4. A left leads to Florencia Bay (9) and Wickaninnish Beach (10) with park headquarters.

(continued, p. 148)

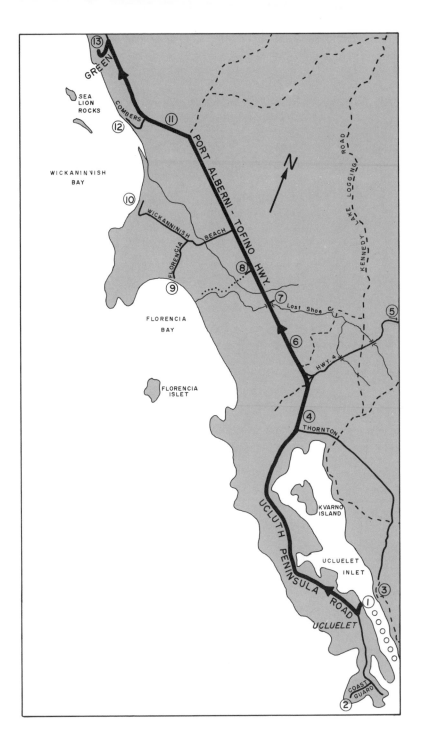

SEA
LION
ROCKS

WICKANINNISH
BAY

WICKANINNISH
BAY

FLORENCIA
BAY

FLORENCIA
ISLET

GREEN

COMBERS

PORT ALBERNI - TOFINO HWY.

N

KENNEDY LAKE LOGGING ROAD

WICKANNINISH BEACH

FLORENCIA

Lost Shoe Cr.

HWY. 4

THORNTON

KVARNO
ISLAND

UCLUELET
INLET

UCLUTH PENINSULA ROAD

UCLUELET

COAST
GUARD

147

17.4 *(10.9)* CAUTION   Bend left by a logging road intersection, following the highway.

17.9 *(11.2)* INTEREST   Rain Forest Nature Trails on both sides of the highway (11).

18.9 *(11.8)* JUNCTION   Go straight ahead on Highway 4. A left leads down to Combers Beach (12) with a view of Sea Lion Rocks offshore.

21.4 *(13.4)* JUNCTION   Turn left for Green Point Campground. Straight ahead on the highway leads to Long Beach and eventually to Tofino.

22.4 *(14.0)* FINISH   Camping at Green Point and trails down to Long Beach (13).

The sand at Long Beach is well packed and hard enough to ride on.

62

**GREEN POINT
RADAR HILL
LOOKOUT
TOFINO**

RATING: Intermediate (5 to 6)
DISTANCE: 22.4 km/14.0 mi

HIGHLIGHTS: Camping at Green Point and Schooner Cove; beach access at Long Beach, Grice, Chesterman and MacKenzie; 360° view from Radar Hill Lookout.
TRAFFIC: Very heavy in summer months.
TERRAIN: Relatively flat in Pacific Rim Park, rolling hills near Tofino.
REPAIRS: Bicycle shop in Port Alberni.
SUPPLIES: Stores in Tofino.
CONNECTIONS: Tour 61.

CHECKPOINTS

km	*(mi)*	
0.0	*(0.0)*	START From the Green Point Campground turnoff (1), continue on Highway 4 (Port Alberni–Tofino Highway) toward Tofino.
1.6	*(1.0)*	DOWNHILL Descend to Long Beach with a beautiful view of the sandy beach.
2.1	*(1.3)*	INTEREST At the bottom of the hill is a short trail left to the beach (2).
3.7	*(2.3)*	JUNCTION Straight ahead past the turnoff right to the airport (3) and Long Beach Picnic Area on the left (4).
4.2	*(2.6)*	INTEREST Access to Long Beach, left (5).
5.6	*(3.5)*	INTEREST Esowista Indian Reserve Arts and Crafts Shop on left (6).
5.8	*(3.6)*	CAMPING Hike-in camping available at Schooner Cove. Trail, left (7).
6.6	*(4.1)*	CAMPING Overflow camping on the left (8); no facilities.
6.9	*(4.3)*	JUNCTION Turn left, following the main highway. Straight ahead leads to a boat launch and picnic area on Grice Bay (9).
10.6	*(6.6)*	JUNCTION Continue on the main highway. A left leads steeply uphill to Radar Hill Lookout and a fabulous view of Pacific Rim (10).

(continued, p. 152)

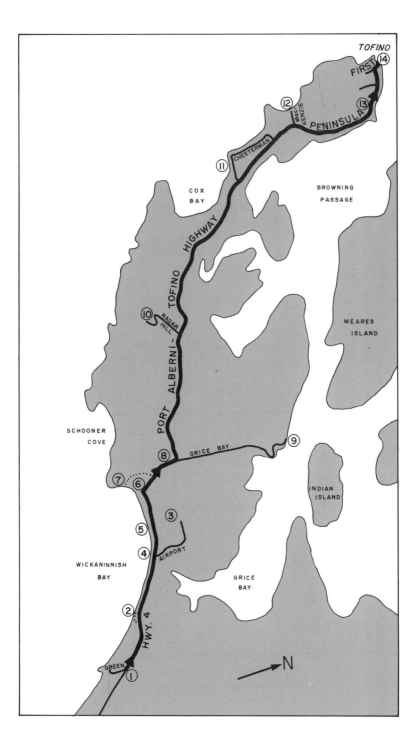

TOFINO

FIRST

PENINSULA

MacKENZIE

CHESTERMAN

COX
BAY

BROWNING
PASSAGE

TOFINO HIGHWAY

PORT ALBERNI-

RADAR
HILL

MEARES
ISLAND

SCHOONER
COVE

GRICE BAY

INDIAN
ISLAND

AIRPORT

WICKANINNISH
BAY

GRICE
BAY

HWY. 4

GREEN

N

11.1 *(6.9)*   INTEREST   Leave Pacific Rim Park on the way to Tofino.

15.8 *(9.9)*   JUNCTION   Continue on the main highway. A left on Chesterman Road leads to Chesterman Beach (11); possible tenting area.

18.2 *(11.4)*   JUNCTION   Straight ahead on the main highway. A left on MacKenzie Road leads to MacKenzie Beach (12), which may be less crowded.

19.8 *(12.4)*   INTEREST   Entering Tofino (13), remain on the main road until town centre.

22.1 *(13.8)*   JUNCTION   Turn right from Peninsula Road (Campbell) onto First Street. A left leads to the hospital.

22.4 *(14.0)*   FINISH   Water access to Tofino docks area (14).

Sea anemones in rocky tidal pools

REGION F   PARKSVILLE/COURTENAY

This region extends from Nanoose Bay near Parksville to Miracle Beach near Courtenay. Two very different types of beaches are found here. Rathtrevor Beach is a long sandy beach that extends into the Strait of Georgia for almost a mile. Qualicum Beach is a small pebble beach. French Creek lies between Qualicum and Parksville, and at the river's mouth is the dock for the Lasqueti Island passenger ferry. Cyclists are more likely to encounter cows than cars on the roads of Lasqueti, all of which are gravel. Also in the area is the Englishman River with an impressive set of upstream waterfalls and some Indian petroglyphs downstream.

About half way between Qualicum Beach and Courtenay is the Buckley Bay Ferry Terminal, the access point to Denman and Hornby islands. These islands must be seen. Especially delightful are the parks on Hornby Island's east tip. Limited camping is available on Denman Island only.

The Comox Valley surrounding Courtenay offers a rolling terrain. Among the farmlands of the Tsolum River are several parks and many beaches, an airforce base and a small naval outpost. Little River to the north of Comox is the terminal for the ferry that connects the island to the Sunshine Coast; many cyclists prefer to leave Vancouver Island at this point to return to Vancouver.

Tour Ratings
Beginner: 69, 70, 71
Intermediate: 63, 64, 65, 66, 72, 75, 76, 77, 78
Advanced: 67, 68, 73, 74, 79

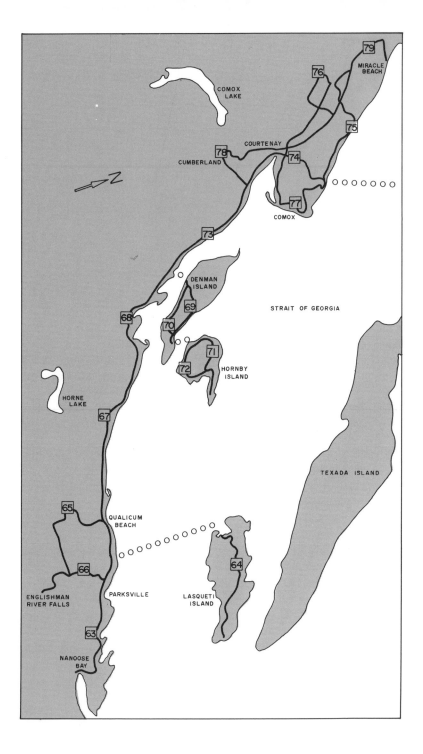

COMOX
LAKE

MIRACLE
BEACH

79

76

75

COURTENAY

78

CUMBERLAND

74

77

COMOX

73

DENMAN
ISLAND

STRAIT OF GEORGIA

69

68

70

71

72

HORNBY
ISLAND

HORNE
LAKE

67

TEXADA ISLAND

65

QUALICUM
BEACH

66

64

ENGLISHMAN
RIVER FALLS

PARKSVILLE

LASQUETI
ISLAND

63

NANOOSE
BAY

63

| NANOOSE BAY
PARKSVILLE
FRENCH CREEK | **RATING:** Intermediate (5 to 6)
DISTANCE: 20.0 km/12.5 mi |

HIGHLIGHTS: Camping and beach access at Rathtrevor Beach Park; hewn log church in Parksville; ferry to Lasqueti Island at French Creek.

TRAFFIC: Very heavy in Parksville, light along Nanoose Bay Road.

TERRAIN: Rolling hills around Nanoose Bay, relatively flat in Parksville.

REPAIRS: Bicycle shop in Parksville.

SUPPLIES: Stores in Nanoose Bay, supermarkets in Parksville.

CONNECTIONS: Tours 52, 53, 65 & 66. Passenger ferry to Lasqueti Island (Tour 64).

CHECKPOINTS

km	*(mi)*	
0.0	*(0.0)*	START From Highway 19 at a point (1) between the Bonell Creek Bridge and the Nanoose Creek Bridge, turn right onto Northwest Bay Road.
0.2	*(0.1)*	CAUTION Cross railway tracks for the first of three times.
0.7	*(0.4)*	UPHILL Cross Nanoose Creek Bridge and head uphill to cross railway again.
2.2	*(1.4)*	CAUTION Just over the hilltop, cross the railway for a third time.
3.2	*(2.0)*	JUNCTION Stay left. A right on Stewart Road leads to Dolphin Beach (2).
5.4	*(3.4)*	CAUTION Cross Northwest Bay Logging Road, going downhill gently. JUNCTION Stay left. A right turn leads to Madrona Point (3). Uphill ahead.
9.6	*(6.0)*	JUNCTION Turn right on Highway 19. A left returns to Nanoose Bay.
11.5	*(7.2)*	CAMPING A right on Rath Road leads to camping at Rathtrevor Beach (4).
12.3	*(7.7)*	CAUTION Bridge over Englishman River, entering Parksville (5)

(continued, p. 158)

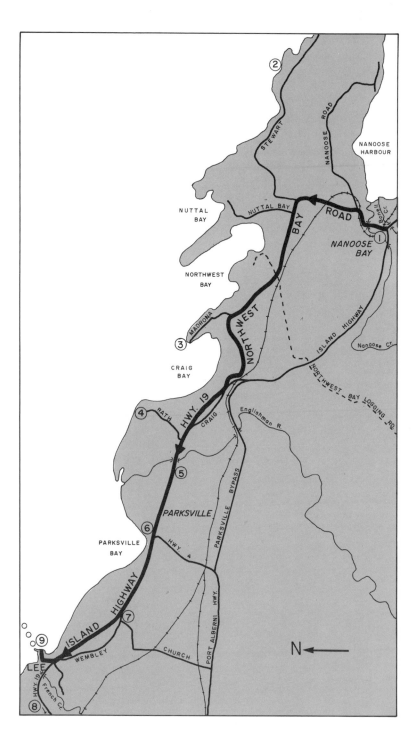

NANOOSE
HARBOUR

②

STEWART
NANOOSE ROAD

Bonell Cr.

NUTTAL BAY

NUTTAL
BAY

ROAD

①

NANOOSE
BAY

BAY

NORTHWEST
BAY

NORTHWEST

ISLAND HIGHWAY

Nanoose Cr.

③

MADRONA

CRAIG
BAY

HWY. 19

NORTHWEST BAY LOGGING RD.

④

RATH

CRAIG

Englishman R.

⑤

PARKSVILLE

PARKSVILLE BYPASS

⑥

PARKSVILLE
BAY

HWY 4

PORT ALBERNI HWY.

ISLAND HIGHWAY

⑦

N ←

⑨

WEMBLEY

CHURCH

LEE

HWY. 19

French Cr.

⑧

157

14.6 *(9.1)* JUNCTION   Continue straight ahead on Highway 19 after the Tourist Information Centre (6). A left on Highway 4 goes to Port Alberni.

16.6 *(10.4)* INTEREST   St. Anne Church on the left along Wembley Road (7).

19.4 *(12.1)* JUNCTION   Turn right on Lee Road for French Creek. Straight on Highway 19 leads across French Creek Bridge to Qualicum Beach (8).

20.0 *(12.5)* FINISH   French Creek and the Centurion passenger ferry dock (9). Catch the Lasqueti Island Ferry here.

Rathtrevor Beach near Parksville, a recommended camping location

64

| FALSE BAY LASQUETI ISLAND SQUITTY BAY | **RATING:** Intermediate (2 to 5) **DISTANCE:** 17.2 km/10.8 mi |

HIGHLIGHTS:	Tea Pot House; Hadley Lake; Island Cemetery; Squitty Bay hillside; side trip to Spanish Cave (private property: inquire at nearby home).
TRAFFIC:	Minimal. Watch for cattle and people on the roads.
TERRAIN:	Rolling hills, some steep gravel sections.
REPAIRS:	Bicycle shop in Parksville.
SUPPLIES:	Very limited store in False Bay. Stock up in Parksville.
CONNECTIONS:	Passenger ferry from French Creek docks. See note below.

CHECKPOINTS

km	*(mi)*	
0.0	*(0.0)*	**START** From the passenger ferry at False Bay (1), peddle up a steep hill on the only road leading from the docks. Turn left at top.
0.8	*(0.5)*	**INTEREST** After passing the post office, notice Mud Bay on the left (2).
1.2	*(0.8)*	**JUNCTION** Tea Pot Corner (3) by the houses with teapot-shaped chimneys. Turn right onto Lasqueti Island Trunk Road. A left leads to Spring Cove (4) and Spanish Cave (5).
2.2	*(1.4)*	**INTEREST** Pete's (Hadley) Lake on the left (6). Uphill ahead.
6.3	*(3.9)*	**INTEREST** Beaver Pond on the right (7). Downhill ahead.
7.1	*(4.4)*	**JUNCTION** Stay on the main road, bending right and then left. Avoid Tucker Bay Road and Richardson Bay and Lake roads at this intersection.
7.4	*(4.6)*	**INTEREST** New community centre on the left (8). Large downhill ahead.
9.7	*(6.1)*	**INTEREST** Lasqueti Island Cemetery on the left (9). Uphill ahead.
15.0	*(9.4)*	**DOWNHILL** Begin descent toward Squitty Bay after passing Copley Road.
16.9	*(10.6)*	**JUNCTION** After a rolling descent, turn right on Squitty Bay Road.
17.2	*(10.8)*	**FINISH** The road ends on a grassy hillside by the bay (10) and near the Squitty Bay dock. Beautiful lunch spot.

NOTE: There are no camping facilities on Lasqueti Island. It is for the most part a wild and undeveloped island. The roads are gravel and the cattle graze on open rangeland which includes the roads. The ferry ride is somewhat expensive because of the extra fare for your bike.

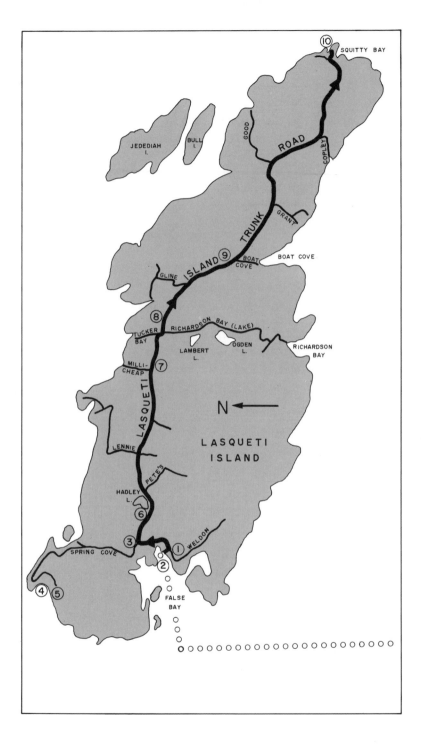

65

**QUALICUM BEACH
HILLIERS
ENGLISHMAN FALLS**

RATING: Intermediate (5)
DISTANCE: 25.2 km/15.8 mi

HIGHLIGHTS: Qualicum Beach; Qualicum Village park; Hamilton Swamp bird sanctuary; camping and hiking at Englishman River Falls Park.
TRAFFIC: May be heavy on Highway 4A between Qualicum Village and Hilliers.
TERRAIN: Rolling hills.
REPAIRS: Bicycle shop in Parksville.
SUPPLIES: Supermarkets in Qualicum Village, store in Errington.
CONNECTIONS: Tours 53, 66 & 67.

CHECKPOINTS

km	*(mi)*	
0.0	*(0.0)*	START From the junction of Highway 19 and 4A in Qualicum Beach (1), take Highway 4A as Memorial Avenue uphill into Qualicum Village.
1.3	*(0.8)*	CAUTION Cross railway into Qualicum Village (2). Turn right on 2nd Ave.
2.0	*(1.2)*	INTEREST Local park on right after left bend (3).
4.7	*(2.9)*	JUNCTION Stay right on Hilliers Road. A left leads to Coombs (4).
5.2	*(3.3)*	INTEREST Stop area on left at local bird sanctuary (5).
7.9	*(4.9)*	CAUTION Cross railway tracks to enter Hilliers (6).
8.5	*(5.3)*	JUNCTION Turn left on Highway 4. A right leads to Qualicum Falls (7).
9.4	*(5.9)*	JUNCTION Turn right on Pratt Road. Continuing on highway leads to Coombs.
10.7	*(6.7)*	CAUTION Bridge over French Creek. Turn left on Grafton ahead.
14.0	*(8.8)*	CAUTION Second bridge over French Creek. Road improves ahead.
18.4	*(11.5)*	JUNCTION Turn right on Errington Road. A left returns to town of French Creek (8).
20.2	*(12.6)*	CAUTION Cross bridge over Swane Creek. Several curves ahead.
22.4	*(14.0)*	CAUTION Bend right across wooden plank bridge over Morison Creek.
24.4	*(15.3)*	INTEREST Entering Englishman Falls Park (9). Camping.
25.2	*(15.8)*	FINISH Parking lot with trails to Englishman Falls (10).

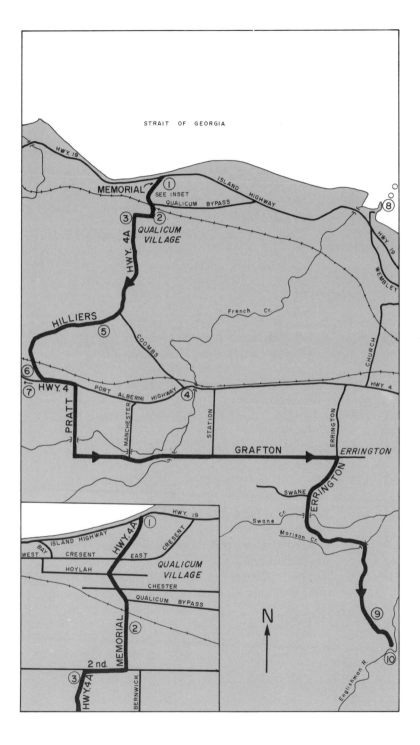

STRAIT OF GEORGIA

HWY. 19

MEMORIAL ①

② SEE INSET
ISLAND HIGHWAY

③ QUALICUM BYPASS

HWY. 4A

QUALICUM
VILLAGE

⑧

HWY. 19

WEMBLEY

French Cr.

HILLIERS

⑤

COOMBS

CHURCH

⑥

⑦ HWY. 4

PRATT

PORT ALBERNI HIGHWAY

MANCHESTER

④

STATION

HWY. 4

GRAFTON

ERRINGTON

ERRINGTON

ERRINGTON

SWANE

Swane Cr.

Morison Cr.

HWY. 19

HWY. 4A

①

ISLAND HIGHWAY

WEST BAY

CRESENT

EAST

CRESENT

QUALICUM
VILLAGE

HOYLAH

CHESTER

QUALICUM BYPASS

MEMORIAL

②

N

2 nd.

③ HWY. 4A

BERNWICK

⑨

⑩

Englishman R.

163

66

ERRINGTON	RATING: Intermediate (5 to
FRENCH CREEK	6)
QUALICUM BEACH	DISTANCE: 14.4 km/8.8 mi

HIGHLIGHTS: Log-hewn church of St. Anne near Parksville; French Creek docks and passenger ferry to Lasqueti Island; park and beach at Qualicum Beach.

TRAFFIC: Heavy on highway between French Creek and Qualicum Beach.

TERRAIN: Rolling hills and relatively flat.

REPAIRS: Bicycle shop in Parksville.

SUPPLIES: Store in Errington, supermarkets in Qualicum Beach.

CONNECTIONS: Tours 63, 65 & 67. Passenger ferry to Lasqueti Island (Tour 64).

CHECKPOINTS

km *(mi)*

0.0 *(0.0)* START   From the town of Errington (1), take Errington Road away from Grafton Road, heading toward Parksville (2).

1.9 *(1.2)* JUNCTION   Turn right on Highway 4. A left leads to Coombs (3).

2.4 *(1.5)* JUNCTION   Turn left on Church Road. Straight on leads to Parksville.

2.8 *(1.7)* CAUTION   Cross railroad, heading downhill. Second set farther ahead.

5.3 *(3.3)* INTEREST   St. Anne Church on the right (4). Turn left on Wembley Road.

7.4 *(4.6)* CAUTION   Merge left onto Highway 19; pass Lee Road and French Creek (5).

8.0 *(5.0)* CAUTION   Cross bridge over French Creek. Follow highway to Qualicum.

14.4 *(8.8)* FINISH   Memorial Park and tourist information on the right (6) in Qualicum Beach. Straight on leads to Courtenay City (7).

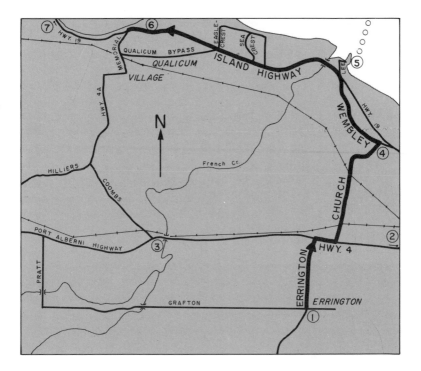

67

| QUALICUM BEACH
QUALICUM RIVER
BOWSER | **RATING:** Advanced (6 to 8)
DISTANCE: 20.5 km/12.8 mi |

HIGHLIGHTS: Plenty of beach and water access; Memorial Park in Qualicum Beach; Qualicum River Fish Hatchery; Qualicum Bay.

TRAFFIC: Heavy.

TERRAIN: Mostly flat with two moderate hills.

REPAIRS: Bicycle shop in Parksville.

SUPPLIES: Stores in Qualicum Beach, Dashwood, Qualicum Bay and Bowser.

CONNECTIONS: Tours 66 & 68.

The annual salmon run at the Qualicum hatchery

CHECKPOINTS

km *(mi)*

0.0 *(0.0)* START From the junction of Highway 19 (Island Highway) and 4A in Qualicum Beach (1), take Highway 19 along the shoreline toward Courtenay.

1.3 *(0.8)* INTEREST Qualicum Beach Memorial Park on the right (2). Beach access.

4.3 *(2.7)* CAUTION Cross the bridge over Little Qualicum River into Dashwood (3).

7.5 *(4.7)* CAUTION Railway crossing after uphill section, relatively flat ahead.

11.2 *(7.0)* CAUTION Cross railroad tracks again, downhill ahead into Dunsmuir (4).

14.9 *(9.3)* INTEREST Qualicum River Fish Hatchery on the left (5).

15.0 *(9.4)* CAUTION Cross the bridge over (Big) Qualicum River to Qualicum Bay (6).

18.9 *(11.8)* CAUTION Cross Nile Creek Bridge and bend sharply left.

20.5 *(12.8)* FINISH Entering the town of Bowser (7). Uphill ahead.

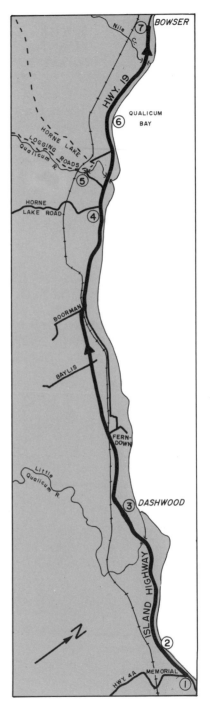

167

68

BOWSER	RATING: Advanced (6 to 8)
FANNY BAY	DISTANCE: 21.3 km/13.3 mi
BUCKLEY BAY	

HIGHLIGHTS: Rosewall Creek Park; Ship Peninsula; Fanny Bay and Buckley Bay; ferry to Denman and Hornby islands.

TRAFFIC: Heavy.

TERRAIN: Rolling hills and relatively flat.

REPAIRS: Bicycle shop in Parksville or Courtenay.

SUPPLIES: Stores in Bowser and Buckley Bay.

CONNECTIONS: Tours 67 & 73. Ferry to Denman Island (Tours 69 & 70).

CHECKPOINTS

km *(mi)*

0.0 *(0.0)* START Follow the main highway uphill through the town of Bowser (1).

1.3 *(0.8)* CAUTION Cross railroad tracks, still heading uphill gently.

6.1 *(3.8)* DOWNHILL Begin a descent into rolling hills.

8.5 *(5.3)* CAUTION Pass Bowser Logging Road and cross Cook Creek Bridge.

10.2 *(6.4)* INTEREST Cross Rosewall Creek Bridge in Rosewall Creek Park (2).

12.2 *(7.6)* CAUTION Pass Rosewall Logging Road and cross railway ahead.

13.1 *(8.2)* CAUTION Bridge over Waterloo Creek beside Mud Bay (3).

15.4 *(9.6)* CAUTION Cross Wilfred Creek Bridge after a logging road crossing.

15.8 *(9.9)* JUNCTION Go straight ahead on Highway 19. A right on Ship Point (Peninsula) Road leads to water access (4) before a small hill.

17.1 *(10.7)* CAUTION Bridge over Cougar (Cowie) Creek. Entering Fanny Bay (5).

18.2 *(11.4)* INTEREST Fanny Bay Pier and "Brico" ship restaurant on the right (6).

19.5 *(12.2)* CAUTION Bridge over Tsable River. Base Flat on the right (7).

21.0 *(13.1)* JUNCTION Turn right for ferry to Denman Island (8). Straight on leads to Courtenay, Comox, Cumberland and Royston.

21.3 *(13.3)* FINISH Buckley Bay Ferry Terminal (9). Catch Denman Island Ferry.

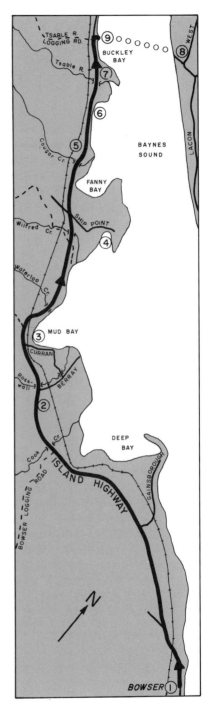

69

DENMAN ISLAND	RATING: Beginner (2 to 4)
FILLONGLEY PARK	DISTANCE: 11.2 km/7.0 mi
EAST POINT	

HIGHLIGHTS: Views from Denman Road; beach access on East Road; camping at Fillongley Park; ferry to Hornby Island.

TRAFFIC: Light except around ferry terminals.

TERRAIN: Steep hills at the start, rolling hills along East Road.

REPAIRS: Bicycle shop in Courtenay.

SUPPLIES: Limited store in Denman Island town, store in Buckley Bay.

CONNECTIONS: Tour 70. Ferry from Buckley Bay (Tours 68 & 73) to Hornby Island (Tours 71 & 72).

CHECKPOINTS

km *(mi)*

0.0 *(0.0)* START   Disembark from the Buckley Bay Ferry and allow all traffic to go first. Ride up a steep hill on the main road (1).

0.5 *(0.3)* INTEREST   Town of Denman Island at the hilltop (2); stay right.

1.0 *(0.6)* JUNCTION   Stay left on Denman Road. A right leads to Metcalf Bay (3).

1.2 *(0.7)* UPHILL   Begin a very steep ascent for 0.4 km. Road is narrow.

1.8 *(1.1)* DOWNHILL   Gradual rolling hill descent for next 3.2 km.

3.6 *(2.2)* INTEREST   Denman Island Cemetery on the right (4).

4.4 *(2.8)* CAMPING   A left on Swan Road leads to camping at Fillongley Park (5).

5.0 *(3.1)* CAUTION   Bend sharp right at the bottom of the hill; follow East Road.

9.0 *(5.6)* JUNCTION   Stay left on East Road. A right on McFarlane Road leads to Metcalf Bay.

11.0 *(6.9)* CAUTION   Bend sharply left down to Gravelly Bay.

11.2 *(7.0)* FINISH   East Point Ferry Terminal (6). Catch ferry to Hornby Island (7).

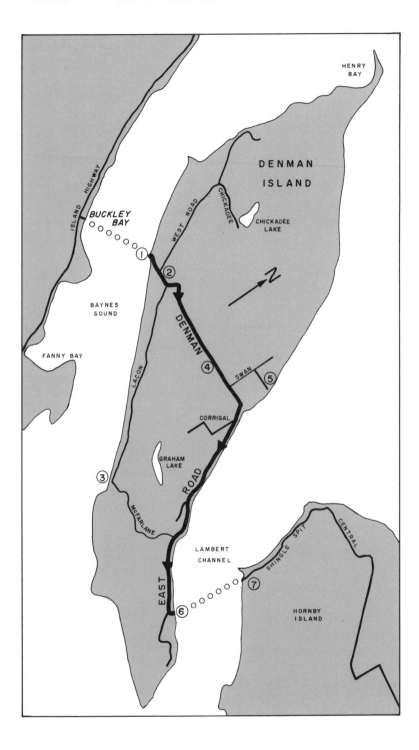

HENRY BAY

DENMAN ISLAND

ISLAND HIGHWAY

BUCKLEY BAY

WEST ROAD

CHICKADEE

CHICKADEE LAKE

①

②

N

BAYNES SOUND

DENMAN

FANNY BAY

LACON

④

SWAN

⑤

CORRIGAL

③

GRAHAM LAKE

ROAD

McFARLANE

SHINGLE SPIT

CENTRAL

LAMBERT CHANNEL

EAST

⑦

⑥

HORNBY ISLAND

70

**EAST POINT
METCALF BAY
DENMAN ISLAND**

RATING: Beginner (2 to 4)
DISTANCE: 11.2 km/7.0 mi

HIGHLIGHTS: Beach access at Metcalf Bay; route makes a nice return trip on dirt roads if you are not pressed for time.
TRAFFIC: Minimal except near ferry terminal.
TERRAIN: Rolling hills.
REPAIRS: Bicycle shop in Courtenay.
SUPPLIES: Store at Denman Island townsite.
CONNECTIONS: Tour 69. Ferry from Hornby Island (Tours 71 & 72) and to Buckley Bay (Tours 68 & 73).

CHECKPOINTS

km   *(mi)*
0.0   *(0.0)*   START   Uphill away from Gravelly Bay and the ferry terminal (1), following East Road. Rolling hills ahead along shoreline.
2.2   *(1.4)*   JUNCTION   Turn left on McFarlane Road. Straight ahead leads to Fillongley Park (2).
2.4   *(1.5)*   UPHILL   Begin uphill into rolling hills. Stay right ahead.
4.3   *(2.7)*   DOWNHILL   Begin downhill with rolling hills and steep sections.
4.9   *(3.1)*   INTEREST   Metcalf Bay (3). Turn right on Lacon Road. Rolling hills ahead.
10.2 *(6.4)*   JUNCTION   Turn left on Denman Road. A right goes back to Fillongley Park and the ferry terminal near East Point.
10.7 *(6.7)*   CAUTION   Steep descent after pasing through Denman Island town (4). Stay left.
11.2 *(7.0)*   FINISH   Denman Island Ferry Terminal (5). Catch ferry to Buckley Bay (6).

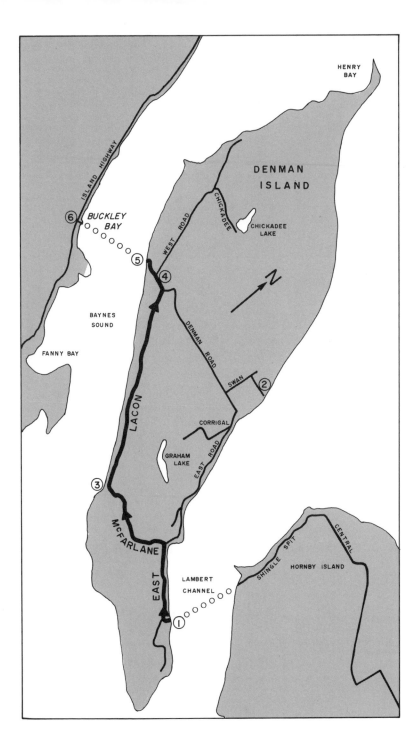

HENRY
BAY

DENMAN
ISLAND

ISLAND HIGHWAY

⑥ BUCKLEY
BAY
ooooooo
⑤

④

CHICKADEE

CHICKADEE
LAKE

WEST ROAD

N

BAYNES
SOUND

DENMAN ROAD

FANNY BAY

SWAN ②

CORRIGAL

LACON

GRAHAM
LAKE

EAST ROAD

③

McFARLANE

SHINGLE SPIT

HORNBY ISLAND

CENTRAL

EAST

LAMBERT
CHANNEL

①ooooooo

71

| HORNBY ISLAND |
| TRIBUNE BAY |
| HELLIWELL PARK |

RATING: Beginner (2)
DISTANCE: 12.8 km/8.0 mi

HIGHLIGHTS:	Picnic area on beach near Tribune Bay; petroglyphs; beach at Whaling Station Bay; Helliwell Park and hiking trails to St. John Point.
TRAFFIC:	Light except near ferry terminal.
TERRAIN:	Rolling hills.
REPAIRS:	Bicycle shop in Courtenay.
SUPPLIES:	Stores in Hornby Island (Shingle Spit) and Tribune Bay (Coop Corner).
CONNECTIONS:	Tour 72. Ferry from Denman Island (Tours 69 & 70).

CHECKPOINTS

km *(mi)*

0.0 *(0.0)* START From the ferry terminal (1) at Hornby Island (Shingle Spit), take Shingle Spit Road uphill.

0.5 *(0.3)* INTEREST Many stopping areas on the left ahead, with good views to Denman Island.

3.2 *(2.0)* CAUTION Bend right onto Central Road. Uphill ahead.

6.7 *(4.2)* INTEREST Pass Hornby Cemetery on right (2) and community hall ahead.

8.5 *(5.3)* JUNCTION Turn left on St. John Road. A right goes to Ford Cove (3). Continuing straight on Salt Spray Road leads to Tribune Bay (4).

9.0 *(5.6)* INTEREST Tribune Bay Park entrance on right (5).

9.3 *(5.8)* JUNCTION Turn right with St. John Road. Straight ahead on Ostby Road leads to a trail to petroglyphs near Tralee Point (6).

12.2 *(7.6)* INTEREST Beach access to Whaling Station Bay on the left (7).

12.3 *(7.7)* JUNCTION Turn right on a dirt road. Straight on leads to Cape Gurney (8).

12.6 *(7.9)* UPHILL Sudden steep hill on Helliwell Road into Helliwell Park (9).

12.8 *(8.0)* FINISH Helliwell parking lot. Hiking trails from here to St. John Point follow the shoreline perimeter above sea cliffs (10).

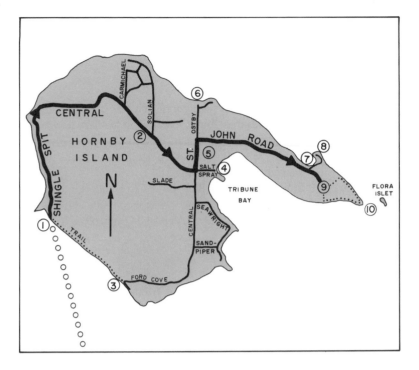

CARMICHAEL

SOLIAN

CENTRAL

HORNBY
ISLAND

N

SHINGLE SPIT

TRAIL

SLADE

ST. OSTBY

⑥

② JOHN ROAD

⑤ SALT SPRAY

④

SEAWRIGHT

CENTRAL

SAND-
PIPER

FORD COVE

③

①

TRIBUNE
BAY

⑦

⑧

⑨

⑩

FLORA
ISLET

72

**TRIBUNE BAY
FORD COVE
HORNBY ISLAND**

RATING: Intermediate (4)
DISTANCE: 7.5 km/4.7 mi

HIGHLIGHTS: An adventurous hiking trail that was once Shingle Spit Road leads from Ford Cove back to the ferry terminal.
TRAFFIC: Minimal. Watch for hikers on the trail.
TERRAIN: Rolling hills. Trail is washed out in a few places.
REPAIRS: Bicycle shop in Courtenay.
SUPPLIES: Stores in Tribune Bay, Ford Cove and Hornby Island (Shingle Spit).
CONNECTIONS: Tour 71. Ferry to Denman Island (Tours 69 & 70).

CHECKPOINTS

km   *(mi)*

0.0   *(0.0)*   START   From Coop Corner in Tribune Bay (1) take Central Road away from St. John Road toward Ford Cove.

0.6   *(0.4)*   UPHILL   Begin fairly steep hill in rolling sections for 2.5 km.

3.1   *(1.9)*   DOWNHILL   Begin very steep descent, with views to Denman Island.

4.5   *(2.8)*   JUNCTION   Turn right on a dirt road. Straight ahead is Ford Cove (2).

4.7   *(2.9)*   CAUTION   Take the right upper fork in the road. Dismount and walk bikes for the next 2.5 km on old road turned trail. Washouts ahead.

5.7   *(3.6)*   CAUTION   Large washout area. Cliffs and views ahead (3).

7.3   *(4.6)*   JUNCTION   At the end of Shingle Spit Trail, turn right on dirt road and then left on paved road past Hornby Island townsite (4).

7.5   *(4.7)*   FINISH   Shingle Spit Ferry Terminal (5). Catch ferry to Denman Island.

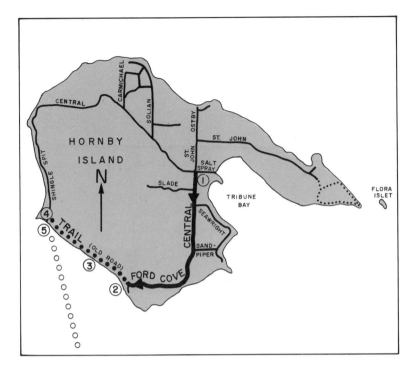

73

**BUCKLEY BAY
UNION BAY
ROYSTON**

RATING: Advanced (6 to 8)
DISTANCE: 16.6 km/10.4 mi

HIGHLIGHTS: Park and picnic area at Buckley Bay; several rest areas and water access spots; Union Bay and Royston.
TRAFFIC: Heavy.
TERRAIN: Flat along the shoreline to Union Bay, then rolling hills.
REPAIRS: Bicycle shop in Courtenay.
SUPPLIES: Stores in Buckley Bay, Union Bay and Royston.
CONNECTIONS: Tours 68, 74 & 78. Ferry from Denman Island into Buckley Bay.

Take a moment to read the Denman Island sign at Buckley Bay ferry terminal.

CHECKPOINTS

km *(mi)*

0.0 *(0.0)* START From the Buckley Bay Ferry turnoff (1), continue on the Island Highway toward Courtenay.

1.9 *(1.2)* INTEREST Local park and picnic area by the water on the right (2).

3.2 *(2.0)* INTEREST Rest area on the right (3). Views of Denman Island.

4.8 *(3.0)* INTEREST Rest area on the right (4). Entering Union Bay ahead.

7.2 *(4.5)* INTEREST Union Bay (5), pier and water access on the right.

8.3 *(5.2)* CAUTION Cross Washer (Hart) Creek. Uphill ahead, leaving Union Bay.

9.8 *(6.1)* CAUTION Cross Bayton Logging Road. Rolling hills ahead.

15.4 *(9.6)* CAUTION Cross Trent River Bridge, entering Royston ahead.

16.6 *(10.4)* FINISH In the centre of Royston at the major crossroad intersection (6): left for Cumberland; straight for Courtenay; right to the beach.

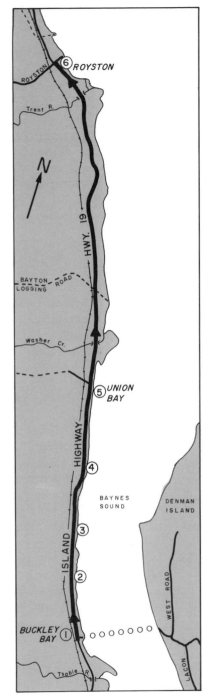

74 | ROYSTON SANDWICK LITTLE RIVER

RATING: Advanced (6 to 9)
DISTANCE: 16.0 km/10.0 mi

HIGHLIGHTS: Museum and parks in Courtenay; beach access at Little River.
TRAFFIC: Heavy near Courtenay.
TERRAIN: Large hill near Sandwick.
REPAIRS: Bicycle shop in Courtenay or Comox.
SUPPLIES: Supermarkets in Courtenay.
CONNECTIONS: Tours 73, 75, 76, 77 & 78. Ferry to Powell River on Sunshine Coast.

CHECKPOINTS

km	*(mi)*	
0.0	*(0.0)*	START From the Royston crossroads (1), continue on the Island Highway toward Courtenay.
0.8	*(0.5)*	CAUTION Cross Comox Lake Logging Road. Downhill gently ahead.
5.3	*(3.3)*	INTEREST Tourist information on right (2) after entering Courtenay.
5.8	*(3.6)*	JUNCTION Turn right on the Courtenay Bypass of the Island Highway. Straight ahead on Cliffe leads to the museum (3).
5.9	*(3.7)*	CAUTION Cross steel deck bridge over Courtenay (Puntledge) River.
6.1	*(3.8)*	JUNCTION Turn left following the Courtenay Bypass and Highway 19. A right leads to Comox (4).
7.8	*(4.9)*	JUNCTION Turn right on Ryan Road. Continuing straight leads to Campbell River (5).
8.3	*(5.2)*	UPHILL Begin steep ascent for next 2.0 km through Sandwick (6).
10.6	*(6.6)*	DOWNHILL Begin gentle descent, bending right.
12.5	*(7.8)*	JUNCTION Turn left on Anderton Road. Straight on leads to the Canadian Armed Forces Base and Airport at Lazo (7).
14.1	*(8.8)*	DOWNHILL Bend right on Ellenor Road downhill into Little River (8).
15.7	*(9.8)*	CAUTION Cross bridge over the Little River after Wilkinson Road.
16.0	*(10.0)*	FINISH Little River Ferry Terminal (9). Catch Powell River Ferry here.

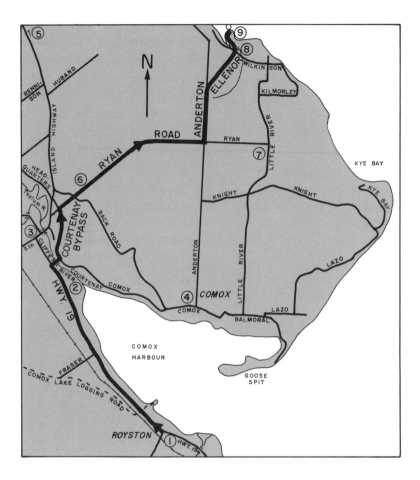

N

5

HUBAND
RENNI-SON
Island Highway

HEAD-QUARTERS
Tsolum R.

RYAN   ROAD
ANDERTON   ELLENOR
9
8
WILKINSON
KILMORLEY

RYAN
7
LITTLE RIVER
KYE BAY

6

COURTENAY BYPASS
BACK ROAD

KNIGHT   KNIGHT
KYE BAY R.

3
5th
CLIFFE
RIVER
COURTENAY

2
COMOX

ANDERTON
LITTLE RIVER
LAZO

4   COMOX

COMOX
BALMORAL
LAZO

HWY. 19

COMOX HARBOUR

FRASER
COMOX LAKE LOGGING ROAD

GOOSE SPIT

ROYSTON   1   HWY. 19A

75

LITTLE RIVER	RATING: Intermediate (5)
KITTY COLEMAN	DISTANCE: 22.4 km/14.0 mi
BEACH	
MERVILLE	

HIGHLIGHTS: Beach access at Little River, Bates and Kitty Coleman; nature trails; camping in Kitty Coleman Beach Park; farmlands around Merville.

TRAFFIC: Heavy on Island Highway 19.

TERRAIN: Rolling hills with many flat sections.

REPAIRS: Bicycle shop in Courtenay or Comox.

SUPPLIES: Store in Merville.

CONNECTIONS: Tours 74, 76 & 77. Ferry from Powell River at Little River.

CHECKPOINTS

km	*(mi)*	
0.0	*(0.0)*	START Follow Ellenor (Anderton) Road away from the Powell River Ferry Terminal at Little River (1).
0.3	*(0.2)*	CAUTION Cross Little River Bridge and turn right on Wilkinson Road.
1.2	*(0.8)*	INTEREST Water access on right (2). Go left uphill on dirt road.
1.7	*(1.1)*	JUNCTION Turn right on Waveland Road. A left leads to Comox (3).
3.9	*(2.4)*	JUNCTION By a second set of radio towers, turn left on Bates Road. A right leads down to Bates Beach (4).
5.1	*(3.2)*	INTEREST Nature trails on both sides of the road (5).
7.6	*(4.8)*	INTEREST Turn right on Coleman Road and then left on Aldergrove Drive. A left on Coleman leads directly to the Island Highway.
9.1	*(5.7)*	INTEREST Follow dirt road down to water and through Kitty Coleman Beach Park (6) along shoreline. Camping.
9.5	*(5.9)*	UPHILL Take Whittaker Road uphill away from the water. Turn left on Left Road and then right on Coleman Road.
13.7	*(8.6)*	JUNCTION Cross the Island Highway onto Poulton Road.
14.8	*(9.2)*	INTEREST Town of Merville (7). Go left on Merville Road.
16.3	*(10.2)*	JUNCTION Turn right on Howard Road. A left leads to village of Headquarters (8).
19.2	*(12.0)*	JUNCTION Turn right on the Island Highway. A left leads to Miracle Beach (9).
22.4	*(14.0)*	FINISH Passing through Merville at Merville Road (10).

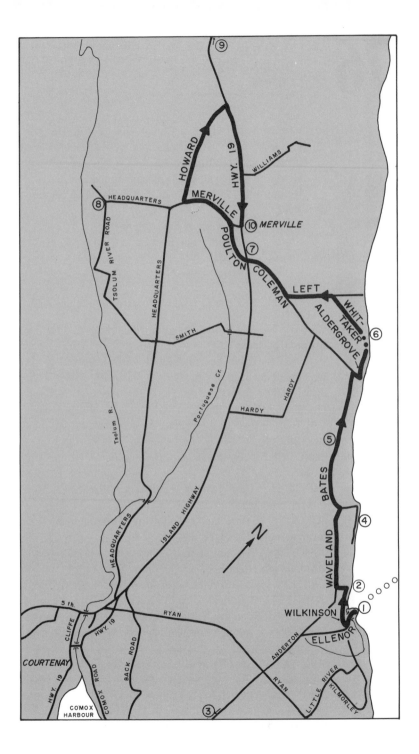

76

MERVILLE	RATING: Intermediate (5)
HEADQUARTERS	DISTANCE: 28.8 km/18.0 mi
COMOX	

HIGHLIGHTS: Farmlands and views of Comox Glacier from Headquarters to Comox; Historical Cairn by the Tsolum River; good views from Back Road.

TRAFFIC: Heavy on the Island Highway and around Courtenay.

TERRAIN: Rolling hills on Back Road, fairly flat on Headquarters Road.

REPAIRS: Bicycle shop in Comox or Courtenay.

SUPPLIES: Store in Grantham, supermarkets in Comox.

CONNECTIONS: Tours 74, 75, 77 & 78.

CHECKPOINTS

km *(mi)*

0.0 *(0.0)* START From Merville (1), continue on the Island Highway toward Courtenay.

0.9 *(0.6)* INTEREST Cross Coleman Road which leads left to Kitty Coleman Beach (2).

2.8 *(1.7)* JUNCTION Turn right on Smith Road near the school in Grantham (3). Continuing on highway leads to Courtenay.

3.3 *(2.1)* CAUTION Bridge over Portuguese Creek. Road bends twice ahead.

5.4 *(3.4)* JUNCTION Cross Headquarters Road on to Tsolum River Road.

10.3 *(6.4)* INTEREST Turn right on Headquarters Road near Headquarters village (4).

12.1 *(7.6)* JUNCTION Turn right, following Headquarters Road. Straight on leads to Merville.

15.6 *(9.7)* JUNCTION Pass Smith and Tsolum River roads, following Headquarters Road.

20.0 *(12.5)* CAUTION Wooden plank bridge over Portuguese Creek.

22.7 *(14.2)* INTEREST Historical cairn by Tsolum River (5). Turn left on Dingwall Road just before it. Uphill to Island Highway.

23.0 *(14.4)* CAUTION Dismount and walk across the Island Highway. Follow Back Road.

23.6 *(14.8)* JUNCTION Cross Ryan Road on Back Road. A left leads to Little River (6).

28.0 *(17.5)* JUNCTION Turn left on Comox Road. A right leads to Courtenay (7).

28.8 *(18.0)* FINISH Comox centre (8) at the crossroads of Comox Avenue and Anderton Road.

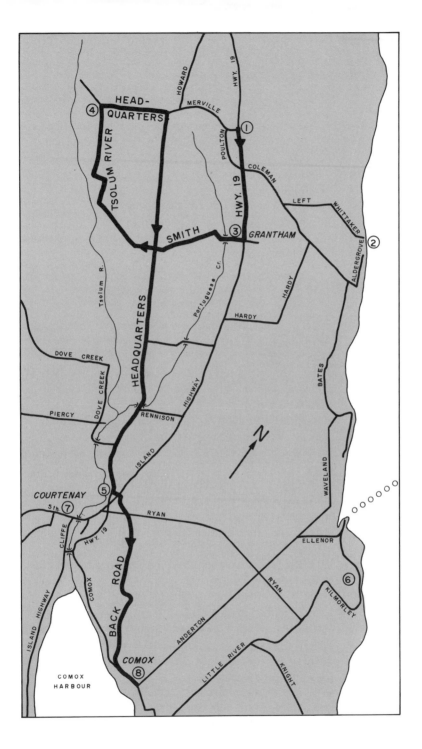

77

COMOX	RATING: Intermediate (5)
LAZO	DISTANCE: 17.3 km/10.8 mi
LITTLE RIVER	

HIGHLIGHTS: Water access in Comox and at Goose Spit; beach access at Lazo and Kin; Canadian Armed Forces Base and Airport; Little River Ferry Terminal.

TRAFFIC: Heavy in Comox.

TERRAIN: Rolling hills.

REPAIRS: Bicycle store in Comox or Courtenay.

SUPPLIES: Supermarkets in Comox, store in Lazo.

CONNECTIONS: Tours 74, 75, 76 & 78. Ferry to Powell River and the Sunshine Coast.

CHECKPOINTS

km *(mi)*

0.0 *(0.0)* START From the crossroads in Comox (1), take Comox Avenue away from Anderton Road and into downtown Comox.

0.7 *(0.4)* JUNCTION Turn left on Port Augusta Street and right on Balmoral Avenue. A right on Port Augusta leads down to the Comox docks (2).

2.1 *(1.3)* JUNCTION Turn left on Torrence and right on Lazo Road. Straight ahead drops down to Goose Spit beach access (3).

3.4 *(2.1)* DOWNHILL After a left turn the road drops downhill toward Cape Lazo.

5.5 *(3.4)* INTEREST Lazo Beach on the right (4).

6.4 *(4.0)* UPHILL Bend left on Knight and go up a steep hill away from the beach.

10.5 *(6.6)* JUNCTION Turn right on Little River Road. A left returns to Comox.

12.1 *(7.6)* INTEREST Lazo (5) and the Canadian Armed Forces Base (6). Go straight.

13.4 *(8.4)* JUNCTION Turn right on Kilmorley Road. Straight leads to Little River.

14.4 *(9.0)* DOWNHILL Turn left and go downhill to reach Kin Beach Park on right (7).

15.8 *(9.9)* JUNCTION Cross Little River Road, going from Booth onto Wilkinson Road.

16.0 *(10.0)* CAUTION Cross bridge over Little River.

16.9 *(10.6)* JUNCTION Turn right on Ellenor (Anderton) Road and cross a bridge. A left leads back to Courtenay (8).

17.3 *(10.8)* FINISH Little River Ferry Terminal (9). Catch Powell River Ferry here.

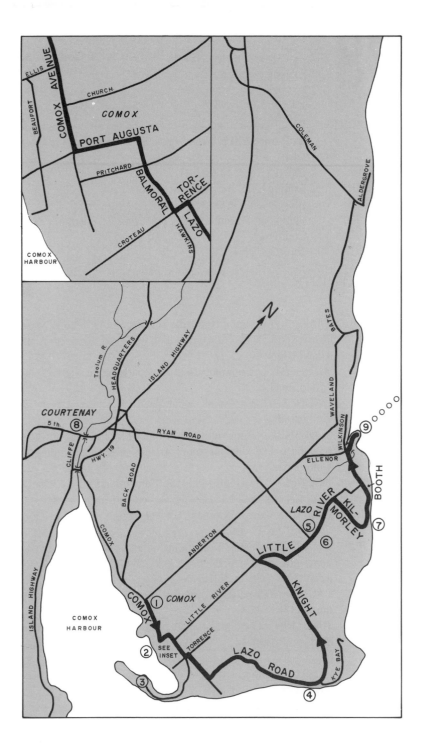

COMOX AVENUE

ELLIS

BEAUFORT

CHURCH

COMOX

PORT AUGUSTA

PRITCHARD

BALMORAL

TOR-
RENCE

LAZO

CROTEAU

HAWKINS

COMOX
HARBOUR

Tsolum R.

HEADQUARTERS

ISLAND HIGHWAY

N

COLEMAN

ALDERGROVE

BATES

WAVELAND

WILKINSON

COURTENAY

5th.

⑧

RYAN ROAD

CLIFFE

HWY. 19

BACK ROAD

ELLENOR

⑨

○○○○○○

LAZO   RIVER

KIL-
MORLEY

BOOTH

⑤

⑥

⑦

ANDERTON

LITTLE

COMOX

ISLAND HIGHWAY

COMOX
HARBOUR

COMOX

① COMOX

LITTLE RIVER

KNIGHT

② SEE
INSET

TORRENCE

LAZO ROAD

TYE BAY

③

④

187

78

ROYSTON	RATING: Intermediate (5)
CUMBERLAND	DISTANCE: 19.5 km/12.2 mi
COURTENAY	

HIGHLIGHTS: Park, museum and cemeteries in Cumberland; camping on Comox Lake; parks, museum and cemetery in Courtenay.

TRAFFIC: Heavy around Courtenay.

TERRAIN: Rolling hills, steep hill after Courtenay.

REPAIRS: Bicycle shop in Courtenay.

SUPPLIES: Stores in Royston and Cumberland, supermarkets in Courtenay.

CONNECTIONS: Tours 73, 74 & 79.

CHECKPOINTS

km	*(mi)*		
0.0	*(0.0)*	START	From the crossroads in Royston (1), take Royston Road uphill across the railroad tracks and away from the Island Highway.
2.1	*(1.3)*	INTEREST	Community hall and park on the left (2) by Minto Road.
6.6	*(4.1)*	INTEREST	Pass small local park (3), entering city of Cumberland.
7.0	*(4.4)*	JUNCTION	Turn right on 4th Street by museum (4). Straight ahead on Dunsmuir Avenue leads to camping at Comox Lake (5).
9.3	*(5.8)*	INTEREST	Bend left following Cumberland Road around a cemetery (6). Stay left after the second cemetery ahead.
13.4	*(8.4)*	CAUTION	Cross Comox Lake Logging Road, heading downhill into Courtenay.
16.6	*(10.4)*	JUNCTION	Turn left on Harmston past many churches and then right on Fifth.
17.1	*(10.7)*	INTEREST	Cross Cliffe; museum on the left (7).
17.4	*(10.9)*	CAUTION	Cross the Courtenay (Puntledge) River; park on the left (8).
17.9	*(11.2)*	JUNCTION	Continue straight on the old highway. A right on Ryan Road leads to the Powell River Ferry at Little River (9).
18.4	*(11.5)*	UPHILL	Continue straight uphill, merging with the New Island Highway Bypass.
19.5	*(12.2)*	FINISH	At the top of the hill are a cemetery and water tower to the right (10).

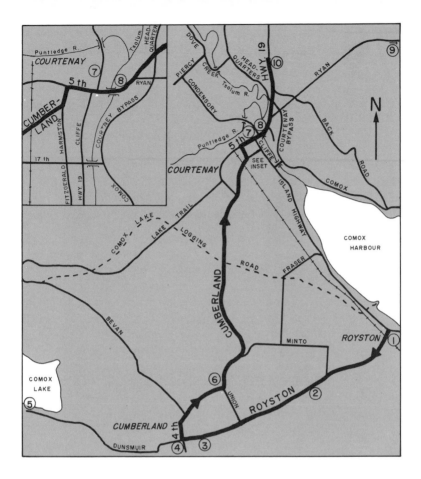

N

79

COURTENAY
BLACK CREEK
MIRACLE BEACH

RATING: Advanced (6 to 8)
DISTANCE: 24.0 km/15.0 mi

HIGHLIGHTS: Farmland and views of Comox Glacier; Black Creek religious community; camping and picnic areas at Miracle Beach.
TRAFFIC: Heavy around Courtenay.
TERRAIN: Gentle rolling hills.
REPAIRS: Bicycle shop in Courtenay or Campbell River.
SUPPLIES: Stores in Grantham, Merville and Black Creek.
CONNECTIONS: Tours 75, 76, 78 & 80.

CHECKPOINTS

km *(mi)*

0.0 *(0.0)* START   From the cemetery and water tower (1) at the hilltop above Courtenay, continue on the Island Highway 19 to Campbell River.

7.0 *(4.4)* INTEREST   Pass through the small town of Grantham (2) at Smith Road.

9.0 *(5.6)* CAUTION   Pass Coleman Road. A right leads to Kitty Coleman Beach (3).

10.1 *(6.3)* INTEREST   Pass through Merville townsite (4) at Merville Road.

13.6 *(8.5)* CAUTION   Pass Howard Road. A left leads to village of Headquarters (5).

16.8 *(10.5)* CAUTION   Bridge over Black Creek. Uphill ahead.

18.7 *(11.7)* INTEREST   Pass through the religious community of Black Creek (6).

20.8 *(13.0)* JUNCTION   Turn right on Miracle Beach Road. Straight on leads to Campbell River (7).

23.2 *(14.5)* CAUTION   Cross bridge over Black Creek and enter Miracle Beach Park (8).

23.7 *(14.8)* CAMPING   Campground on the right (9).

24.0 *(15.0)* FINISH   Beach and water access at Miracle Beach (10) on Elma Bay.

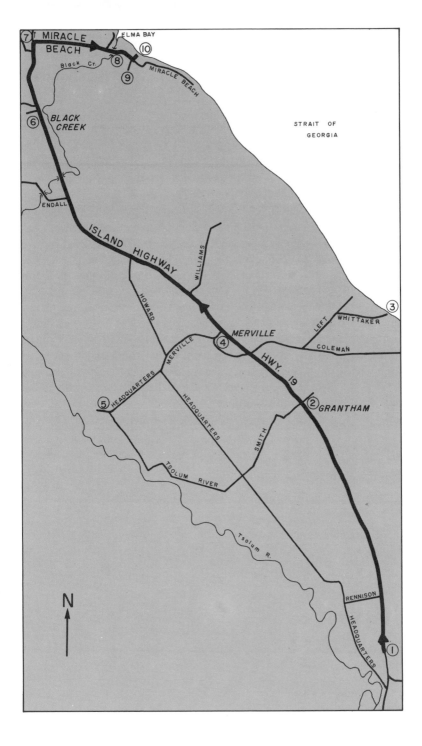

STRAIT OF
GEORGIA

ELMA BAY

⑦ MIRACLE
BEACH

Black Cr.

⑩

⑧

⑨ MIRACLE BEACH

⑥ BLACK
CREEK

ENDALL

ISLAND HIGHWAY

WILLIAMS

HOWARD

③

LEFT WHITTAKER

④ MERVILLE

COLEMAN

MERVILLE

HWY. 19

HEADQUARTERS

⑤ HEADQUARTERS

HEADQUARTERS

② GRANTHAM

SMITH

TSOLUM RIVER

Tsolum R.

RENNISON

N

HEADQUARTERS

①

REGION G

CAMPBELL RIVER/ STRATHCONA

This region includes all the travellable roads within Strathcona Provincial Park and the area from Gold River in the west to Campbell River in the east. The highway from Campbell River to Gold River passes through some spectacular high country. The main beauty here consists of the opportunity to ride along the shores of two huge man-made lakes with snow-capped peaks towering above you. There are many campsites within the park. Several short hiking trails lead to small waterfalls and many of the longer trails take you into alpine meadows high above timberline.

At Gold River there is a chance to visit Nootka Island by boat and see the point where Captain Cook first landed on Vancouver Island. The museum in downtown Campbell River has a fine collection of Indian artifacts.

Two islands at the north tip of the Strait of Georgia are easily reached by ferry from Campbell River. The island of Quadra has parks, beaches, a lighthouse and an Indian village with a museum and petroglyph displays. Small Cortes Island is reached by ferry from Quadra and is the most primitive of the accessible Gulf Islands. Its roads are mostly gravel and services are few. But its beach areas are appealing and the cyclist will not have to contend with crowds or cars.

Tour Ratings
Intermediate: 81, 82, 83, 84, 87, 88
Advanced: 80, 85, 86, 89, 90

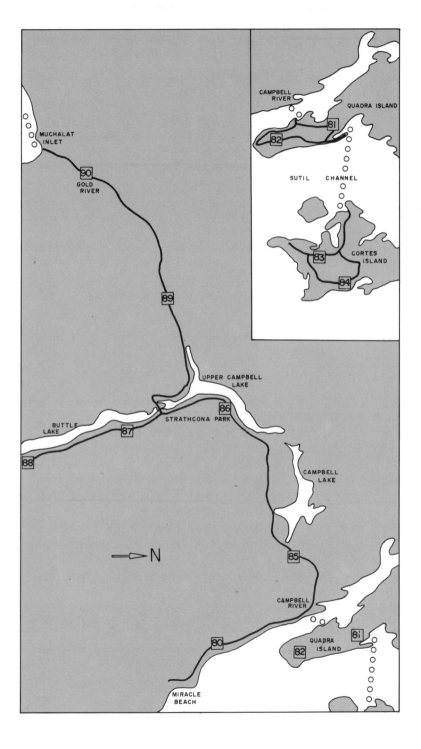

MUCHALAT
INLET

90
GOLD
RIVER

89

CAMPBELL
RIVER

81

82

QUADRA ISLAND

SUTIL   CHANNEL

83

CORTES
ISLAND

84

UPPER CAMPBELL
LAKE

86

BUTTLE
LAKE

87

STRATHCONA PARK

88

CAMPBELL
LAKE

N

85

CAMPBELL
RIVER

82

QUADRA
ISLAND

81

80

MIRACLE
BEACH

80 MIRACLE BEACH OYSTER BAY CAMPBELL RIVER

RATING: Advanced (6 to 8)
DISTANCE: 24.0 km/15.0 mi

HIGHLIGHTS: Beach access at Saratoga, Oyster Bay, Shelter Point and Campbell River; park, museum/library in Campbell River.
TRAFFIC: Heavy around Campbell River.
TERRAIN: Flat with hills at Campbell River.
REPAIRS: Bicycle shop in Campbell River.
SUPPLIES: Stores in Oyster River, Oyster Bay, Shelter Point and Campbell River.
CONNECTIONS: Tours 79, 85 & 91. Ferry to Quadra Island (Tours 81 & 82).

CHECKPOINTS

km   *(mi)*

0.0   *(0.0)*   START   From the Miracle Beach turnoff (1), continue on Highway 19.

1.6   *(1.0)*   INTEREST   Turn off right to Saratoga Beach (2). Continue straight.

1.9   *(1.2)*   CAUTION   Bridge over the Oyster River. Entering Oyster River town (3).

5.3   *(3.3)*   INTEREST   Entering Oyster Bay, plenty of beach access ahead (4).

5.8   *(3.6)*   INTEREST   Rest area on the right (5) by Oyster Bay.

11.7   *(7.3)*   INTEREST   Beach access on the right (6) in Shelter Bay.

16.3   *(10.2)*   JUNCTION   Continue straight ahead for Campbell River. A left on Erikson leads to the airport (7).

19.0   *(11.9)*   INTEREST   Big Rock Park on the right (8).

20.2   *(12.6)*   INTEREST   Entering Campbell River; local park and swimming area on the right (9).

20.8   *(13.0)*   INTEREST   Cross the 50th parallel (10). Uphill steeply ahead.

23.8   *(14.9)*   JUNCTION   Turn right by a large park for the ferry terminal. Straight on leads past the museum and library (11) toward Port Hardy.

24.0   *(15.0)*   FINISH   Quadra Island Ferry Terminal on the right (12).

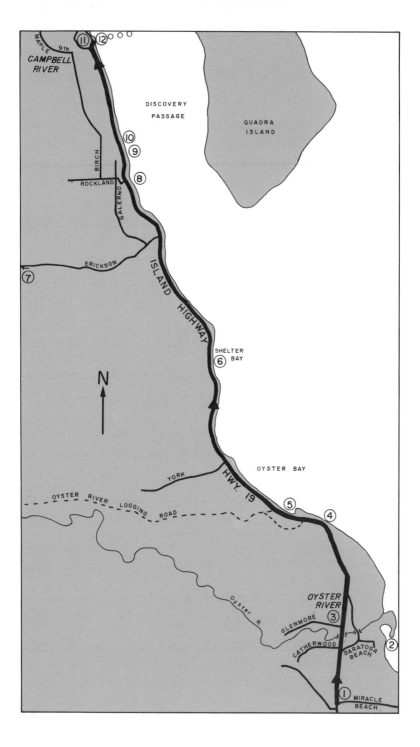

CAMPBELL RIVER

MAPLE

9th

⑪ ⑫ ○ ○ ○

DISCOVERY PASSAGE

QUADRA ISLAND

⑩
⑨

BIRCH

ROCKLAND ⑧

GALERNO

ERICKSON

⑦

ISLAND HIGHWAY

SHELTER BAY ⑥

N

OYSTER BAY

YORK

HWY. 19

OYSTER RIVER LOGGING ROAD

⑤

④

Oyster R

OYSTER RIVER

GLENMORE ③

CATHERWOOD

SARATOGA BEACH

②

① MIRACLE BEACH

81

QUATHIASKI COVE HERIOT BAY REBECCA SPIT	RATING: Intermediate (5) DISTANCE: 13.6 km/8.5 mi

HIGHLIGHTS: Buildings in Quathiaski Cove; Blenkin Memorial Park; Heriot Bay Inn; Rebecca Spit Park (no camping allowed).

TRAFFIC: Minimal, except around ferry terminals.

TERRAIN: Rolling hills.

REPAIRS: Bicycle shop in Campbell River.

SUPPLIES: Small store at Heriot Bay, large store at Quathiaski Cove.

CONNECTIONS: Tour 82. Ferry to Cortes Island (Tours 83 & 84).

CHECKPOINTS

km *(mi)*

0.0 *(0.0)* START At Quathiaski Cove Ferry Terminal (1), allow the traffic to go first. Follow Quathiaski Cove Road and then Harper Road.

1.0 *(0.6)* CAUTION Bend sharp right near the school onto Heriot Bay Road.

1.3 *(0.8)* JUNCTION Turn left on West Road for Heriot Bay. Continuing straight ahead leads to Cape Mudge Road and the lighthouse (2).

3.0 *(1.9)* INTEREST After the hilltop, Blenkin Memorial Park on the right (3).

6.9 *(4.3)* JUNCTION Turn right with the main road to enter Heriot Bay (4). A left leads to the north section of the island.

7.7 *(4.8)* JUNCTION Turn right on Heriot Bay Road. Straight ahead is the Heriot Bay Ferry Terminal (5) and the ferry to Cortes Island.

9.8 *(6.1)* JUNCTION Turn left for Rebecca Spit. Straight on continues to Cape Mudge.

11.0 *(6.9)* INTEREST Enter Rebecca Spit Park and continue on dirt road. (6) Camping is available on the Drew Harbour Indian Reserve.

13.6 *(8.5)* FINISH The dirt road becomes a trail and ends at the tip of the spit.

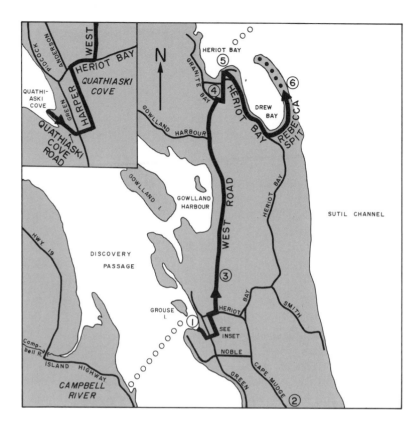

WEST
HERIOT BAY
QUATHIASKI
COVE

HERIOT BAY

QUATHI-
ASKI
COVE

QUATHIASKI
COVE
ROAD

N

HERIOT BAY

(5)

(4)

(6)

GRANITE BAY

GOWLLAND HARBOUR

DREW
BAY

HERIOT BAY

REBECCA SPIT

GOWLLAND I.

GOWLLAND
HARBOUR

WEST ROAD

SUTIL CHANNEL

HWY 19

DISCOVERY
PASSAGE

HERIOT BAY

(3)

GROUSE
I.

(1)

HERIOT

BAY

SMITH

SEE
INSET

NOBLE

Camp-
bell R.

ISLAND HIGHWAY

CAMPBELL
RIVER

GREEN

CAPE MUDGE

(2)

82

REBECCA SPIT	**RATING:** Intermediate (5)
CAPE MUDGE	**DISTANCE:** 18.1 km/11.3 mi
QUATHIASKI COVE	

HIGHLIGHTS: Rebecca Spit Park; views from Heriot Bay Road; Island Cemetery; Cape Mudge Lighthouse; Indian village of Yaculta; museum and church.

TRAFFIC: Minimal, except around ferry terminals.

TERRAIN: Rolling hills with a couple of steep descents.

REPAIRS: Bicycle shop in Campbell River.

SUPPLIES: Store in Quathiaski Cove, supermarkets in Campbell River.

CONNECTIONS: Tour 81. Ferry to Campbell River.

CHECKPOINTS

km *(mi)*

0.0 *(0.0)* START From the junction by Rebecca Spit Park (1), continue straight ahead on Heriot Bay Road. Rolling hills up ahead.

5.1 *(3.2)* INTEREST Small cemetery on the left (2).

5.4 *(3.4)* JUNCTION Stay left following Cape Mudge Road. Heriot Bay Road goes right downhill and back to Quathiaski Cove.

9.4 *(5.9)* JUNCTION Turn right on Joyce Road and then right on Lighthouse Road. A left leads down to Francisco Point (3).

11.0 *(6.9)* DOWNHILL Begin steepening descent on dirt road toward Cape Mudge.

12.4 *(7.8)* INTEREST At the bottom of the hill is Cape Mudge Lighthouse and petroglyph trail to left (4). Go right on dirt road.

13.2 *(8.3)* INTEREST When dirt road ends, continue to walk bikes along the beach (5). Pick up the dirt road again after 0.6 km and then onto pavement.

14.6 *(9.1)* INTEREST In Yaculta (6) are the Kwakiutl Indian Museum, Indian village school, Petroglyph Park and Walker Memorial Church and cemetery.

16.4 *(10.2)* UPHILL Following Green Road away from Yaculta, start up a steep hill.

16.8 *(10.5)* DOWNHILL Go downhill steeply into Quathiaski Cove (7) toward the ferry.

18.1 *(11.3)* FINISH At the Ferry Terminal (8), catch the ferry for a ride across Discovery Passage to Campbell River (9).

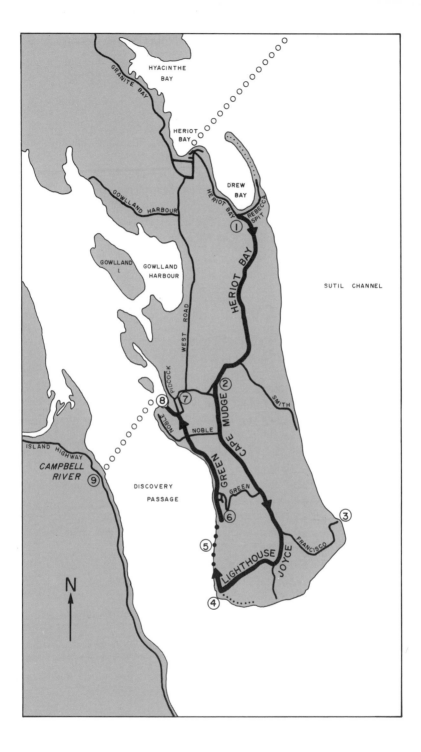

HYACINTHE BAY

GRANITE BAY

HERIOT BAY

GOWLLAND HARBOUR

GOWLLAND HARBOUR

GOWLLAND L

DREW BAY

HERIOT BAY

REBECCA SPIT

①

HERIOT BAY

SUTIL CHANNEL

WEST ROAD

PIDCOCK

②

SMITH

⑦

⑧

NOBLE

NOBLE

CAPE MUDGE

GREEN BAY

GREEN

ISLAND HIGHWAY

CAMPBELL RIVER

⑨

DISCOVERY

PASSAGE

⑥

⑤

③

FRANCISCO

LIGHTHOUSE

JOYCE

④

N

199

83 | WHALETOWN MANSONS LANDING SMELT BAY | **RATING:** Intermediate (4 to 5)
DISTANCE: 20.0 km/12.5 mi

HIGHLIGHTS: Whaletown cemetery and schoolhouse; Gorge Harbour; Gunflint and Hague lakes; Mansons Landing and Lagoon; camping at Smelt Bay Park.
TRAFFIC: Minimal, except near ferry terminal.
TERRAIN: Rolling hills; several are quite steep, especially near the ferry terminal.
REPAIRS: Bicycle shop in Campbell River.
SUPPLIES: Limited stores in Whaletown, Gorge Harbour and Mansons Landing.
CONNECTIONS: Tour 84. Ferry to Quadra Island (Tour 81).

CHECKPOINTS

km *(mi)*
0.0 *(0.0)* START   From the Whaletown Ferry Landing (1), follow Harbour Road uphill. Let traffic go first.
1.4 *(0.9)* JUNCTION   Turn right on Carrington Bay Road. A left leads to the cemetery (2).
2.6 *(1.6)* INTEREST   Old schoolhouse on the left (3).
2.7 *(1.7)* JUNCTION   Turn left on Whaletown Road for Gorge Harbour. A right leads to the small village of Whaletown (4).
4.0 *(2.5)* INTEREST   Pass Hunt and Robertson roads. Both lead to Gorge Harbour (5).
8.0 *(5.0)* UPHILL   Bend left away from the water and go uphill across a small creek.
8.6 *(5.4)* JUNCTION   Turn right uphill on Gorge Harbour Road toward Mansons Landing. Straight ahead and uphill leads to Squirrel Cove (6).
12.3 *(7.7)* JUNCTION   Turn right on Seaford Road for Mansons Landing. A left leads to Squirrel Cove and Cortes Bay (7).
12.6 *(7.9)* INTEREST   Gunflint Lake on the left (8).
15.0 *(9.4)* INTEREST   Just after a creek bridge look left for Hague Lake Trail (9).
15.3 *(9.6)* JUNCTION   Turn left for Smelt Bay. A right leads down to Mansons Landing and beach park (10). No camping.
17.0 *(10.6)* JUNCTION   Pass Cemetery Road, following Manson Road. A left on Bartholemew Road leads to Cortes Bay.
19.4 *(12.1)* INTEREST   At bottom of hill is Smelt Bay (11); turn left.
20.0 *(12.5)* FINISH   At Smelt Bay Park (12). Camping.

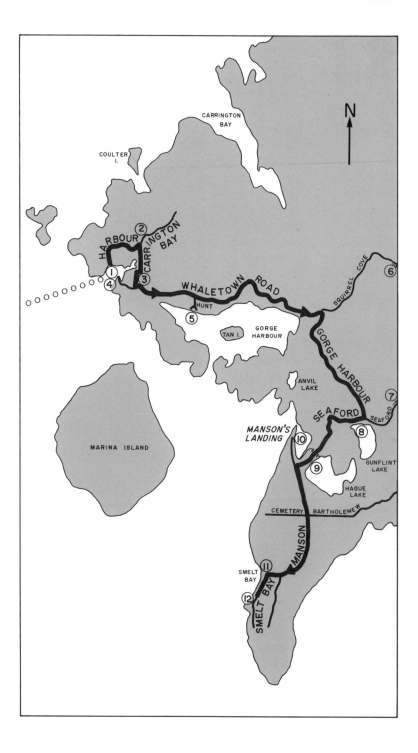

N

CARRINGTON
BAY

COULTER
I.

CARRINGTON BAY

HARBOUR

WHALETOWN ROAD

HUNT

TAN I.

GORGE
HARBOUR

SQUIRREL COVE

GORGE HARBOUR

ANVIL
LAKE

MARINA ISLAND

SEAFORD

SEAFORD

MANSON'S
LANDING

GUNFLINT
LAKE

HAGUE
LAKE

CEMETERY   BARTHOLEMEW

MANSON

SMELT
BAY

SMELT BAY

84 | MANSONS LANDING SQUIRREL COVE WHALETOWN | RATING: Intermediate (4 to 5)
DISTANCE: 25.6 km/16.0 mi

HIGHLIGHTS:	Cortes Bay; views from Squirrel Cove Road; Squirrel Cove; Gorge Harbour; Whaletown schoolhouse and cemetery; Whaletown Ferry Terminal.
TRAFFIC:	Minimal, except near ferry terminal.
TERRAIN:	Rolling hills; many are steep near Cortes Bay and the ferry terminal.
REPAIRS:	Bicycle shop in Campbell River.
SUPPLIES:	Limited stores in Squirrel Cove, Gorge Harbour and Whaletown.
CONNECTIONS:	Tour 83. Ferry to Quadra Island (Tour 81).

CHECKPOINTS

km	*(mi)*	
0.0	*(0.0)*	**START** From the junction of Cemetery Road and Manson Road (1), take Bartholemew Road downhill with steep rolling hills ahead.
3.2	*(2.0)*	**JUNCTION** Go straight on Cortes Bay Road. A right on Bartholemew leads to Cortes Bay and pier.
3.5	*(2.2)*	**INTEREST** Cortes Bay on the right (2). Ascend through rolling hills.
5.4	*(3.4)*	**JUNCTION** Turn right on Seaford Road for Squirrel Cove. Left leads to Gunflint Lake (3) and Mansons Landing (4).
7.0	*(4.4)*	**JUNCTION** Turn left on Squirrel Cove Road into more rolling hills. A right leads to Calwell Cove (5). Stay on the main dirt road.
11.0	*(6.9)*	**INTEREST** Squirrel Cove (6). Follow main road through village.
17.1	*(10.7)*	**JUNCTION** Go straight downhill; pass Gorge Harbour Road which leads left to Gunflint Lake and Mansons Landing.
21.8	*(13.6)*	**INTEREST** Pass Hunt and Robertson roads. Both lead to Gorge Harbour (7).
23.0	*(14.4)*	**JUNCTION** Turn right on Carrington Bay Road past the small schoolhouse (8). Straight on leads to Whaletown (9).
24.2	*(15.1)*	**JUNCTION** Turn left on Harbour Road for the ferry terminal. Straight ahead is the island cemetery (10).
25.6	*(16.0)*	**FINISH** At the bottom of the steep hill is the Whaletown Bay Ferry Terminal (11) and the ferry to Heriot Bay and Quadra Island.

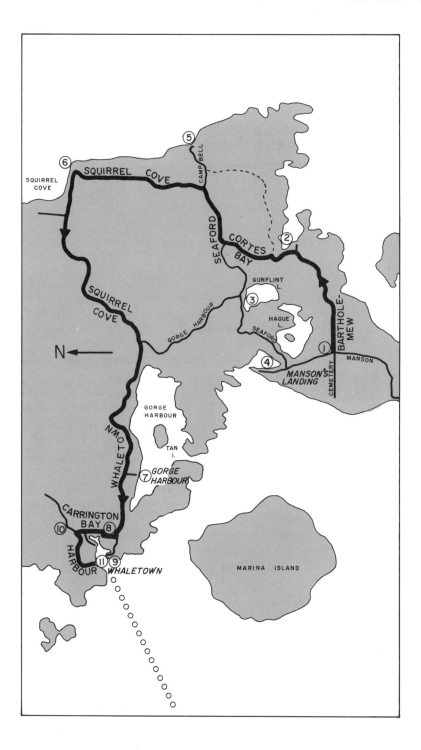

SQUIRREL COVE

SQUIRREL COVE

CAMPBELL

SEAFORD

CORTES BAY

GUNFLINT L.

HAGUE L.

SEAFORD

BARTHOLE-MEW

MANSON

MANSON'S LANDING

CEMETERY

N

SQUIRREL COVE

GORGE HARBOUR

GORGE HARBOUR

TAN I.

WHALETOWN

GORGE HARBOUR

CARRINGTON BAY

HARBOUR

WHALETOWN

MARINA ISLAND

⑤ ⑥ ② ③ ① ④ ⑦ ⑩ ⑧ ⑪ ⑨

85

CAMPBELL RIVER	RATING: Advanced (5 to 8)
ELK FALLS	DISTANCE: 17.4 km/10.9 mi
ECHO LAKE	

HIGHLIGHTS: Museum in Campbell River; Quinsam River Hatchery near Campbellton; camping at Elk Falls; McIvor Lake picnic area; Echo Lake.
TRAFFIC: Light. Watch for logging trucks at crossings.
TERRAIN: Rolling hills with a few steep sections.
REPAIRS: Bicycle shop in Campbell River.
SUPPLIES: Supermarkets in Campbell River and Campbellton.
CONNECTIONS: Tour 86 & 91.

CHECKPOINTS

km *(mi)*

0.0 *(0.0)* START From Quadra Island Ferry Terminal (1) near Tyee Mall and the museum/library (2), turn right on Discovery Crescent.

0.3 *(0.2)* INTEREST Merge with the Island Highway. Tourist Information on left (3).

1.6 *(1.0)* INTEREST Enter Campbellton (4), following the Island Highway.

2.6 *(1.6)* JUNCTION Continue straight ahead, following Highway 28 toward Gold River. A right on Island Highway leads to Sayward and Port Hardy.

2.9 *(1.8)* INTEREST Quinsam Road goes left to a fish hatchery (5). Continue straight ahead on Highway 28.

3.7 *(2.3)* CAUTION Cross major logging road. Water access on the right.

4.2 *(2.6)* CAMPING After the bridge over Quinsam River, Elk Falls Campground is reached by a left into the park (6).

5.0 *(3.1)* UPHILL Stay left on the main road; avoid the power plant entrance. Begin a steep ascent with excellent views of Campbell River.

7.0 *(4.4)* JUNCTION Stay left on the main road. Straight ahead leads to the Elk Falls Viewpoint and the John Hart Dam (7).

10.6 *(6.6)* INTEREST Continue on Highway 28. Turn left to picnic area at McIvor Lake (8).

14.1 *(8.8)* UPHILL After passing some lakes, start up a relatively steep hill.

17.4 *(10.9)* FINISH Access to Echo Lake on the left. Excellent lunch stop (9).

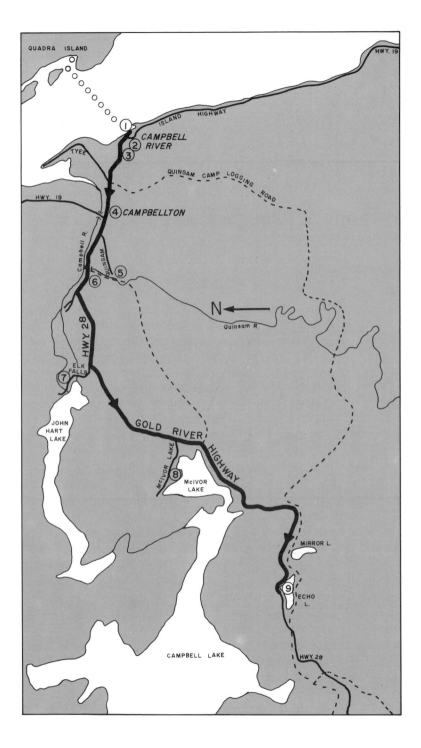

86

ECHO LAKE	RATING: Advanced (8)
UPPER CAMPBELL	DISTANCE: 35.7 km/22.3 mi
LAKE	
STRATHCONA PARK	

HIGHLIGHTS: Echo Lake and Snakehead Lake rest areas; views along Upper Campbell Lake; camping on Buttle Lake.
TRAFFIC: Light. Watch for logging trucks at crossings.
TERRAIN: Rolling hills with a few steep sections.
REPAIRS: Bicycle shop in Campbell River.
SUPPLIES: Campbell River or Gold River.
CONNECTIONS: Tours 85, 87 & 89.

CHECKPOINTS

km	*(mi)*		
0.0	*(0.0)*	START	From Echo Lake (1), continue on Highway 28 to Gold River.
1.9	*(1.2)*	CAUTION	Cross major logging road beside Quinsam Camp (2).
3.8	*(2.4)*	CAUTION	Cross major logging road. Rolling hills ahead.
8.8	*(5.5)*	INTEREST	Small rest area beside Snakehead Lake (3).
9.8	*(6.1)*	CAUTION	Bridge over small creek. Rolling hills and uphill.
11.8	*(7.4)*	DOWNHILL	Begin downhill section, which becomes steep toward the end.
14.7	*(9.2)*	JUNCTION	Continue straight on past the turnoff to Strathcona Dam (4).
18.1	*(11.3)*	CAUTION	Cross the small logging road that you have been following.
18.6	*(11.6)*	INTEREST	Upper Campbell Lake and lagoon on left (5).
18.9	*(11.8)*	CAUTION	Road follows the lakeshore, becoming curved and narrow.
26.9	*(16.8)*	INTEREST	Strathcona Lodge on the right (6).
32.8	*(20.5)*	INTEREST	Entering Strathcona Park. End of the rolling hills section.
33.9	*(21.2)*	JUNCTION	Turn right, following the main highway to Gold River. Buttle Lake Road continues straight ahead toward Western Mines site.
34.1	*(21.3)*	CAUTION	Cross a single-lane wooden plank bridge over Campbell River.
34.9	*(21.8)*	JUNCTION	Turn left to enter campground area. Continuing straight on main highway leads through park to Gold River.
35.7	*(22.3)*	FINISH	Buttle Lake Campground (7).

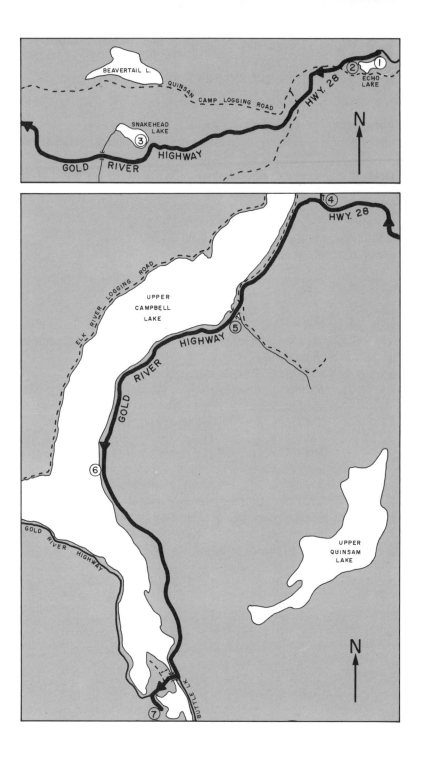

87

**STRATHCONA PARK
LUPIN FALLS
AUGERPOINT TRAIL**

RATING: Intermediate (5)
DISTANCE: 20.8 km/13.0 mi

HIGHLIGHTS: Water access to Buttle Lake at many spots; good views from the cliffy sections of road; short hike to Lupin Falls and long hike to Augerpoint.

TRAFFIC: Watch for industrial traffic from Western Mines at the road end.

TERRAIN: Rolling hills with three sections of cliffs.

REPAIRS: Bicycle shop in Campbell River.

SUPPLIES: Campbell River or Gold River.

CONNECTIONS: Tours 86 & 88.

CHECKPOINTS

km *(mi)*

0.0 *(0.0)* START   From the junction of Buttle Lake Road and Highway 28 (1), go straight ahead on Buttle Lake Road, avoiding bridge on right.

0.5 *(0.3)* INTEREST   Park Headquarters on the right (2).

1.3 *(0.8)* INTEREST   Buttle Lake boat launch on right (3). Drinking water just ahead.

4.2 *(2.6)* CAUTION   Road follows many curves along cliff face, with rolling hills.

5.4 *(3.4)* INTEREST   Lupin Falls Nature Trail (4) and bridge over small creek.

5.6 *(3.5)* UPHILL   Rolling hills along more cliffs; winding road.

12.2 *(7.6)* CAUTION   Cliff section with curves and rolling hills.

20.8 *(13.0)* FINISH   Augerpoint Hiking Trail on the left (5) and a stopping area to the right with good views across the lake to Marble Peak.

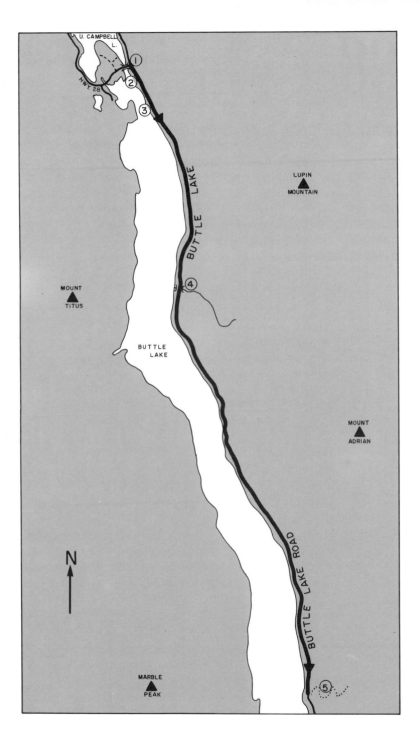

U. CAMPBELL L.

HWY 28

BUTTLE LAKE

LUPIN MOUNTAIN

MOUNT TITUS

BUTTLE LAKE

MOUNT ADRIAN

N

MARBLE PEAK

BUTTLE LAKE ROAD

88 | AUGERPOINT TRAIL RALPH RIVER MYRA FALLS | **RATING:** Intermediate (5) **DISTANCE:** 16.6 km/10.4 mi

HIGHLIGHTS:	Water access at many points along Buttle Lake; camping at Ralph River; short hike up Shepherd Creek and long hike to Flower Ridge; Myra Falls.
TRAFFIC:	Watch for industrial traffic from Western Mines at the road end.
TERRAIN:	Rolling hills with large hill up to Myra Falls turnoff.
REPAIRS:	Bicycle shop in Campbell River.
SUPPLIES:	Campbell River or Gold River.
CONNECTIONS:	Tour 87.

CHECKPOINTS

km *(mi)*

0.0 *(0.0)* START   From Augerpoint Hiking Trail (1), continue straight ahead on Buttle Lake Road.

2.7 *(1.7)* INTEREST   Ralph River boat launch on the right (2).

5.9 *(3.7)* CAUTION   At the hill bottom, cross the bridge over Ralph River.

6.1 *(3.8)* CAMPING   Ralph River Campground on right (3); Shepherd Creek Hiking Trail on left. Rolling hills ahead.

10.1 *(6.3)* INTEREST   Cross Henshaw Creek Bridge and Flower Ridge Hiking Trail (4).

14.9 *(9.3)* CAUTION   After a considerable stretch of rolling hills, cross bridge over Buttle Lake and Thelwood Creek.

15.4 *(9.6)* UPHILL   Start up a steep hill with excellent views along the lake.

16.3 *(10.2)* JUNCTION   Turn right onto a dirt road leading to Myra Falls. The paved road continues to Western Mines (5).

16.6 *(10.4)* FINISH   Leave your bike beside the radio shack and walk down the trail to visit Myra Falls (6). Camping is no longer permitted here.

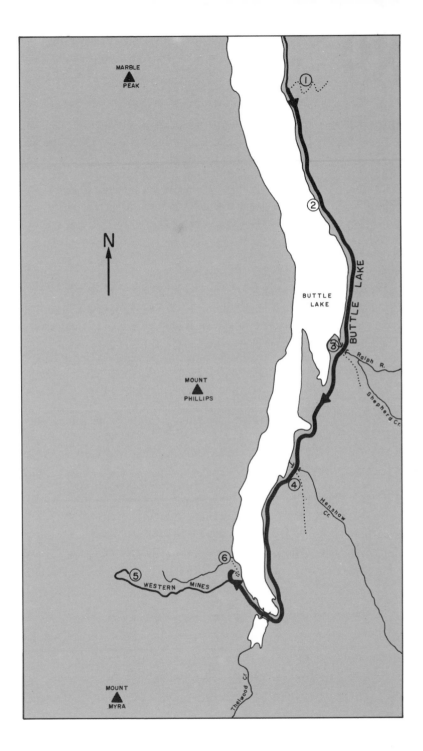

N

MARBLE
PEAK

BUTTLE
LAKE

BUTTLE LAKE

Ralph R.

Shepherd Cr.

MOUNT
PHILLIPS

Henshaw Cr.

WESTERN MINES

MOUNT
MYRA

Thelwood Cr.

89

| STRATHCONA PARK |
| ELK RIVER VALLEY |
| DRUM LAKE |

RATING: Advanced (8)
DISTANCE: 24.6 km/15.4 mi

HIGHLIGHTS: Camping on Buttle Lake; rest area on Upper Campbell Lake; short hike to Lady Falls and long hike along Elk River; rest area at Drum Lake.
TRAFFIC: Light. Watch for logging trucks at crossings.
TERRAIN: Rolling hills, generally uphill toward Crest Lake.
REPAIRS: Bicycle shop in Campbell River.
SUPPLIES: Campbell River or Gold River.
CONNECTIONS: Tours 86 & 90.

CHECKPOINTS

km *(mi)*

0.0 *(0.0)* START   From the Buttle Lake Campground entrance (1), continue straight ahead on Highway 28 toward Gold River. Rolling hills ahead.

7.7 *(4.8)* INTEREST   Boat launch and rest area (2) on Upper Campbell Lake.

12.5 *(7.8)* UPHILL   Leaving the lake and heading up the Elk River Valley.

13.8 *(8.6)* CAUTION   Bridge over Filberg Creek. More rolling hills ahead.

16.5 *(10.3)* INTEREST   Lady Falls Hiking Trail and Cervus Creek Bridge (3).

19.7 *(12.3)* CAUTION   Cross logging road and Elk River Bridge.

22.9 *(14.3)* CAUTION   Small bridge over Drum Creek.

23.5 *(14.7)* INTEREST   Elk River Hiking Trail (4).

24.6 *(15.4)* FINISH   Rest area beside Drum Lake (5).

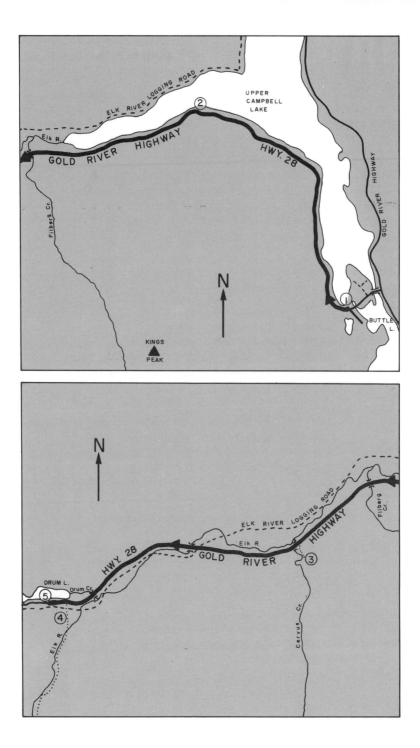

90 DRUM LAKE / GOLD RIVER / MUCHALAT INLET

RATING: Advanced (8)
DISTANCE: 30.6 km/19.1 mi

HIGHLIGHTS: Rest Area at Drum Lake; camping along Gold River; boat ride to Captain Cook's landing place on Nootka Island; Gold River mill tours.
TRAFFIC: Light. Watch for logging trucks at crossings.
TERRAIN: Rolling hills, mostly downhill after Crest Lake.
REPAIRS: Bicycle shop in Campbell River.
SUPPLIES: Gold River.
CONNECTIONS: Tour 89. MV Uchuck passenger ferry to Friendly Cove.

CHECKPOINTS

km	(mi)	
0.0	*(0.0)*	START Continue to follow Highway 28 from Drum Lake Rest Area (1).
1.4	*(0.9)*	CAUTION Bridge over Drum Creek by small lake.
1.9	*(1.2)*	INTEREST Leaving Strathcona Park by Crest Lake (2).
2.7	*(1.7)*	CAUTION Wooden bridge over Crest Creek.
3.4	*(2.1)*	CAUTION Logging road crossing and bridge over water pipeline.
4.6	*(2.9)*	CAUTION Bridge over Heber River. Logging road crossings and more creek bridges ahead. Rolling terrain.
15.7	*(9.8)*	INTEREST Entering Gold River (3); steepening downhill.
16.2	*(10.1)*	JUNCTION Turn left past the R.C.M.P. Station and go downhill through the town. A right leads to Woss Camp, 78 km on logging roads.
17.1	*(10.7)*	CAUTION At the bottom of the hill, cross a narrow bridge over Gold River.
18.6	*(11.6)*	CAUTION Cross major logging road. Rolling hills ahead.
20.3	*(12.7)*	INTEREST Picnic area beside Gold River (4), just after logging road.
21.3	*(13.3)*	CAMPING Gold River Campground on the left (5); another one ahead.
24.0	*(15.0)*	INTEREST Stopping area among cliffs; good view (6).
27.0	*(16.9)*	CAMPING Gold River Campground on the left (7). Flat ahead.
29.8	*(18.6)*	JUNCTION After a small creek bridge, go straight ahead to dock at Muchalat Inlet, avoiding the right turn to mill (8).
30.6	*(19.1)*	FINISH Highway 28 ends at the edge of Muchalat Inlet (9). Catch the ferry and take a day to explore Nootka Sound.

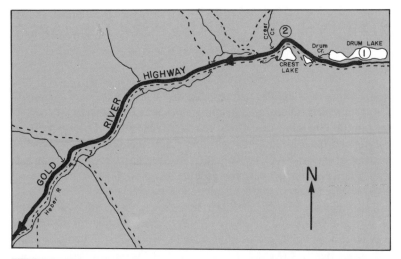

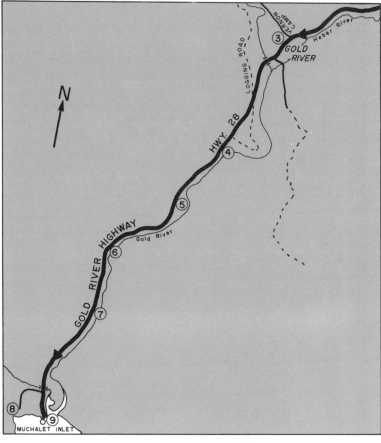

REGION H   NIMPKISH/PORT HARDY

Few cyclists reaching this point venture beyond the immediate vicinity of Campbell River, choosing to return southward to Victoria or to cross by ferry to the Sunshine Coast for a return to Vancouver. Those who strike out beyond the Sayward area will find a newly paved highway winding through a wilderness of dense forests and raging rivers. The Nimpkish Valley is without major services, and the trip from Sayward to Port Mac-Neill is recommended only for hardy, experienced cyclists.

The Nimpkish Valley is the site of major logging operations, and almost all logs are transported on a local railway system. Portions of the railroad may be seen along the route of travel, and a major side trip to the booming grounds at Beaver Cover allows you to observe the railway and log-sorting process.

Two islands lie offshore from Port MacNeill, and a short ferry trip will take you to a pair of separate cultures: Malcolm Island with its remnant Scandinavian population and a small museum; and Cormorant Island just outside Alert Bay where the Nimpkish Indian Reserve is situated. This reserve boasts the world's tallest totem pole. It is important to respect private land on both islands; public beach access and camping are limited.

At the end of this tour lies the city of Port Hardy and a major ferry terminal, which can serve as a starting point for a trip farther north to Prince Rupert and the Queen Charlotte Islands. It is also possible during some off-season periods to board a ferry for Tsawwassen near Vancouver, thus permitting a one-way trip from one end of Vancouver Island to the other.

Tour Ratings
Beginner: 94, 102, 103
Intermediate: 101, 105, 108
Advanced: 91, 92, 93, 95, 96, 97, 98, 99, 100, 104, 106, 107

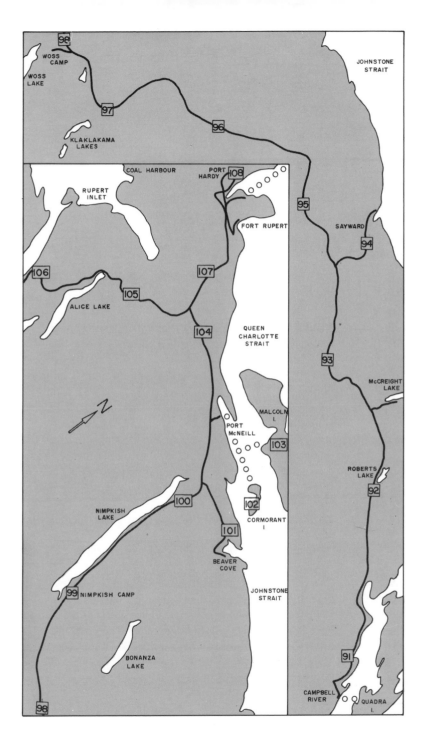

217

91

| CAMPBELL RIVER DUNCAN BAY BLOEDEL | RATING: Advanced (6 to 8) DISTANCE: 16.6 km/10.4 mi |

HIGHLIGHTS: Quinsam Hatchery outside Campbellton; museum/ library in Campbell River; Duncan Bay Beach; Seymour Narrows Viewpoint; Race Point.

TRAFFIC: Heavy between Campbell River and Campbellton. Watch for logging trucks.

TERRAIN: Mostly rolling hills.

REPAIRS: Bicycle shop in Campbell River.

SUPPLIES: Supermarkets in Campbell River and Campbellton.

CONNECTIONS: Tour 85 to Gold River. Ferry to Quadra Island.

CHECKPOINTS

km *(mi)*

0.0 *(0.0)* START From Quadra Island Ferry Terminal (1) near Tyee Mall and the museum/library (2), turn right on Discovery Crescent.

0.3 *(0.2)* INTEREST Merge with Island Highway. Tourist Information on left (3).

1.6 *(1.0)* INTEREST Enter Campbellton (4), following the Island Highway.

2.6 *(1.6)* JUNCTION Turn right across a narrow bridge over the Campbell River. Straight on leads to the hatchery, Strathcona and Gold River.

3.5 *(2.2)* UPHILL Abrupt but short uphill section followed by rolling hills.

6.4 *(4.0)* CAUTION Cross Duncan Bay Logging Road. Continue on highway.

7.0 *(4.4)* INTEREST View of the Duncan Bay Mill (5) after the water pipeline.

7.8 *(4.9)* CAUTION Logging road crossing. Continue on highway.

8.3 *(5.2)* INTEREST Beach access on right at bottom of hill (6).

13.1 *(8.2)* INTEREST Seymour Narrows Viewpoint (7) and road to Race Point (8). Sign tells the story of Ripple Rock (9).

14.6 *(9.1)* CAUTION Bridge over Mohun Creek; water access to Josephine Flat (10).

16.6 *(10.4)* FINISH Cross the Bloedel Logging Road (11) near Menzies Bay.

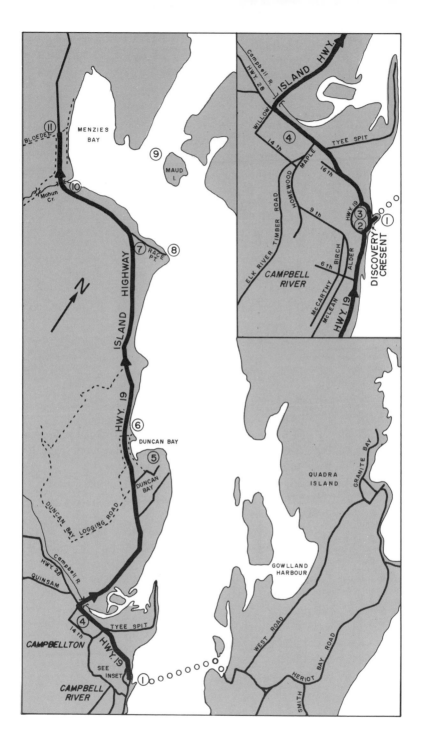

92

| BLOEDEL
ROBERTS LAKE
McCREIGHT LAKE | RATING: Advanced (8)
DISTANCE: 29.4 km/18.4 mi |

HIGHLIGHTS: Rest area at Roberts Lake; camping at McCreight (Bear) Lake; Old Logging Railway Trestle along Rock Bay Road; historical sign.

TRAFFIC: Watch for logging trucks and industrial traffic.

TERRAIN: Rolling hills with initial steep hill.

REPAIRS: Bicycle shop in Campbell River.

SUPPLIES: Campbellton or Sayward.

CONNECTIONS: Tours 91 & 93.

CHECKPOINTS

km *(mi)*

0.0 *(0.0)* START Cross the Bloedel Logging Road (1) near Menzies Bay.

0.8 *(0.5)* UPHILL Begin a long and moderate uphill grade for 6.7 km.

11.2 *(7.0)* DOWNHILL Begin a moderate grade down for about 5.0 km.

15.8 *(9.9)* INTEREST Roberts Lake on the right (2).

18.4 *(11.5)* INTEREST Rest area and viewpoint on the right (3).

21.8 *(13.6)* INTEREST Sandy area and water access to Roberts Creek.

25.3 *(15.8)* JUNCTION Turn right off the main highway onto Rock Bay Road to reach McCreight Lake. Continuing straight leads to Sayward.

28.5 *(17.8)* CAMPING Several B.C. Forestry Service primitive sites exist in this area (4).

29.1 *(18.2)* INTEREST Rock Bay Road was once a logging railroad grade; parts of the original trestles remain here along the lake edge.

29.4 *(18.4)* FINISH Sign tells the history of J.F. McCreight, B.C.'s first premier (5). Bicycle travel not recommended beyond this point.

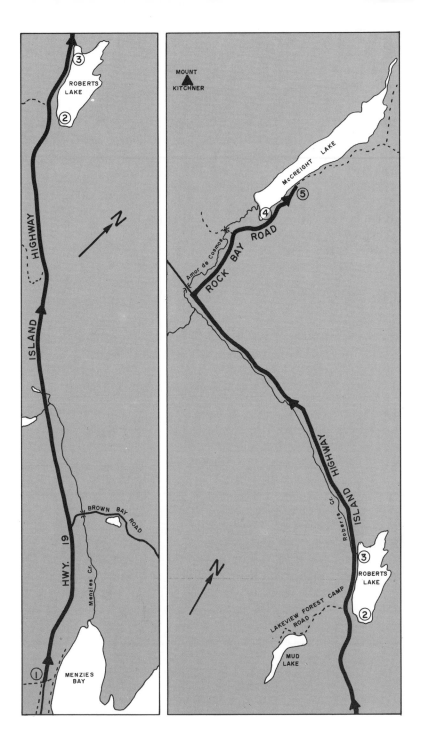

ROBERTS
LAKE

③

②

N

ISLAND HIGHWAY

BROWN BAY ROAD

HWY. 19

Menzies Cr.

①

MENZIES
BAY

MOUNT
KITCHNER

McCREIGHT LAKE

④ ⑤

Amor de cosmos

ROCK BAY ROAD

ISLAND HIGHWAY

Roberts Cr.

N

③

ROBERTS
LAKE

②

LAKEVIEW FOREST CAMP ROAD

MUD
LAKE

93

McCREIGHT LAKE	RATING: Advanced (8)
BIG TREE CREEK	DISTANCE: 24.0 km/15.0 mi
SALMON RIVER	

HIGHLIGHTS: Big Tree Creek Rest Area; Dalrymple Creek Nature Trail; water access areas at Salmon and White rivers; camping at Elk Creek.

TRAFFIC: Heavier near the Sayward turnoff.

TERRAIN: Rolling hills, generally downhill into the Salmon River Valley.

REPAIRS: Bicycle shop in Campbell River.

SUPPLIES: Limited supermarket in Sayward.

CONNECTIONS: Tours 92, 94 and 95. Kelsey Bay Ferry Terminal is closed.

CHECKPOINTS

km *(mi)*

0.0 *(0.0)* START From the Rock Bay Road turnoff to McCreight Lake, continue north on the Island Highway. Turn right coming from the lake.

0.2 *(0.1)* CAUTION Cross a narrow bridge over Amor de Cosmos Creek (1).

4.8 *(3.0)* CAUTION Cross Big Tree Logging Road.

5.8 *(3.6)* INTEREST Cross bridge over Big Tree Creek; rest area on right (2).

5.9 *(3.7)* DOWNHILL 2.2 km descent, with good views of the Salmon River Valley.

14.5 *(9.1)* INTEREST Dalrymple Creek Nature Trail on the right (3).

14.7 *(9.2)* UPHILL Moderate uphill grade for 1.9 km.

16.6 *(10.4)* DOWNHILL Gentle downhill grade for 2.9 km.

20.2 *(12.6)* CAUTION Bridge over Stowe Creek.

21.6 *(13.5)* CAUTION Narrow bridge over the Salmon River (4).

22.9 *(14.3)* JUNCTION Turn left on the Old Island Highway. A right leads to Sayward; straight ahead leads to Port Hardy.

23.0 *(14.4)* CAMPING A quick right on Dyea Road leads to B.C. Forest Service sites (5).

23.2 *(14.5)* CAUTION Cross the bridge over the White River and stay left.

24.0 *(15.0)* FINISH The Old Island Highway ends at the old bridge over the Salmon River, now closed to traffic. Water access here (6).

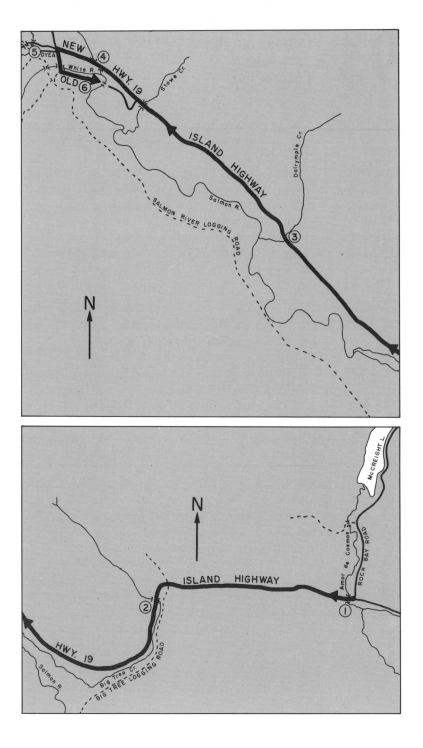

223

94

SALMON RIVER	RATING: Beginner (3)
SAYWARD	DISTANCE: 12.0 km/7.5 mi
KELSEY BAY	

HIGHLIGHTS: Link & Pin Logging Museum; Cable Cookhouse; cemetery; lots of water access; old B.C. Ferries Terminal (now closed); beach.
TRAFFIC: Moderate in Sayward Centre. Watch out for logging trucks.
TERRAIN: Flat with several creek bridge crossings.
REPAIRS: Bicycle shop in Campbell River.
SUPPLIES: Limited stores in Sayward and Kelsey Bay.
CONNECTIONS: Tours 93 & 95. Kelsey Bay Ferry Terminal is closed.

CHECKPOINTS

km *(mi)*

0.0 *(0.0)* START   From the New Island Highway, follow the Sayward/Kelsey Bay turnoff to the right (1).

1.0 *(0.6)* CAUTION   Narrow bridge over the Salmon River.

1.1 *(0.7)* INTEREST   Link & Pin Museum and Cable Cookhouse on the left (2).

2.4 *(1.5)* INTEREST   Sayward Cemetery on the right (3).

3.2 *(2.0)* CAUTION   Wooden plank bridge over Springer Creek.

6.2 *(3.9)* CAUTION   Bend left sharply and then cross a single-lane wooden plank bridge over the Salmon River. Second smaller bridge ahead.

7.4 *(4.6)* CAUTION   Cross and then parallel Kelsey Bay Logging Road.

10.1 *(6.3)* INTEREST   Entering Sayward, with local park and lake on the left (4).

10.7 *(6.7)* INTEREST   Large logging camp on the right (5).

11.7 *(7.3)* INTEREST   Old B.C. Ferry Corporation Terminal on the right (6).

12.0 *(7.5)* FINISH   Water access by Kelsey Bay Pier at the end of the road (7).

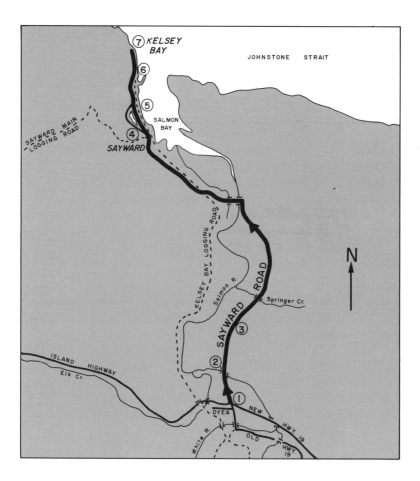

95

SALMON RIVER	RATING: Advanced (9)
ADAM RIVER	DISTANCE: 20.5 km/12.8 mi
ROONEY LAKE	

HIGHLIGHTS: Camping at Elk Creek; Keta Lake Rest Area; Rooney Lake Picnic Area.

TRAFFIC: Watch for logging trucks and other industrial traffic.

TERRAIN: Steep hills.

REPAIRS: Bicycle shop in Campbell River or Port Hardy.

SUPPLIES: Limited stores in Sayward.

CONNECTIONS: Tours 93, 94 & 96. Kelsey Bay Ferry Terminal is closed.

CHECKPOINTS

km *(mi)*

0.0 *(0.0)* START   At the intersection of the New Island Highway and the Old Island Highway (1), take the New Island Highway (Highway 19) toward Port Hardy.

0.8 *(0.5)* CAUTION   Cross bridge over Elk Creek. Camping area (2).

1.1 *(0.7)* UPHILL   Pass beneath logging road and begin steep ascent for 6.7 km.

5.9 *(3.7)* CAUTION   Cross narrow bridge over a small creek.

8.3 *(5.2)* CAUTION   Cross Adam River Logging Road, shortly after grade levels out.

9.0 *(5.6)* INTEREST   Rest area beside Keta Lake (3).

9.8 *(6.1)* DOWNHILL   Pass beneath logging road and begin rolling hills descent.

18.5 *(11.6)* CAUTION   Cross the bridge over the Adam River at the hill bottom (4).

18.7 *(11.7)* UPHILL   Begin moderate uphill grade for next 4.0 km.

19.0 *(11.9)* CAUTION   Cross minor logging road, continuing uphill.

20.0 *(12.5)* JUNCTION   Turn right on paved road leading to Rooney Lake. Continuing straight on the highway leads to Port Hardy.

20.5 *(12.8)* FINISH   Rooney Lake Picnic Area (5).

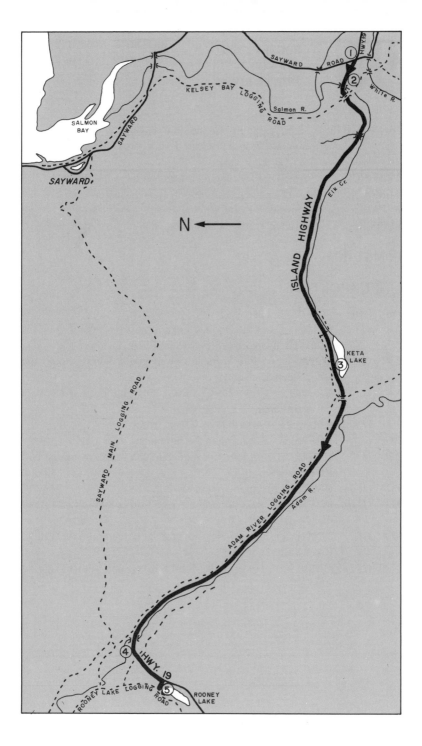

SAYWARD ROAD

HWY 19

KELSEY BAY LOGGING ROAD

Salmon R.

SALMON BAY

White R.

SAYWARD

N

ISLAND HIGHWAY

Elk Cr.

SAYWARD MAIN LOGGING ROAD

KETA LAKE

ADAM RIVER LOGGING ROAD

Adam R.

HWY 19

ROONEY LAKE LOGGING ROAD

ROONEY LAKE

96

| ROONEY LAKE
EVE RIVER
TSITIKA RIVER | **RATING:** Advanced (9)
DISTANCE: 27.4 km/17.1 mi |

HIGHLIGHTS: Open camping in the Eve River Valley; Eve/Tsitika Summit; rest area at the Eve River Bridge; bridge over the Tsitika River.

TRAFFIC: Watch out for logging trucks and other industrial traffic.

TERRAIN: Long steady hill climbs, steep in places.

REPAIRS: Bicycle shop in Campbell River or Port Hardy.

SUPPLIES: Limited stores in Sayward, very limited store in Woss Camp.

CONNECTIONS: Tours 95 & 97.

CHECKPOINTS

km	*(mi)*	
0.0	*(0.0)*	START From the Rooney Lake turnoff, travel uphill on the Island Highway away from Adam River (1).
2.4	*(1.5)*	DOWNHILL Pass beneath Montague Logging Road and begin steep descent.
5.6	*(3.5)*	CAUTION Cross the Eve River Logging Road. Relatively flat in this area.
7.4	*(4.6)*	CAUTION Cross the Eve River Bridge.
7.6	*(4.7)*	INTEREST Rest area to the right along a logging road (2).
7.7	*(4.8)*	UPHILL Begin long but moderate ascent following the Eve River Valley.
16.2	*(10.1)*	CAUTION Logging road crossing.
17.8	*(11.0)*	INTEREST Pass through the Eve/Tsitika Summit, 500 m at the top (3).
17.8	*(11.1)*	DOWNHILL Begin long but gradual descent into the Tsitika River Valley.
27.4	*(17.1)*	FINISH Bridge over the Tsitika River and Tsitika Logging Road (4).

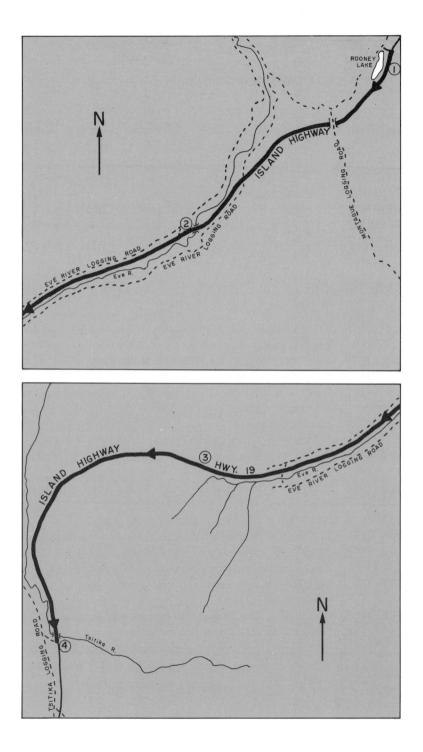

N

ROONEY
LAKE

①

ISLAND HIGHWAY

MONTAGUE LOGGING ROAD

②

EVE RIVER LOGGING ROAD

Eve R.

EVE RIVER LOGGING ROAD

ISLAND HIGHWAY

HWY. 19

③

Eve R.

EVE RIVER LOGGING ROAD

N

TSITIKA LOGGING ROAD

④

Tsitika R.

97

TSITIKA RIVER	**RATING:** Advanced (8)
HOOMACK LAKE	**DISTANCE:** 18.2 km/11.4 mi
WOSS CAMP	

HIGHLIGHTS: Croman Lake; Davie River Bridge; camping at Klakla-kama Lake; Hoomack Lake Rest Area; high railway bridge at Woss Camp. See note below.

TRAFFIC: Watch out for logging trucks and other industrial traffic.

TERRAIN: Rolling hills and relatively flat.

REPAIRS: Bicycle shop in Campbell River or Port Hardy.

SUPPLIES: Very limited store at Woss Camp.

CONNECTIONS: Tours 96 & 98. Rough road to Gold River (67 km) not recommended.

CHECKPOINTS

km *(mi)*

0.0 *(0.0)* START From the Tsitika River Bridge, continue on the Island Highway (1).

2.2 *(1.4)* CAUTION Logging road crossing. Rolling hills ahead.

4.3 *(2.7)* INTEREST Croman Lake on the left (2).

5.9 *(3.7)* JUNCTION Remain on the highway. A left on the logging road leads to Davie River Bridge (3) and Klaklakama Lake campsites (4 & 5).

8.5 *(5.3)* DOWNHILL Gentle downhill grade for 1.5 km.

10.0 *(6.3)* INTEREST Rest area beside Hoomack Lake (6). Rolling hills ahead.

11.8 *(8.0)* CAUTION Cross Lukwa Creek Bridge and two logging roads.

13.6 *(8.5)* CAUTION Cross Woss/Lukwa Logging Road.

14.9 *(9.3)* INTEREST Small lake on the left (7); access is difficult.

16.5 *(10.3)* JUNCTION Turn left on paved road into Woss townsite (8). Continuing straight on the highway leads to Port Hardy.

17.1 *(10.7)* CAUTION Cross railway tracks and go downhill to the logging offices.

17.6 *(11.0)* CAUTION Cross second set of railroad tracks and turn left.

18.2 *(11.4)* FINISH The high logging railroad bridge over the Nimpkish River (9) should not be ridden on. Dismount and walk across.

NOTE: Camping is also available on Woss Lake (10). Follow the signs from the high bridge and check in at the forestry offices to obtain permission and directions.

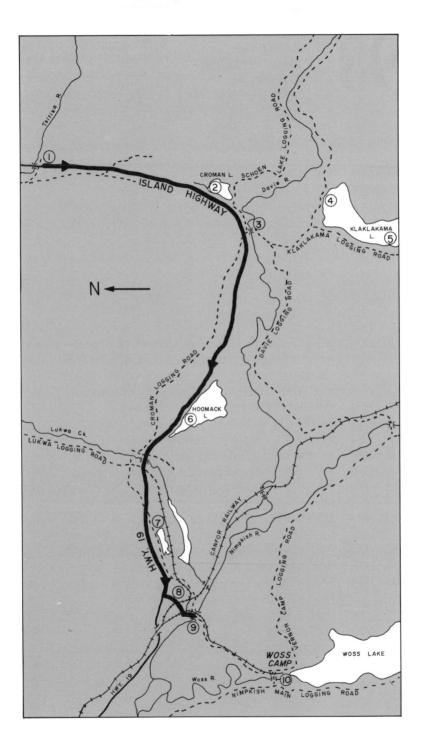

231

98

**WOSS CAMP
UPPER NIMPKISH
RIVER
STEELE CREEK**

RATING: Advanced (8)
DISTANCE: 20.6 km/12.9 mi

HIGHLIGHTS: Gold Creek Rest Area; public drinking water; Zeballos turnoff.
TRAFFIC: Watch out for logging trucks and other industrial traffic.
TERRAIN: Rolling hills with one fairly steep hill.
REPAIRS: Bicycle shop in Campbell River or Port Hardy.
SUPPLIES: Limited stores at both Woss Camp and Nimpkish Camp, ahead.
CONNECTIONS: The rough route to Zeballos (45 km) connects by passenger ferry to Gold River.

CHECKPOINTS

km   *(mi)*
0.0   *(0.0)*   START   From the Woss Camp turnoff, continue downhill on the Island Highway toward the Nimpkish River Valley. Turn left coming from Woss (1).
1.3   *(0.8)*   CAUTION   Pass under the Canfor Logging Railway.
1.8   *(1.1)*   CAUTION   Cross bridge over Gold Creek.
1.9   *(1.2)*   INTEREST   Gold Creek Rest Area on the right (2).
6.1   *(3.8)*   INTEREST   Drinking water stop on the left (3).
7.4   *(4.6)*   UPHILL   Begin fairly steep climb up for 2.9 km.
8.5   *(5.3)*   CAUTION   Pass under the Canfor Logging Railway.
17.1   *(10.7)*   INTEREST   Roadside cliffs and rest area beside a small lake (4).
17.4   *(10.9)*   DOWNHILL   After crossing a logging road, descend steeply for 1.8 km.
19.5   *(12.2)*   CAUTION   Pass under the Canfor Logging Railway.
20.0   *(12.5)*   CAUTION   Cross the Steele Logging Road.
20.6   *(12.9)*   FINISH   Cross Steele Creek Bridge with the railway on the right. Zeballos turnoff on the left just ahead (5).

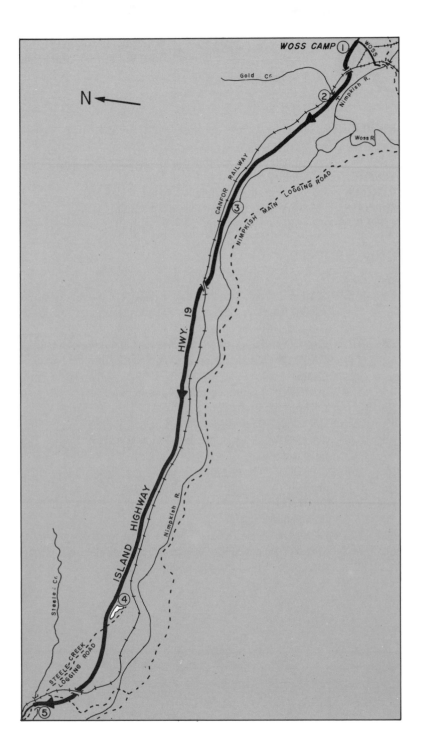

N

WOSS CAMP ①
Woss
Gold Cr.
②
Nimpkish R.
Woss R.
CANFOR RAILWAY
③
NIMPKISH MAIN LOGGING ROAD
HWY. 19
ISLAND HIGHWAY
Nimpkish R.
Steele Cr.
④
STEELE CREEK LOGGING ROAD
⑤

99

STEELE CREEK
NIMPKISH CAMP
NIMPKISH LAKE

RATING: Advanced (8)
DISTANCE: 18.7 km/11.7 mi

HIGHLIGHTS: Fabulous views of Nimpkish Lake and River; roadside rest area.
TRAFFIC: Watch out for logging trucks and other industrial traffic.
TERRAIN: Rolling hills.
REPAIRS: Bicycle shop in Campbell River or Port Hardy.
SUPPLIES: Very limited store at Nimpkish Camp.
CONNECTIONS: Tours 98 & 100.

CHECKPOINTS

km *(mi)*

0.0 *(0.0)* START   From Steele Creek Bridge (1), continue on the Island Highway, cross the Zeballos Logging Road, and climb steadily for 6.0 km.

1.8 *(1.1)* CAUTION   Pass beneath logging road and railroad trestles.

6.2 *(3.9)* CAUTION   Cross major logging road leading to Nimpkish Camp.

8.5 *(5.3)* JUNCTION   Continue straight on the highway. A left leads to Nimpkish Camp (2).

8.6 *(5.4)* CAUTION   Pass under Canfor Logging Railway.

9.3 *(5.8)* CAUTION   Cross bridge over Kinman Creek. Rolling hills up ahead.

10.9 *(6.8)* CAUTION   Cross bridge over Storey Creek. More uphill ahead.

14.4 *(9.0)* CAUTION   Cross bridge over Noomas Creek. Still more uphill ahead.

17.0 *(10.6)* DOWNHILL   Descend for about 1.2 km; terrain flattens out.

18.7 *(11.7)* FINISH   Roadside rest area shortly after Nimpkish Lake sign (3).

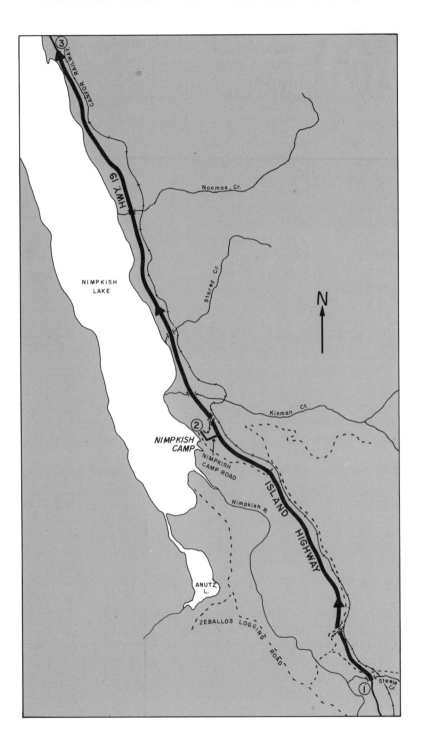

100

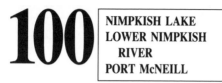

NIMPKISH LAKE
LOWER NIMPKISH
RIVER
PORT McNEILL

RATING: Advanced (8)
DISTANCE: 25.4 km/15.9 mi

HIGHLIGHTS: Camping at Cheslakees; primitive campsites on the Lower Nimpkish River; Port McNeill Ferry to Cormorant and Malcolm islands.

TRAFFIC: Heavy in Port McNeill.

TERRAIN: Rolling hills with some steep sections.

REPAIRS: Bicycle shop in Campbell River or Port Hardy. Limited in Port McNeill.

SUPPLIES: Supermarkets in Port McNeill, very limited store in Nimpkish Camp.

CONNECTIONS: Tours 99, 101, 102, 103 & 104. Ferry to Alert Bay and Sointula.

CHECKPOINTS

km *(mi)*

0.0 *(0.0)* START From the roadside rest area at Nimpkish Lake (1), continue uphill on the Island Highway for 4.0 km.

4.0 *(2.5)* DOWNHILL Descend for 1.0 km, and continue on the flats.

6.6 *(4.1)* UPHILL Ascend for 6.4 km through rolling hills.

11.2 *(7.0)* CAUTION Cross major logging road leading to Beaver Cove (2).

13.0 *(8.1)* DOWNHILL Steady descent for 2.2 km, then flat for a short distance.

15.4 *(9.6)* JUNCTION Remain on main highway, bending left. A right leads to Beaver Cove and railway booming grounds.

16.0 *(10.0)* CAMPING A small dirt road leads left to a primitive campground (3).

16.8 *(10.5)* CAUTION Long, narrow bridge over Lower Nimpkish.

17.0 *(10.6)* INTEREST Rest area on the far right side (4). Swimming not recommended.

17.1 *(10.7)* UPHILL Rolling hills ascend for the next 5.3 km.

19.5 *(12.2)* INTEREST New airport on the right (5).

22.4 *(14.0)* JUNCTION Turn right for Port McNeill and the island ferry. Straight ahead leads to Port Hardy and the Bear Cove Ferry Terminal.

24.0 *(15.0)* DOWNHILL After crossing the main logging road, follow Campbell Way downhill steeply into Port McNeill (6)

25.4 *(15.9)* FINISH Service to Alert Bay on Cormorant Island and Sointula on Malcolm Island from Island Ferry Terminal (7).

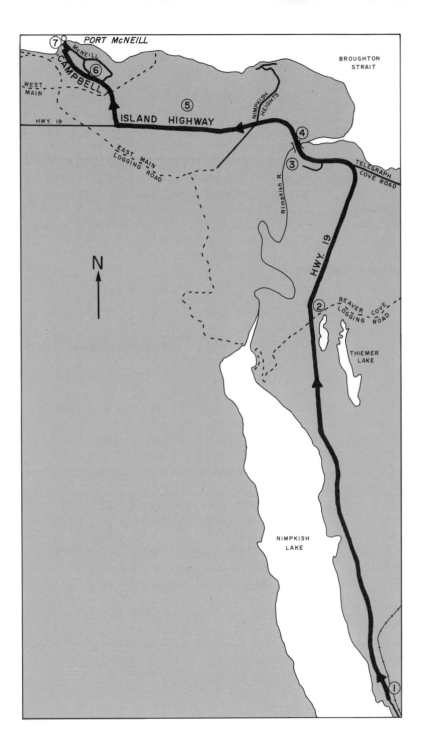

101

| LOWER NIMPKISH RIVER KOKISH RIVER BEAVER COVE | **RATING:** Intermediate (5) **DISTANCE:** 11.5 km/7.2 mi |

HIGHLIGHTS: Possible primitive camping by the Kokish River; log booming and sorting facility at Beaver Cove; Canfor Logging Railway operations.

TRAFFIC: Watch out for logging trucks and other industrial traffic.

TERRAIN: Rolling hills with one large hill in the middle.

REPAIRS: Bicycle shop in Campbell River or Port Hardy. Limited in Port McNeill.

SUPPLIES: Supermarkets in Port McNeill.

CONNECTIONS: Tour 100.

CHECKPOINTS

km *(mi)*

0.0 *(0.0)* START At the turnoff from the main highway, go right to Beaver Cove/Telegraph Cove. (1).

0.8 *(0.5)* CAUTION Cross wooden plank bridge, with second one just ahead.

1.1 *(0.7)* UPHILL Begin fairly steep series of grades for 4.1 km.

5.3 *(3.3)* DOWNHILL Begin rolling hills down for about 2.6 km.

7.9 *(4.9)* CAUTION Cross logging road and begin uphill again.

8.4 *(5.2)* DOWNHILL Extremely steep descent for 0.8 km.

9.4 *(5.8)* CAUTION Slow down to cross wooden plank bridge at the hill bottom.

10.2 *(6.4)* CAUTION Turn left and travel along the logging road.

10.4 *(6.5)* CAUTION Cross narrow wooden bridge over the Kokish River (2).

10.9 *(6.8)* CAUTION Turn right across the Canfor Logging Railway.

11.5 *(7.2)* FINISH Beaver Cove Logging Operations, log sorting and booming facility (3). Public displays and tours available.

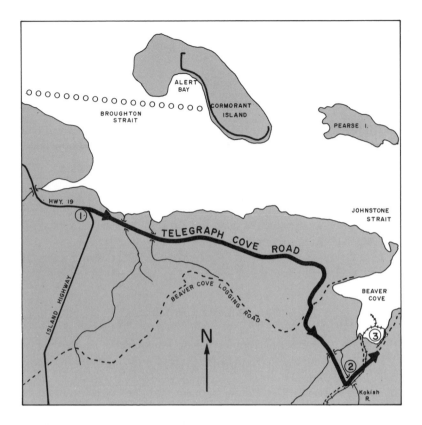

102

ALERT BAY CORMORANT ISLAND NIMPKISH RESERVE

RATING: Beginner (1 to 3)
DISTANCE: 1.9 km/1.2 mi

HIGHLIGHTS: Beach access; Nimpkish Museum; totem poles and long house; burial grounds and totem poles; interesting buildings in Alert Bay Town.

TRAFFIC: Minimal, except near ferry terminal.

TERRAIN: Flat by the water, steep hills everywhere else.

REPAIRS: None.

SUPPLIES: Very limited stores in Alert Bay. Try Port McNeill.

CONNECTIONS: Ferry from Port McNeill and to Sointula.

CHECKPOINTS

km *(mi)*

0.0 *(0.0)* START   Disembark from the ferry and allow traffic to go ahead (1).

0.1 *(0.1)* JUNCTION   Turn left for the Nimpkish Indian Reserve. A right leads to an Indian cemetery (2) and the beach at Gordon Bluff (3).

1.1 *(0.7)* INTEREST   Follow the main road right. Just ahead are the health centre and museum (4).

1.6 *(1.0)* INTEREST   At the top of the hill is the world's tallest totem pole and the Nimpkish Long House (5).

1.7 *(1.1)* DOWNHILL   Follow the dirt road downhill to the water.

1.9 *(1.2)* FINISH   Stony beach (6). View to Malcolm Island.

NOTE: Please respect the Nimpkish Indian Reserve as private land. Do not trespass upon the sacred burial grounds. Camping is unavailable on Cormorant Island. However, it may be possible to tent on the school grounds (7), but check with the Alert Bay R.C.M.P. detachment first.

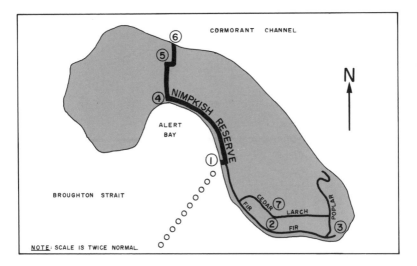

CORMORANT CHANNEL

NIMPKISH RESERVE

ALERT BAY

BROUGHTON STRAIT

CEDAR

FIR

LARCH

FIR

POPLAR

N

NOTE: SCALE IS TWICE NORMAL.

Totem poles at the Nimpkish sacred burial grounds in Alert Bay

241

103 SOINTULA MALCOLM ISLAND KEMPS BEACH

RATING: Beginner (1 to 3)
DISTANCE: 4.6 km/2.9 mi

HIGHLIGHTS: Beach access; Sointula Museum; cemetery; Kemps Beach Picnic Area.
TRAFFIC: Minimal, except near ferry terminal.
TERRAIN: Flat by the water, hilly everywhere else.
REPAIRS: Hardware store in Sointula.
SUPPLIES: Large store opposite the ferry landing.
CONNECTIONS: Ferry from Port McNeill and to Alert Bay.

CHECKPOINTS

km *(mi)*

0.0 *(0.0)* START   Disembark from the ferry and allow traffic to go ahead (1).

0.1 *(0.1)* JUNCTION   Turn right on First Street. A left leads past the museum (2) to the beach at Rough Bay (3). Take First Street out of town.

0.5 *(0.3)* INTEREST   Pass the cemetery on the right (4), leaving town on a dirt road.

3.2 *(2.0)* JUNCTION   Continue straight ahead, along the water's edge. Stay off the logging roads on the left.

4.6 *(2.9)* FINISH   Kemps Beach Picnic Area on the right (5). No camping.

NOTE: Camping is not allowed on Malcolm Island unless you can make special arrangements with the local residents.

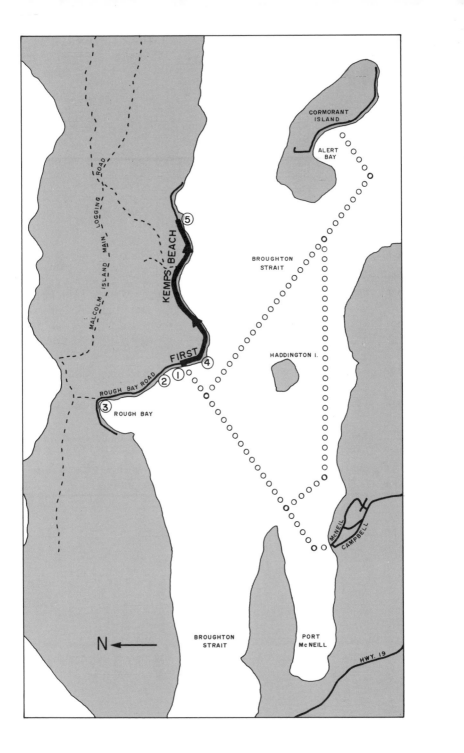

CORMORANT
ISLAND

ALERT
BAY

BROUGHTON
STRAIT

MALCOLM ISLAND MAIN LOGGING ROAD

KEMPS BEACH

⑤

FIRST

④

② ①

ROUGH BAY ROAD

③ ROUGH BAY

HADDINGTON I.

McNEILL

CAMPBELL

N

BROUGHTON
STRAIT

PORT
McNEILL

HWY. 19

104

PORT McNEILL	RATING: Advanced (8)
BROUGHTON STRAIT	DISTANCE: 20.0 km/12.5 mi
BEAVER LAKE	

HIGHLIGHTS: Viewpoint of Broughton Strait; Misty Lake Rest Area; Beaver Lake Picnic Area.
TRAFFIC: Heavy near Port McNeill. Watch out for logging trucks.
TERRAIN: Rolling hills with some long flat sections.
REPAIRS: Bicycle shop in Port Hardy.
SUPPLIES: Stores in Port McNeill.
CONNECTIONS: Tours 100, 105 & 107.

CHECKPOINTS

km   *(mi)*

0.0   *(0.0)*   START   Continue on the Island Highway toward Port Hardy from the Port McNeill turnoff (1). Turn right coming from Port McNeill.

1.0   *(0.6)*   CAUTION   Cross East Main Logging Road, flat and straight ahead.

3.5   *(2.2)*   CAUTION   Cross West Main Logging Road, downhill for 1.9 km.

8.6   *(5.4)*   CAUTION   Sharp left bend and then bridge over Cluxewe River.

12.2   *(7.6)*   INTEREST   Broughton Strait Viewpoint on the right (2).

16.0   *(10.0)*   INTEREST   Misty Lake Rest Area on the right (3).

18.6   *(11.6)*   INTEREST   Thermal Power Plant on the left (4).

19.1   *(11.9)*   CAUTION   Cross bridge over the Keogh River.

19.6   *(12.2)*   JUNCTION   Turn left for Port Alice. Straight on leads to Port Hardy.

20.0   *(12.5)*   FINISH   Beaver Lake Picnic Area (5).

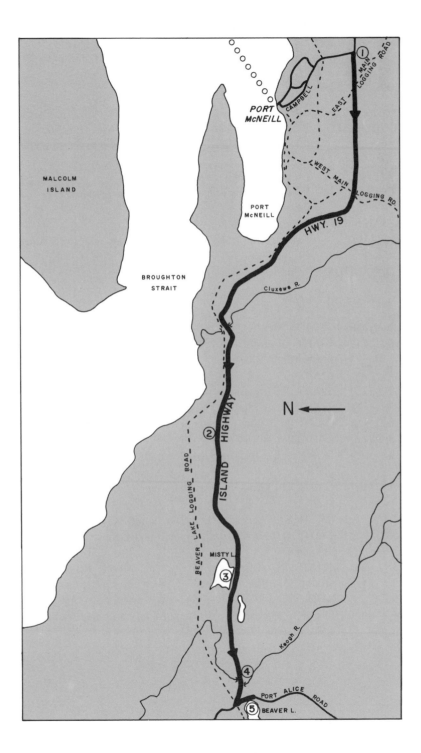

MALCOLM
ISLAND

BROUGHTON
STRAIT

PORT
McNEILL

PORT
McNEILL

CAMPBELL

MAIN LOGGING ROAD

EAST MAIN

WEST MAIN

LOGGING RD.

HWY. 19

Cluxewe R.

ISLAND HIGHWAY

BEAVER LAKE LOGGING ROAD

N

MISTY L.

Keogh R.

PORT ALICE ROAD

BEAVER L.

① ② ③ ④ ⑤

105

BEAVER LAKE	RATING: Intermediate (5)
WAUKWAAS CREEK	DISTANCE: 14.2 km/8.9 mi
MARBLE RIVER	

HIGHLIGHTS: Beaver Lake Picnic Area; Sara Lake; water pipeline following road; Alice Lake; Marble River Rapids; camping at Marble River.

TRAFFIC: Light, but watch for industrial traffic.

TERRAIN: Rolling hills with a steep descent to Marble River and Alice Lake.

REPAIRS: Bicycle shop in Port Hardy.

SUPPLIES: Stores in Port McNeill, Port Hardy and Port Alice (Rumble Beach).

CONNECTIONS: Tours 104, 106 & 107.

CHECKPOINTS

km *(mi)*

0.0 *(0.0)* **START** From Beaver Lake (1), continue on Port Alice Road toward Port Alice, away from the Island Highway intersection.

3.7 *(2.3)* **CAUTION** Logging road crossing. Rolling hills ahead.

6.7 *(4.2)* **CAUTION** Bridge over Waukwaas Creek (2).

7.0 *(4.4)* **CAUTION** Major intersection of West Main Logging Road.

7.3 *(4.6)* **CAUTION** Bridge over small creek.

9.4 *(5.9)* **DOWNHILL** Rolling hills down to Alice Lake, steep in places.

9.7 *(6.1)* **CAUTION** Cross Rupert Inlet Logging Road. Sharp right bend ahead.

12.0 *(7.5)* **INTEREST** Access to Sara Lake on the left (3).

13.6 *(8.5)* **CAUTION** Narrow bridge over Marble River beside Alice Lake (4).

13.7 *(8.6)* **JUNCTION** Turn right to enter the Marble River Campground (5). Straight ahead on the main road leads to Port Alice.

14.2 *(8.9)* **FINISH** Marble River Campground; primitive campsites and trail to rapids.

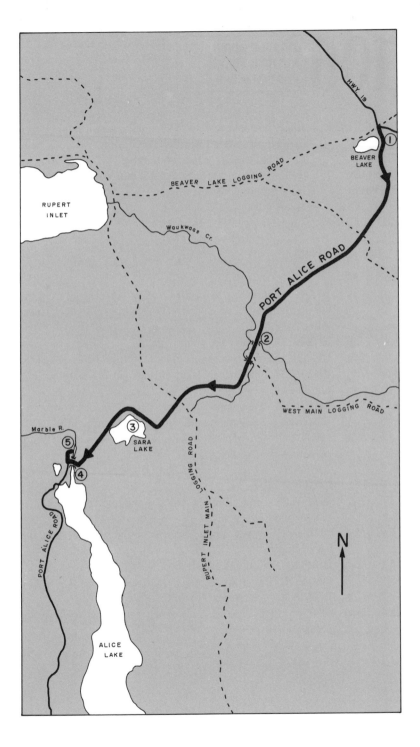

BEAVER LAKE

HWY 19

BEAVER LAKE LOGGING ROAD

RUPERT INLET

Waukwaas Cr.

PORT ALICE ROAD

WEST MAIN LOGGING ROAD

Marble R.

SARA LAKE

RUPERT INLET MAIN LOGGING ROAD

PORT ALICE ROAD

N

ALICE LAKE

106 MARBLE RIVER RUMBLE BEACH PORT ALICE

RATING: Advanced (7)
DISTANCE: 21.4 km/13.4 mi

HIGHLIGHTS: Alice Lake and several other small lakes; Rumble Beach Park on Neroutsos Inlet; Port Alice Mill.
TRAFFIC: Light, but watch for industrial traffic.
TERRAIN: Rolling hills with a steep descent into Rumble Beach.
REPAIRS: Bicycle shop in Port Hardy.
SUPPLIES: Stores in Rumble Beach.
CONNECTIONS: Tour 105.

CHECKPOINTS

km *(mi)*

0.0 *(0.0)* START   Follow the main road to Port Alice away from the campground at Marble River (1). Rolling hills ahead near Alice Lake.

1.4 *(0.9)* INTEREST   Small lake on the right (2).

1.9 *(1.2)* UPHILL   Begin short steep climb away from Alice Lake (3).

4.6 *(2.9)* INTEREST   Pass small lake on the right (4). Rolling hills ahead.

5.7 *(3.6)* INTEREST   Pass same lake again. Excellent views ahead.

11.8 *(7.4)* DOWNHILL   Begin long steep drop to Neroutsos Inlet.

13.6 *(8.5)* CAUTION   Cross Nequilipaulis Logging Road after sharp corners.

14.5 *(9.1)* CAUTION   At the bottom of the hill merge left with Jeune Landing Road.

15.0 *(9.4)* INTEREST   Enter Rumble Beach (5) and Port Alice Municipality.

16.6 *(10.4)* INTEREST   Water access and park on the right (6). Leaving town ahead.

18.1 *(11.3)* UPHILL   Rolling hills for 1.3 km.

19.5 *(12.2)* CAUTION   Narrow bridge over Jahonaal Creek.

20.2 *(12.6)* DOWNHILL   Steep descent for 0.5 km to Port Alice.

21.4 *(13.4)* FINISH   Port Alice Mill (7) at the end of the road. Water access.

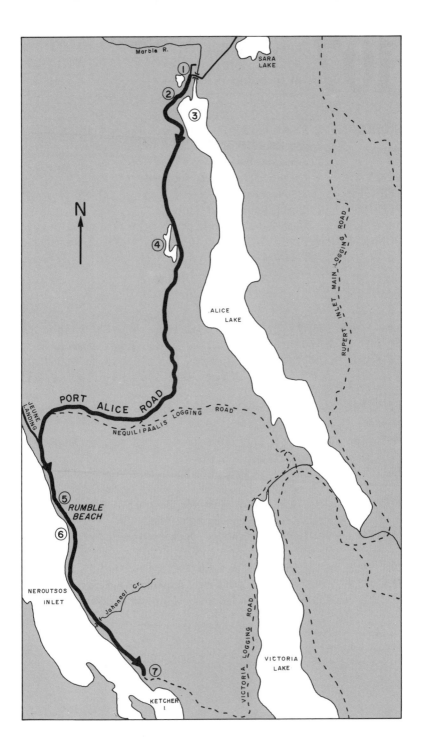

N

Marble R.

SARA
LAKE

ALICE
LAKE

RUPERT INLET MAIN LOGGING ROAD

PORT ALICE ROAD

JEUNE
LANDING

NEQUILIPAALIS LOGGING ROAD

⑤ RUMBLE
BEACH

⑥

NEROUTSOS
INLET

Jahonaai Cr.

VICTORIA LOGGING ROAD

VICTORIA
LAKE

⑦

KETCHER
I

107

| BEAVER LAKE |
| FORT RUPERT |
| BEAR COVE |

RATING: Advanced (8)
DISTANCE: 20.8 km/13.0 mi

HIGHLIGHTS: Beaver Lake Picnic Area; side trips to Fort Rupert and Port Hardy; Bear Cove Rest Area and points of interest; Bear Cove ferries.
TRAFFIC: Congested around ferry terminal.
TERRAIN: Rolling hills.
REPAIRS: Bicycle shop in Port Hardy.
SUPPLIES: Small stores in Fort Rupert, supermarkets in Port Hardy.
CONNECTIONS: Tours 104, 105 & 108. Ferry to Prince Rupert and Tsawwassen/Vancouver.

CHECKPOINTS

km *(mi)*

0.0 *(0.0)* START From Beaver Lake Picnic Area (1), return to the Island Highway intersection. Turn left from the parking lot.

0.5 *(0.3)* JUNCTION Turn left on the Island Highway for Port Hardy and Bear Cove. A right leads back to Port McNeill and Nimpkish Lake.

6.1 *(3.8)* CAUTION Logging road crossing near Keogh Creek. Rolling hills ahead.

11.7 *(7.3)* JUNCTION Stay left on the main highway. A right leads to Fort Rupert (2).

15.2 *(9.5)* CAUTION Go straight on across portion of the Old Island Highway.

16.2 *(10.1)* JUNCTION Turn right for Bear Cove Ferry Terminal. Straight ahead continues to Port Hardy (3).

16.3 *(10.2)* CAUTION Cross bridge over a small creek. Rolling hills up ahead.

20.5 *(12.8)* INTEREST Rest area and point of interest on the left (4).

20.8 *(13.0)* FINISH Bear Cove Ferry Terminal (5). Ferries to Prince Rupert year-round and seasonal trips back to Vancouver.

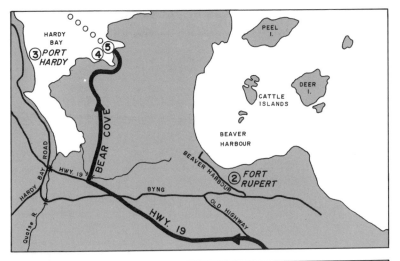

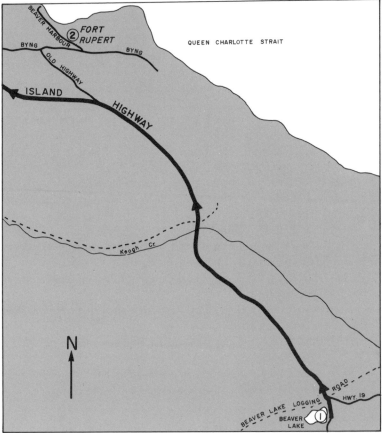

108

PORT HARDY **QUATSE RIVER** **FORT RUPERT**	**RATING:** Intermediate (5) **DISTANCE:** 17.6 km/11.0 mi

HIGHLIGHTS: Park and beach in Port Hardy; Port Hardy Museum; Hardy Bay Rest Area; camping on the Quatse River; park and beach in Fort Rupert.

TRAFFIC: Heavy in Port Hardy centre.

TERRAIN: Rolling hills and winding roads.

REPAIRS: Bicycle shop in Port Hardy.

SUPPLIES: Supermarkets in Port Hardy, small stores in Fort Rupert.

CONNECTIONS: Tour 107. Ferry to Prince Rupert and Tsawwassen/Vancouver.

CHECKPOINTS

km *(mi)*

0.0 *(0.0)* **START** From the Bear Cove Ferry Terminal turnoff (1), continue straight ahead on the main highway toward Port Hardy.

1.1 *(0.7)* **CAUTION** Cross the Quatse River Bridge, following the Island Highway.

1.3 *(0.8)* **JUNCTION** Cross Hardy Bay Road. Go straight ahead and uphill.

2.1 *(1.3)* **CAUTION** Cross Holberg Logging Road. Rolling hills descend ahead.

2.9 *(1.8)* **CAUTION** Cross the bridge over Glenlion River.

3.5 *(2.2)* **INTEREST** Follow the main road downhill, entering Port Hardy (2).

4.8 *(3.0)* **INTEREST** Turn left on Rupert Street, right on Seaview Drive and right on Market Street to reach small park and beach in the city (3).

5.8 *(3.6)* **INTEREST** Pass the local museum, following Market Street through town (4).

6.6 *(4.1)* **INTEREST** Hardy Bay Rest Area left (5). Leave town on Hardy Bay Road.

8.5 *(5.3)* **JUNCTION** Cross New Island Highway, following Hardy Bay Road.

9.4 *(5.9)* **JUNCTION** Stay left at a triangular intersection for Fort Rupert. A right leads to Coal Harbour (6), 13.6 km.

(continued, p. 254)

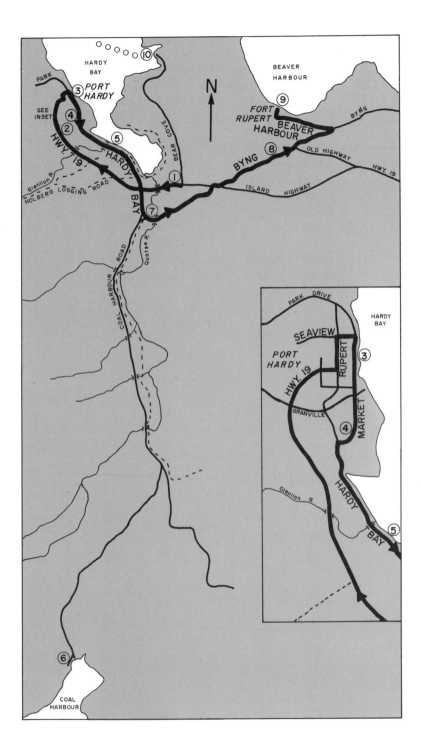

HARDY BAY

○○○○○○ (10)

PARK

PORT HARDY

(3)

SEE INSET

(4)

(2)

(5)

HWY. 19

HARDY BAY

Glenlion R.

HOLBERG LOGGING ROAD

Qualse R.

COAL HARBOUR ROAD

(7)

(1)

BEAR COVE

N

BYNG

(8)

ISLAND HIGHWAY

BEAVER HARBOUR

FORT RUPERT

(9)

BEAVER HARBOUR

BYNG

OLD HIGHWAY

HWY. 19

(6)

COAL HARBOUR

PARK DRIVE

SEAVIEW

PORT HARDY

HWY. 19

GRANVILLE

RUPERT

(3)

MARKET

(4)

HARDY BAY

Glenlion R.

HARDY BAY

(5)

9.6 *(6.0)*   CAMPING   Municipal Campground on the left by the Quatse River (7).

9.9 *(6.2)*   CAUTION   Bridge over the Quatse River. Rolling hills up ahead.

12.0 *(7.5)*   JUNCTION   Cross New Island Highway, following Byng Road to Fort Rupert. A left leads to the ferry; a right, to Port McNeill.

13.6 *(8.5)*   INTEREST   Fort Rupert Cemetery on the left (8).

14.4 *(9.0)*   JUNCTION   Continue straight on for Fort Rupert. A right leads to the highway.

15.5 *(9.7)*   DOWNHILL   Bend sharp left and drop down into the town of Fort Rupert.

17.3 *(10.8)*   INTEREST   Turn right by a public park, school and playing fields.

17.6 *(11.0)*   FINISH   Beach and park on Beaver Harbour (9). Nice place to spend spare time before returning to Bear Cove (10) to catch a ferry.

FURTHER READING

Bicycling Magazine. *Basic Bicycle Repair*. Emmaus, PA: The Rodale Press, 1980.

————. *Basic Riding Techniques*. Emmaus, PA: The Rodale Press, 1979.

Forester, John. *Bicycle Transportation*. Cambridge, MA and London: The MIT Press, 1983.

————. *Effective Cycling: A Handbook for Safe, Fast Bike Travel*. 4th Ed., 1981. Available from Custom Cycle Fitments, 726 Madrone Ave., Sunnyvale, CA 94086.

Krausz, John, Vera van de Krausz and Paul Harris, eds. *The Bicycling Book: Transportation, Recreation, Sport*. New York: The Dial Press, 1982.

Smith, Ken, ed. *The Canadian Bicycle Book*. Toronto: D.C. Heath Canada, 1972.

INDEX

(by route number)

255

10|18